Teaching Tips for Accounting Cases

by

Sylvie Deslauriers, PhD, MSc

FCPA, FCA, CGA, FCMA, CPA (FL)

Professor of Accounting

at the University of Québec at Trois-Rivières, Canada

Translated by Tradek

AB + Publications

Teaching Tips for Accounting Cases
by Sylvie Deslauriers, PhD

Graphics and Cover design: Sabina Kopica

P.O. Box 38
St-Alban
Canada
G0A 3B0
418-268-3099 (phone)
418-268-3044 (fax)
info@ABplusPublications.com
www.ABplusPublications.com

ISBN 978-0-97380-385-3

Legal deposit: 2012
Library and Archives Canada
Bibliothèque et Archives nationales du Québec

Printed in Québec, Canada

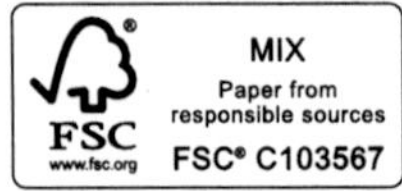

French version:
Trucs payants pour enseigner les cas, AB + Publications.
© 2012 ISBN 978-0-97380-386-0

Teaching Tips
for Accounting Cases

For a greater Success!
Dr. Sylvie Deslauriers

PREFACE

Dear Colleagues,

After more than 27 years of experience both in university teaching and in the marking of professional exams, it is with complete confidence that I am able to make the present book available to you. My objective in doing so is simply to share my lifetime knowledge and experience with a view to contributing to the betterment of training in accounting.

I am very much aware that case teaching is a real challenge for a teacher dealing with student apprenticeship, a lengthy activity marked by periods of soul-searching and insecurity. As the students look ahead to the moment when they will have to write a professional accounting exam, we must find the best ways of assisting them.

To resolve cases, one needs a wide range of knowledge, together with an ability to adapt to constantly changing situations. Since each case is unique to itself, each case provides its own challenges. This means that the teaching of case resolution requires the acquisition of an ongoing ability: not to overdo things, but to go just as far as necessary. This demands constant readjustment in order to achieve the right balance.

Through the use of two cases, one short, one long, which will be found in the Appendix to this volume, I wish to follow up on the ideas presented in my book *Accounting for Success The Guide to Case Resolution*, and at the same time provide a series of *Teaching Tips for Accounting Cases.*

I am happy to share with you the working strategies I have developed and hope they will contribute to the success of your own work.

Dr. Sylvie Deslauriers

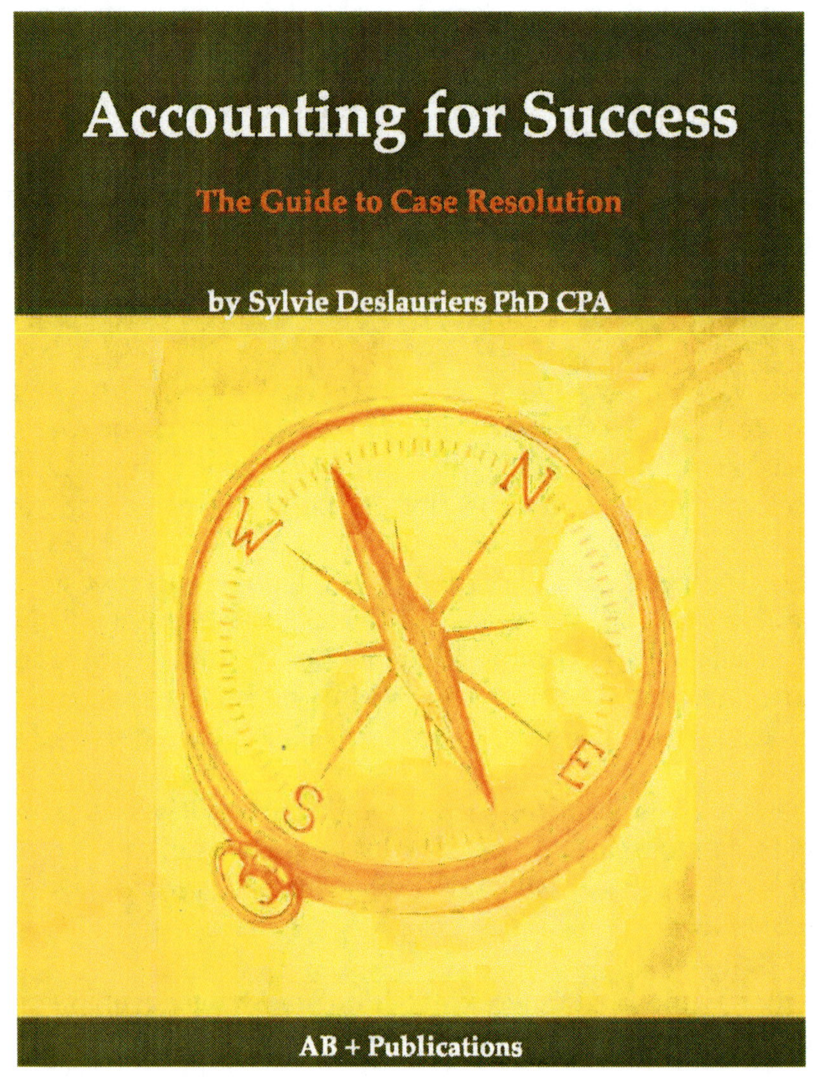

Accounting for Success The Guide to Case Resolution

AB + Publications, 271 pages. © 2010 ISBN 978-0-97380-384-6

CONTENTS

CONTENTS (continued)

EXHIBITS

Part 1
Reading and annotating a case

The relevance of the response will be directly related to your understanding of the assignment.

Accounting for Success, 2010, p. 8

Part 1

Reading and annotating a case

"The challenge is to spend enough time reading and annotating a case in order to understand it properly, while leaving enough to resolve it."

This section is designed to assist students in reading and annotating cases and, to this end, provides three objectives: learning how to determine case parameters rapidly; knowing what to take into consideration when reading a case; and determining the most efficient way of annotating a case.

Objective: Learning how to determine case parameters rapidly

Each case is unique. When it comes to resolving problems or issues, one must identify the specifics of each case as speedily as possible. I believe that students who can clearly and sufficiently isolate these parameters significantly increase their chances of success. When reading through a case, it is important to constantly remind oneself to:

- Bring out those aspects of the CONTEXT that will affect the response.

  CASES A and B: The accounting resources to be used are the International Financial Reporting Standards (IFRS).

- Be aware of the impact of the ROLE, since this is what determines the angle from which problems or issues will be examined.

  CASE B: The accountant from the Finance Department "participates" in the work of the internal audit group. Since he is not an employee of the Internal audit Department, he should not be performing tasks that are not normally assigned to him. (B5)

- Understand the work to be done or the various REQUIREMENTS so as to provide a relevant discussion.

  CASE A: One is required to establish performance "measures" congruent with corporate "objectives." (A5)

N.B.: Part 2 deals with the planning of a response.

TIP: Suggest to the students that they identify the various case parameters in some specific way. I know from experience that it is very useful to note them down all together in one spot, on a work sheet.

Objective: Knowing what to take into consideration when reading a case

Since a case has to be resolved within a limited—indeed, restricted—time frame, it must be read in such a way as to identify its important components as speedily and as fully as possible. When presented with the case, I would suggest the following steps: 1- A preliminary look through the information supplied and 2- An in-depth reading of the text and the exhibits.

1- Preliminary look through the information supplied

It is essential that, right from the start, students pick out the benchmarks that will take them through each step of their reading. The first thing to do is to read the "Required" section, when identified as such. It is to be found between the case text and the exhibits, and usually contains the general terms of what must be done. Subsequently, they should attempt to follow up on the various requirements by picking out every sentence or paragraph that provides extra information as to what is expected. In order to do this as early as possible, each paragraph of the case text should be looked over briefly. I believe it is essential that, right from the start, students should read at one and the same time all the information concerning what is required, because this is the referential framework that will color the rest of their reading. Then, a little later, the various requirements should be classified according to their relative importance.

> The last paragraph of the CASE B text reads as follows: "John has asked you to drop everything to respond to the issues raised in the email." The student therefore has to go to Exhibit I, which contains the email, in order to obtain the list of the various requirements. Since this page is important, it should be read immediately.
>
> The student must pay attention to each word and understand that he has just been provided with important facts, that is to say that his response must deal mainly with what is asked in this email. Of course, other requirements might come up elsewhere in the case, but, initially, the main part of the requirements is to be found in Exhibit I.

TIP: Suggest to the students that they copy the important words of each requirement on a separate page. This will allow them to focus on <u>each</u> word and better grasp the meaning of the requirement.

OR

TIP: Suggest to the students that they identify the various case requirements differently, in order to be able to locate them speedily once their reading is completed.

TIP: Make the students aware that explanatory paragraphs are often located towards the end of the text, that they often refer to their role, sometimes begin with quotation marks, refer to a problem or issue, or can be presented as a question that needs to be answered.

The second step—if this has not already been taken—is to determine exactly what role to play, since this will affect how the case information is read and interpreted. A quick glance over the final paragraphs of the text will usually allow students to determine their role. And, while resolving problems or issues, they must constantly adopt the right personality.

In CASE B, the accountant works in the Finance Department. This is an in-house position, which means that the problems or issues to be resolved need to be considered from this point of view.
Consequently, when the student prepares the audit plan, he will need to check out what is really relevant for the company by focusing on the accuracy of the Canadian Radio-television and Telecommunications Commission (CRTC) Fee calculations. He must certainly not analyze events from the point of view of an external auditor (a role often played in case simulations).

The ultimate reflex prior to a detailed reading of the case is to briefly examine the content of the exhibits in order to become familiar with the material available. I suggest to students that they skim through each of the exhibits—rather than reading every detail—so as to build up an initial broad picture.

TIP: Invite a colleague to come to your class and then have each of you, playing different roles, explain your approach to resolve the problems or issues of a specific case.

TIP: Advise the students to look at the Index to Exhibits, where available, and to check out titles and subtitles.

Taking into account the questions to be resolved that have already been identified, a brief examination of the contents of the CASE B exhibits allows the student to rapidly determine, amongst other things, that:

- Exhibit II, which contains a reporting document, is the subject of a specific question.
- Exhibits II, III and IV contain information concerning 2009 and 2010.
- Exhibit IV provides the information necessary to evaluate operating performance relative to competitors.
- The Fees payable to CRTC is dealt with in two exhibits, V and VI, confirming the importance of this subject, which is in fact open to an explicit and detailed requirement.
- Chief Executive Officer's presentation in Exhibit VII will probably be useful as regards more than one subject, since the Committee's request for a report came up following his presentation.
- Information provided in Exhibit VII as to SableTel's "future" will serve mainly to comment on the strategic plan and to evaluate the budget.

2- In-depth reading of the case text and exhibits

The first paragraphs of a case usually provide the entity's background or characteristics, and the student should pinpoint anything that can help resolve problems or issues. One has to consider the specifics of the context, such as the size of the entity, the industry, the key success factors, the strengths, weaknesses, opportunities and threats, the objectives and biases of the stakeholders, the constraints, business management practices, managerial behavior, etc.

TIP: Ask the students how the interpretation of information is modified when the role is changed. For example, an external auditor and a chief accountant will not proceed in the same way when analyzing accounting policies.

TIP: Help students rapidly identify key elements in the exhibits, such as the mention of a "Third notice" in the CRTC letter presented in Exhibit V. (B13)

TIP: Point out to students that one needs to pinpoint anything that is different or unusual, i.e. "that is not found in all cases."

TIP: Suggest that they make a chart when information is difficult to grasp or when many parties are involved. Or again, suggest that they draw a time line in order to follow key events, when keeping track of the dates is essential or complicated.

In CASE B, it is important to note that, amongst other things,

- StarNova is a publicly traded company, subject to specific accounting, legal and tax rules that differ from those applicable to private enterprises.
- Star Nova expects a 15% return on investment, and this will influence the evaluation of operating performance and the analysis of the strategic plan.
- SableTel is strictly regulated by the CRTC, and its survival depends on the renewal of its operating license.

As he reads on, the student should continue to identify the work he has to do, by keeping an eye open for any indication suggesting a requirement by the employer, the client or other party involved. One needs to check for anything different or changing, more especially during the current year, and to bring out the current and new problems or issues. In other words, one needs to identify all the questions that are pending—all the main subjects and subtopics waiting to be resolved—because, *a priori* at least, they all have to be settled.

CASE A

A sentence such as "The payroll staff at CYOF, Kim, is concerned about how he is going to process payments in future" should attract the student's attention. (A4) A "payroll processing" section will then be added to the list of requirements.

By experience, I know that students find it difficult to identify implicit problems or issues. To do so, they need to collect the case facts that will help them make such identification, for example, that management's integrity is questionable, that financial information was manipulated, that the ability of the entity to continue as a going concern is uncertain, that the cash flow is insufficient, or that the external auditor lacks independence. To identify an implicit problem or issue, one must pick up and collect the various case facts that lead down the same path, and be able to take a step back in order to offer an overall interpretation of the whole matter.

> In CASE A, various facts or hints lead the student to bring up the possibility of fraudulent behavior by the previous controller. This implicit issue is contained within the explicit requirement to "analyze recent issues that should be dealt with on a timely basis." (A5)

> In CASE B, many indications lead one to believe that senior management at SableTel does not have the skills required to return the company to profitable operations. It is normal that an accountant working in the Finance Department should pick up on this more implicit issue, since the Committee would like further information and analysis. (B5) Additionally, we know that "typically, StarNova expects all of its businesses to generate a 15% return on investment."

TIP: Ask the students to draw up a list of all the case facts that lead to the identification of an implicit problem or to the resolution of a specific subject. Point out that "implicit" problems or issues fit in with one or other of the "explicit" requirements, within the framework of the role to be played.

TIP: Suggest to your students that they should make a habit of standing back at some point when reading a case, and take the time to ask themselves whether the various facts have anything in common. For example, on many occasions the Chief Executive Officer at SableTel was unable to answer questions that were quite essential. One needs to put the facts together, even if this means going back and rereading some parts of the case. (CASE B)

While reading the case, the student must continuously improve his understanding of its different parameters (context, role, requirements) and make sure he picks up all the facts relevant to the resolution of the case. When several exhibits must be read, I would suggest that students begin by looking at the financial statements provided, in order to bring out the key elements as shown below. Personally, when there are financial statements in the exhibits, I refer to them regularly while reading the case. Thus, as soon as I read than StarNova expects to generate a 15% return on investment, I make a calculation and find out that the current return is 4.5%. (B8) After reading all the exhibits, I skim through the financial statements once more to make sure that I have fully integrated the information provided.

Items to highlight in the financial statements	Examples (CASE B, Exhibit III)
Basic information	– DRAFT/2010 unaudited – Year ended August 31
The most significant items (in terms of changes and percentage)	– Cash is very low. Accounts receivable have more than doubled. Trade and other payables have also significantly increased. – Inventory has increased substantially, but is made up of items that have a short life.
The items that are at the greatest risk (those whose future benefits are least certain or that require an estimate of the situation)	– Significant research and development (R&D) costs have been capitalized for the first time. – The impact of Hurricane Baylee on SableTel's activities is yet to be determined.
Unusual items	– In September 2009, SableTel paid $2.5 million for inventory, which it purchased at a substantial discount. – The $2,500,000 government grant is a non-recurring event.
Inconsistencies and contradictions	– Accounts receivable have more than doubled while revenue has decreased. – We turned the corner from a loss in 2009 to profitable operations in 2010 while the total revenue has slightly diminished.
Non-compliance with accounting standards, laws, business practices, etc.	– Inventory is not measured at the lower of cost and net realizable value.
Key ratios (more especially those of interest to a creditor or to management)	– The actual return on investment must be compared with the objective of 15%. – The working capital is less than 1.0 and the situation has deteriorated since 2009.

TIP: Warn the students against automatisms, for example automatically calculating four to six ratios for each financial statement provided. Taking into account the case parameters, they must learn how to rapidly determine what can be useful.

TIP: Show the students financial statements in order to discuss how to interpret financial information; go back over cases that have already been analyzed and make comparisons.

TIP: Draw the students' attention to contradictions, to "what is going wrong" or to what appears to differ from what is found in a "standard" entity, by taking a closer look at the items specific to the industry.

It seems essential to me that one read the entire case before planning out a response and dealing with the various requirements. I find myself regularly making this point because many students simply glance at specific exhibits or don't even bother to read the last pages or paragraphs. This is an especially damaging attitude when an exhibit contains a whole range of subjects thrown together huggermugger, i.e. where one can find ideas about different subjects, one example being Exhibit VII of CASE B.

I therefore urge my students to focus on active and attentive reading right up to the last word of the case! They need to pay particular attention to case facts referring to one and the same subject, whichever part of the case they are in. They need to pick out and mention every type of link. In fact, case reading is never strictly linear, since one generally has to go back to earlier parts in order to fully understand what is happening. For example, those elements that need to be considered when analyzing the reporting document in Exhibit II will essentially be found in Exhibit III. When reading the case, one needs to examine these two exhibits concomitantly. (B6 à B10)

TIP: Carry out a survey amongst the students (via Doodle, for example) in order to find out how much reading time they devote to a case. They should be reading in depth but leaving themselves enough time to draft a suitable response.

TIP: Use examples to show the danger of reading too fast or of not reading all the case exhibits prior to drafting. A student who reads too fast and, for example, fails to realize that "accuracy" is the key assertion in the audit plan is likely to write an over-detailed response. (B5)

TIP: Point out to students the presence of key case facts in the final paragraphs of an exhibit, or in the last exhibit itself.

Objective: Determining the most efficient way of annotating a case

When I go over the text and exhibits of a case that has been resolved by my students, I constantly come up against the surprising fact that almost nothing has been written on the case itself. And yet, I consider it essential to find ways of classifying the information read, so as to facilitate the retrieval of relevant facts when planning out and drafting the response.

There are various ways of annotating a case, starting with the simple underlining of significant words, going on to the use of work sheets, and finally to the preparation of a detailed and complete checklist. Each case is unique, and each student, as he goes through simulation after simulation, develops his own methodology. How one annotates cases depends, amongst other things, on the length of the case in question, since the longer the case, the more the annotations are necessary. It also depends on the direct or indirect nature of what is required, on the complexity of the problems or issues to be dealt with, on how the information is presented and, finally, on the ability of the student to remember the information provided. All of which means that when the case facts relating to a given subject are scattered throughout the case, a more elaborate annotation system will be necessary.

TIP: Provide the students with genuine examples of student annotations written on a case. This exercise is especially interesting when carried out using an interactive whiteboard (IWB), since this allows one to directly annotate the case.

TIP: Ask your students how they dissected and classified the case facts. Ask them, a posteriori, how they might have better classified the information provided therein.

One needs to remember that what is written on the case text itself is not considered to be part of the response, whereas work sheets or checklists are. This means one should minimize the number of annotations written on the case and opt rather for the use of separate sheets of paper. I would suggest that students underline or encircle those words or expressions in the case that they deem to be significant. Personally, when I do a case simulation, I use the left-hand margin to note down the requirements to which the information relates, along with the problem or issue involved. When possible I indicate the importance of the subject. As for the right-hand margin, that is where I enter brief remarks or key words that allow for speedy retrieval of information, such as: quantitative – qualitative, past – future, net income – cash flow, period – year, name of the company, division, country, strategic – operational, strength – weaknesses – opportunities – threats, parts *a), b)*, etc. To sum up, annotations of the case text and exhibits are used, amongst other things, to:

Objective of annotation	**Examples**
– pick up all the requirements and subjects that need to be dealt with;	– After noting accounting errors in the financial statement, the student realizes that there is an implicit requirement with regard to unresolved "accounting issues." (CASE B, Exhibit III)
– highlight the important words and elements;	– The fact that the controller "gave his notice at the same time GFI purchased CYOF" is an indication worth considering. (A3) This action will certainly impact the firm's activities. – The fact that the Committee was "confused" by the results for 2010 means that they did not expect them to be so exceptional. (B3) One should therefore prepare to look for "what is going wrong."
– determine the links between the various pieces of information regarding the same subject;	– The very fact that the controller's departure was "quick" indicates that there are probably mistakes to pick out—whether deliberate or not. The following case facts will confirm that the "mistakes" were deliberate. (A4) – Reading that there was a "high turnover in the Sales Department" (B16) is information that links up with the fact that they were paid less than their competitors (B19).

Objective of annotation	Examples
– indicate the problem or issue to which the information relates;	– The trends and variance analysis in Exhibit 1 serve to identify the relevant performance measures. (A6) – Some information is applicable to more than one problem or issue. For example, the content of Note 6 regarding Hurricane Baylee (B10) is relevant to the analysis of the accounting issue regarding impairment of the network. It also allows one to comment on the reporting document, and to evaluate the likelihood of the result being achieved.
– evaluate objectively the information read;	– B9: Some expenses were paid to a related party. This does not automatically mean that there will also be "revenue" from related parties. Of course, one may wonder, but an objective reading will show that there is no mention of revenue in the case.
– give a preliminary opinion as to the importance of a problem or issue.	– The symbol "++" or the mention "IMP" is placed next to important elements, whether on the case itself, on work sheets or on the checklist. (CASES A and B)

TIP: Suggest to students that they read a paragraph completely before annotating it. Otherwise they are in danger of underling everything in yellow!

TIP: Point out to the students that all annotations are valid, providing they are short and useful. Examples could include "!", "?", "WOW", "$", "bias", "again", "Why?", "WRONG", "fishy", "obj.", "tax", "check", etc.

TIP: Show examples where "what is not written doesn't exist." For example, noting that the supplier is located more than 250 km (155 miles) away does not necessarily mean that he uses pesticides in growing produce. Not complying with an agreement criterion does not automatically mean that the other criteria are not respected. (A4) In the same way, the fact that they are not aware of any "new" lawsuit does not mean there were no "previous" lawsuits that are still pending. (B6)

Apart from the annotations on the case itself, the student can note down his observations on work sheets or on a partial or overall checklist. The method used will depend on the circumstances.

Since CASE A is short, the student will not need sophisticated work sheets. Some will not use any at all. However, as indicated above, my own experience tells me that it is very useful to pick out or jot down the essential case parameters (context, role, requirements). Doing so helps one to remain focused on the essential elements. When one examines the annotations on CASE A (A3 to A6) as a whole, the following will be noticed:

- The role stands out clearly.
- Throughout the reading stage, the elements specific to the context were listed at the very end of the case. (A5) For example, the fact that the clients are willing to pay a premium price for local, organic products is a key element one needs to remember.
- In the left-hand margin, the problems and issues are mentioned, along with their corresponding reference *a)* or *b)*. The importance of certain subjects is also indicated.
- In the right-hand margin, one finds a number of useful ideas, such as the distinction between short-term (ST) and medium-term (MT), along with the structure of the discussion regarding the accounting treatment of the first building and the presence of certain key words, "lawyer?" being one of them.

When dealing with a long (4-5 hour) case, one should consider preparing work sheets or a more detailed checklist. This allows for information to be classified according to the problems or issues that have to be resolved and for all the case information on a given subject to be found in the same place, thus facilitating the later drafting of the response.

Because CASE B is long, the student needs to find the most efficient way of classifying the information. Apart from annotating the case itself as he read on (B3 à B22), he used a work sheet. (B23)

When examining the annotations in CASE B, we notice the following:

- The role stands out clearly.
- The various requirements are listed in Exhibit I. The references to the pages or exhibits concerned are clearly indicated.
- In the left-hand margin, the matter to keep in mind while reading the case is identified (e.g. "check for errors!" in the notes to the financial statements). Or again, direct reference to the key words of the requirement is made (e.g. "comments + suggestions" on the reporting document in Exhibit II).
- Throughout the reading process, the items specific to the context were listed at the very end of the case, on a separate sheet. For example, one key element was the fact that the "industry is strictly regulated." (B23)
- A number of links between the various pieces of information are identified from one page to the next. (e.g.: B11, B16, B19)

CASE B (continued)

- All the information needed for the resolution of certain problems or issues is centralized in one and the same part of the case. For example, one may notice that the reporting document is presented in Exhibit II. Since the important items of information necessary to prepare comments on this report are all located in the same spot, there is no need to re-list them on a separate sheet. The same goes with respect to the evaluation of operating performance, which is essentially founded on Exhibits III and IV and the variance analysis, the latter being based on pages B15 to B17.
- As for the case facts needed for the evaluation of budgeted information, they are scattered pretty much throughout the case. One needs, on the one hand, to fully understand the actual results and, on the other hand, to pick out all the facts that can be used to assess the likelihood of the expected results being achieved (revenues or expenses). In such a situation, an efficient way of annotating the case is to bring all the case facts together in one place. (B23) That way, nothing is forgotten, the interrelationships can be brought out, and the ranking of subjects by their order of importance is facilitated. It would be useful to go through the same steps with the information regarding the strategic plan, since it too is spread over several pages in Exhibit VII.

TIP: Provide your students with a range of genuine examples of checklists--or of work sheets--and discuss their usefulness. When using a computer to draft the response, the preparation of work sheets can be speeded up thanks to the copy/paste function.

TIP: Stress those situations where recopying everything is pointless, for example when the subject is not complex (ratio analysis--B11) or when all the necessary information can be found in one and the same exhibit (e.g. the method of calculation of the CRTC Fee--B12).

TIP: Check out students' case simulations, so that you can comment on how they annotate and classify the information. Be on the look-out for different, efficient and original ways of annotating a case.

TIP: Take the time to show students that there are different ways of annotating a case and that it can vary from one situation to the next and also depend on one's personal style.

I believe it is important to encourage your students to try out different ways of annotating and organizing case information. Some may mark up the case facts with different colors, while others summarize the facts on work sheets or on checklists, reflecting different approaches and levels of thoroughness. Another strategy that is often effective is to tabulate the information so that the similarities and differences are brought out. For example, the characteristics that are specific to different means of financing will be more prominent.

Part 2
Planning out the response

> **The response plan is essential in order to deal properly with each required subject.**

Accounting for Success, 2010, p. 52

Part 2
Planning out the response

"The challenge is to determine exactly the depth to which each subject will be discussed, while ensuring that all of them receive sufficient coverage."

This section is designed to assist students in planning out their case response and, to this end, provides three objectives: structuring the response; determining the importance of problems or issues; and establishing a response plan.

Objective: Structuring the response

The case response, whatever its length, is usually structured as follows:

1- Presentation page containing the "Date, To, From, Subject" header.

Although this first page gives a more professional look to the response, one needs to remember that it is not really taken into consideration when it comes to marking. However, it does remind one of the essential case parameters and serves as a guide for students. Since they do not always know how to start, this is a good start-off.

The Subject may be short or more detailed, as necessary. I myself use it to summarize the various requirements of the case, which helps me avoid losing sight of what has to be done. This is also where I list the main problems or issues to be solved, by order of their importance.

Example of a Presentation page (CASE A)

MEMO

Date:

To: President of GFI

From: CGA, Controller per *interim*

Subject: Integration of the new division

a) Issues to be dealt with on a timely basis:

Lawsuit
Suppliers' agreement (bio, 250 km) (ST)
Ethical issue regarding former controller
Accounting for buildings
Suppliers' agreement (MT)

b) Steps through transition:

Communication to employees
Performance measures
Payroll processing and spreadsheets (ST)
Suggested incentives
Business continuity (MT)

TIP: Bring out those specifics of the case that make it necessary to reshuffle the Presentation page header--Date, To, From, Subject--so as to adapt the form to fit any particular requirement. For example, it might be useful to indicate the name and address of the recipient in a "letter to the creditor."

TIP: Provide examples of students wasting time drafting overlong introductions to the report required.

2- Solving problems or issues

I am referring here to the actual text of the response, which usually starts on a new page where each new problem or issue is introduced. A very useful way of organizing one's thoughts is to regularly include headings and subheadings that detail the problem or issue to be solved, along with the subject or aspect that needs to be dealt with. A clear heading provides the reader with a rapid focus while at the same time helping the student minimize unnecessary repetitions of the case. Thus, it would be preferable to write the heading "Obsolescence provision" rather than "Inventory." (CASE B) Or again, a heading such as "Supplier adherence to terms of agreement" is preferable to "Suppliers." (CASE A)

TIP: Provide examples of responses that lack organization or, for example, where the subjects are dealt with every which way.

TIP: Show that the use of headings such as "ANALYSIS", "PROBLEM SOLVING" or "NEW DIVISION" is quite useless; provide examples where the headings and subheadings are used in such a way as to make the discussion clear and facilitate understanding of the ideas put forward.

When the case is long, I would suggest that one thinks in terms of providing an "overall" integrative conclusion, the type of conclusion usually found on the last page of the response text.

N.B.: Part 4 is more concerned with conclusions and recommendations.

3- Exhibits

In most cases, the exhibits are made up essentially of the various calculations required for the response. However, under certain circumstances one may find it useful to include part of the qualitative analysis in an exhibit, more generally in the form of a table. This table can include a list of the strengths, weaknesses, opportunities and threats, a list of the risks and opportunities associated with an investment project, or the major sections of an implementation plan (who, what, when, how much).

TIP: Tell your students not to erase or cross out the ideas contained in their worksheets as they transfer them into the body of their response. You never know! When the response is drafted on a computer, it is better to "copy/paste" than to "cut/paste."

4- Work sheets and checklist

Work sheets are generally read by the marker, since they constitute an integral part of the response. Occasionally, though not often, the assessment of a response is enhanced thanks to the ideas contained in the work sheets and checklist.

Objective: Determining the importance of problems or issues

The various problems or issues to be resolved should always be ranked according to their order of importance. It should not be necessary to explain that the more important subjects require a greater in-depth level of analysis.

The student who manages to work out the relative importance of the subjects will stand a better chance of success, since he will be better able to estimate how much time should be devoted to each one. One therefore needs to check out the information provided and determine what elements are important, within the case parameters (context, role, requirements). Of course, an employer or client may offer an opinion on certain subjects, but it is up to the student to take the various elements into consideration. For example, the Director of Operations may have said "not to worry about the lawsuit because it was initiated before GFI purchased CYOF, so GFI would not be responsible for any of the legal implications." (A4) One must realize that this is not true, and that this subject is important.

When determining the importance of the problems or issues to be discussed, I would suggest applying the following criteria:

Criteria to take into account	Examples
Amount of money involved	Given the 65 million dollar revenue and the scale of the other issues, such as the possible impact of Hurricane Baylee, the "cross-functional access to the files," which would cost $50,000, is not an important issue. (CASE B)
Time factor	In the short term one needs to comply with the conditions set out in the agreement with the current suppliers. In the medium term one needs to establish an ongoing validation process. The first subject is a priority and requires that the student go into greater depth than does the second. (CASE A)

Criteria to take into account	Examples
The specifics of the industry	In order to function, SableTel must hold an operating license (B3), which the CRTC has threatened to revoke! (B13) This, therefore, should be treated as a priority, all the more so since SableTel is the key to the growth strategy of the StarNova business. (B5)
Associated risks	The lawsuit initiated by a client constitutes a major risk. Apart from its financial impact, one should understand that it could lead to other lawsuits being initiated for the same reason. This lawsuit could also cause irremediable damage to CYOF's brand. (CASE A)
Role to play	Since the role requires the student to work in the Finance Department, i.e. as an insider, it is not surprising that tax issues are of lesser or little importance. (CASES A and B)

TIP: Discuss with the students how to determine the importance of a problem or issue, taking into account the various criteria that need to be considered at one and the same time.

TIP: Encourage your students to work out the importance of a given subject as they read through the case. Remind them not to lose sight of the requirements.

TIP: Point out that the presence of an important item in the financial statements does not automatically mean that it is an important subject. That will depend on the case facts!

Personally, at the planning stage, I separate the problems or issues to be discussed into three categories: (1) those that are important, (2) those of lesser importance, and (3) those that are of little importance (or secondary). From experience, I know that to write a successful case it is essential to deal with <u>all</u> the important subjects and with <u>most</u> of the others. Subjects of little importance may be set aside or dealt with very speedily. For example, if there are six accounting issues to be discussed, and 30 minutes to write about them, it would hardly be appropriate to automatically allocate five minutes to each one. One needs to be very attentive when determining the relative importance of each subject.

Thus, as we show below, using CASE B, a student may decide that the accounting treatment of the government grant is an important subject. On the other hand, he may find it of lesser importance to discuss the presentation of this grant in the financial statements. This means that we need to individually assess each aspect and subtopic of a problem or issue. The fact that the subject of the grant matters does not mean that all grant-related aspects are also important.

Subject	Aspects to be analyzed	Importance of the aspect to be analyzed
Inventory	– Determining whether or not to record a provision – Estimating the writedown amount	– important – important
Research and Development	– Determining whether the 2010 costs can be capitalized – Knowing what to do with the 2009 costs – Discussing the presentation in the financial statements	– important – of little importance – of lesser importance*
Government grant	– Determining whether the grant must be recognized – Discussing the presentation in the financial statements	– important – of lesser importance*
Mobile network	– Determining whether or not to record an impairment – Determining whether this is an individual asset or a cash-generating unit – Determining the recoverable amount AND estimating the impairment loss	– important – important – of lesser importance
CRTC Fees	– Correcting the accounting error	– of lesser importance
Deferred revenues	– Recording billing in advance	– of little importance

* In general, presentation in the financial statements is an aspect of little importance. However, taking into account the impact on subsequent analyses, such as performance evaluation (ratios), it is more important in this case.

CASE A: The information regarding accounting for the buildings is presented prior to that regarding the lawsuit. However, given the risks associated with the lawsuit, it is not surprising that this subject is discussed prior to the accounting issue.

TIP: Mention to your students that the order in which subjects are presented in the text or in the exhibits attached to a case rarely corresponds to their importance.

TIP: Point out to the students that they need to deal with each major requirement in a case, whatever conclusion or recommendation they came up with in an earlier part. For example, the fact that a recommendation has been made to reject an investment project does not preclude a discussion of the means of financing that must be retained, if this was requested. After all, the employer or client may still opt for a decision other than one recommended. If there has been a request to examine how the investment project can be financed, then this is what must be done!

In the short CASE A, one has to "identify and analyze the problems that should be dealt with on a timely basis." Consequently one should organize the problems or issues according to their immediacy. Of course, one has to deal with all the requirements, for example, the accounting for the two buildings, but one needs to first look into those problems or issues that represent the greatest risk for the entity.

Objective: Establishing a response plan

Whether the case is short or long, I think it is essential to establish a response plan. This means one needs to pause for breath between reading the case and drafting the response in order to make sure one is going down the right path. The response plan must include the list of problems and issues to be discussed, along with the list of the main subjects to be dealt with, taking the importance of each one into account. Those of little importance are usually omitted.

Most students work out their response plan in writing, while others do it in their heads. This will depend both on the length and complexity of the case and on individual personalities. However, my own experience has shown me that taking the time to write things down is really helpful when it comes to planning out one's response. This is particularly true when one has little case experience, and imperative when dealing with a long case.

TIP: For each case discussed with the students, provide them with an adequate response plan.

TIP: Explain to your students that it is not always easy--especially when simulating one's first cases--to make an accurate assessment of the importance of a subject. When one is asking oneself whether a subject is important, or of lesser importance, then that subject should be written into their case agenda.

TIP: Explain to the students how to make use of the annotations, the work sheets or the checklist in order to draw up their response plan.

The sequencing of the subjects must be considered when drawing up a response plan, since the analysis of one problem or issue is a common prerequisite to the analysis of another. This means one should, amongst other things, take into account the interrelationships between subjects, based on the fact that the options to be discussed may be complementary or even mutually exclusive, and that a calculation may be applicable to more than one subject.

In the long CASE B, the sequencing of the subjects requiring resolution is significantly affected by the interrelationships between them. Indeed, the acquisition of reliable and precise information is a prerequisite to:
- the estimate of the error in the calculation of the CRTC Fee;
- the evaluation of operating performance (ratios);
- the analysis of the variance between results;
- the evaluation of the likelihood of the budgeted results being achieved.

This means, therefore, that the analysis of accounting errors must take place very early in the case resolution process. Even though everyone agrees that the renewal of the CRTC license is a priority issue, one still needs to be able to evaluate the CTRC Fee calculation error using precise financial information. Consequently, the review of the CRTC Fee, which is a key aspect, will be presented at the very beginning of the response, but the analysis of the accounting issues come first. Additionally, the recalculation of the CRTC Fee must precede the preparation of the audit plan (risk analysis, approach and procedures) in order to bring out what is relevant for purposes of the analysis.

CASE B

Once the rank of the priority element, i.e. the determination of an accurate CRTC Fee, has been established, one needs to decide on the order in which the discussion of the following problems and issues will take place. First, stepping back a little, one will realize that there is a need to analyze both the "past" items (ratios, reporting document, variances) and the "future" items (strategic plan, budget). Logically, one will discuss these subjects in the order of their time frame, since observations regarding what is "past" can help better evaluate the "future." In the second place, one needs to determine whether certain problems and issues can affect the resolution of others. For example, first evaluating operating performance (ratios) and analyzing variances will make it easier to comment on the reporting document. Additionally, starting off by commenting on the strategic plan will certainly allow one to better evaluate the likelihood of the budgeted results being achieved.

Basically, when planning out his report, the student needs to be fully aware of the overall time allotted to him, which must be distributed between the various subjects according to their importance. Whether calculated mentally or on paper, one should have a clear idea of roughly how many minutes can be devoted to each requirement or subject. The time budget must be realistic.

TIP: Point out to the students, with the help of examples, that the order of importance of the subjects will not necessarily determine the order in which they are written about.

CASE B

I believe it essential to be aware, for example, that roughly 25 minutes (and not 45) are available to comment on SableTel's reporting document. Knowing that some 12 subjects can be discussed (comments and suggestions for improvements), one must also be aware that this allows about 2 minutes per subject, which is not really much. This means that the student needs to identify the most important subjects, so as to be able to deal with them at greater length (say, 4-5 minutes per subject). If we suppose that the student manages to provide an adequate discussion of four subjects in, say, 20 minutes, that leaves him about 5 minutes to come up with an analysis of one or two supplementary subjects.

TIP: Structure a response plan for a 4-5 hour case and share it with the students once the case simulation is concluded.

OR

TIP: Allow the students to read the case, draw up a response plan as a group (or in teams of two students), then ask them to draft the response.

OR

TIP: Distribute the response plan to the students when they are simulating a long case. The distribution can take place when the case reading is completed, just before beginning the drafting period. This is an especially useful strategy when they are simulating a long case for the first time.

TIP: Do exercises illustrating the planning of a short case. Alternatively, take one section from a long case, for example accounting for the new operations of the period, and allocate time amongst the various parts involved.

When I establish a response plan—which I generally enter under Subject on the Presentation page—I take the time to work out the reason for analyzing each problem or issue. In other words, I make an *a priori* determination of the response structure and of the type of conclusion or recommendation I am aiming at.

For example, if the question is: "What is the likelihood of the result being achieved?" (B5), one needs to come to a lucid conclusion: Is it likely? YES or NO? One needs to adopt a clear position, in line with the analysis. Or, faced with the following requirement, "Discuss the steps that can be taken to assist in the transition of the new employees" (A5), one must certainly provide a "list of" pragmatic recommendations.

N.B.: Part 11 is more concerned with response structures.

It is not always easy to determine what calculations are required to resolve a case. On the one hand, calculations take up a lot of time. On the other, one needs to make an accurate estimate of what is the least that must be done for the case to be successful. My own observations tell me that students have a lot of trouble planning out their calculations. In general, I would say that they overdo calculations and underestimate the amplitude of the task before them. I would suggest that they take into consideration the number of components required, such as adjustments to the restated profit (loss), since this might make it easier for them to plan out their time.

CASE B

SableTel operating performance evaluation requires the calculation of ratios––adjusted or not––that must be analyzed subsequently. A student may estimate that calculating each ratio, for two years, will take him 2 minutes, maybe 3 if he has to adjust the figures. Aware that he has about 10 minutes to make his calculations, he is already aware that he will have to determine which four or five main ratios must be analyzed.

TIP: With respect to each problem or issue to be discussed, bring out the major features of the response structures; ask your students whether they can identify the final "outcome" for each section.

TIP: Bring out the specific or difficult components in the preparation of calculations, such as working out revenue in a forecasted cash flow statement.

TIP: Help your students work out the time they will need to make a "standard" calculation, such as that of restated profit (loss), or of a "net present value." This will become a basic reference when they have to draw up a time budget.

One has to admit that sticking to a response plan is not easy, especially if the student is a perfectionist. My own experience has taught me that the best students tend to want to present a perfect response with respect to one or two subjects—generally those at the top the list—which leaves them with no choice but to ignore those remaining. Of course, if they do not cover all the essential subjects, their incomplete response prevents them from achieving the passing standard. Such students, therefore, must work out how deeply they need to go into a subject, while ensuring that they treat each important problem or issue adequately. One must also remember that a student who does not manage to complete his analyses and who does not have enough time to make suggestions or recommendations cannot generally achieve the passing standard.

In the short CASE A, the drafting time between *a)* and *b)* needs to be planned out. Of course, the planning out can be purely mental, but it must take place in order to ensure that all the important problems or issues are covered. An approximately 20-minute reading of this case leaves the student with some 75-80 minutes to draft his response. Since there are ten subjects to be dealt with, the student needs to recognize, at least *a priori*, that he has an average of 7-8 minutes for each subject. Though timing one's writing to the nearest minute is not essential, it should be clear that any extra time devoted to one specific subject will diminish the time available for the others. This is where the student has to come to terms with the fact that more time is required for certain subjects, such as the suppliers' agreement, accounting for buildings, and performance measures. On the other hand, even though they are important, some subjects—such as the lawsuit and communication with employees—require less writing time. Also, MT subjects can be covered faster than ST ones.

TIP: Make the students aware of the need to discuss every important subject in their response. If they have made a mistake in time allocation, advise them on how to select and handle the subjects yet to be resolved in the time remaining.

TIP: Encourage your students to develop an instinctive approach when it comes to organizing a response. Of course, they can work out a detailed response plan, but they also need to develop a sense of the priorities and of how to make the best use of the time allotted.

TIP: Provide students with examples where the response was not in line with an organized response plan and discuss with them what that means when it comes to assessing their responses. For example, the student may have evaluated the past activities (2010) and the budgeted results for 2011 in the same section (CASE B). This will make it difficult to determine the depth of the analysis of each separate subject.

TIP: Suggest to your students that they keep a few minutes "in hand" so that they can include a subject they had not been anticipated, or make up for the excess time they spent on another subject. For example, when simulating a long case, suggest they reserve 10 minutes or so to cope with unexpected extras.

As indicated above, since CASE B is long, I believe it essential to draw up a response plan. If you take a look at the one offered as an exhibit (B24), you will notice that:

- Its reading time is set at 90 minutes, which is reasonable. Normally, reading time runs from a quarter (75 minutes) to a third (100 minutes) of the full amount of time allotted for a simulation (300 minutes).
- For a given subject, the time allotted for a quantitative analysis is determined separately from that for its qualitative analysis.
- The approximate time allotted for each subject is reasonable; it is a good idea to provide for the time span of the longer subjects.
- The time allocated to each problem or issue is determined on an overall basis, by dividing up the total available time (in writing or in one's head) between the various aspects that need to be discussed.
- The major features of the response structure are brought out. Thus, as concerns performance evaluation, we find "calculation of ratios; time/industry comparison; analysis/interpretation" (B48) and, with respect to the strategic plan analysis, "P-I-R (problem-impact-recommendation)."
- Since this is a long case, the drafting of an "overall" conclusion is to be anticipated. This reminds the student that he needs to step back and ask himself whether the specifics of the case require that he write a synthesis-type commentary.
- Some extra time is allowed for in order to compensate for any oversight or calculation error, or for any faulty planning of a problem or issue.

TIP: Ensure that your students realize that the time budget needs to be respected, without too much leeway. With practice they will usually acquire an instinctive feeling of how much time they are taking, without needing to constantly check their watches!

TIP: Remind your students that the response plan is not strictly linear. This means that they should not assume that once they have completed writing on a subject they can forget about it and move on to the next one. Whether qualitative or quantitative, an idea related to a subject already covered can pop up at any time, even when you are in the middle of resolving the next ones.

Part 3
Drafting relevant ideas

If an idea, a sentence or a paragraph is applicable without any change to all cases or to any entity, this means that your response is not sufficiently integrated with the specifics of the case.

Accounting for Success, 2010, p. 73

Part 3
Drafting relevant ideas

"The challenge is to demonstrate one's theoretical knowledge while integrating it into the specifics of the case."

This section is designed to assist students in drafting relevant ideas and, to this end, provides three objectives: learning how to integrate ideas; knowing how to take the case facts into account; and ensuring that one's ideas are adequate.

Objective: Learning how to integrate ideas

Resolving a case requires that one provide a response that is unremittingly integrated into the case and its specific context. This means that each analysis, argument, piece of advice, conclusion or recommendation must respond directly to the needs expressed by the intended recipient of the report. This is not an easy task for students, more especially if they are still in the throes of their first case simulations. On the one hand, a case refers to a number of distinct subjects, subjects that are generally taught independently one of the other. Thus, for example, one may need to remember the criteria that must be met for an intangible asset arising from development to be recognized, or remind oneself that there is a specific accounting standard applicable to investment property. Additionally, considerable understanding is required to treat a subject realistically in a specific context. One has to be very familiar with the underlying theory (standards, rules, regulations, laws, principles, etc.) and be able to stand back and determine what will be useful in the case under consideration. For example, making an evaluation of the financing availability may be necessary to assess the criterion of availability of the financial resources required to complete the Wireless Technology Project. (CASE B)

TIP: Regularly provide your students with indicators that help them remember key concepts (e.g. the use of assertions in an audit program); take the time to remind them of the main concepts underlying subjects they have not been fully understood.

TIP: Allow students direct access to the various reference volumes during the case simulation, at least for the first cases.

TIP: Go back over the concepts that characterize a particularly difficult subject and develop short scenarios that allow practice at integrating theory and case facts.

TIP: Reveal in advance to students the main subjects to be dealt with in the following case. They may thus review them prior to the simulation so that, once into it, they can focus more on how to resolve the problems or issues.

Reading the CASE B makes it evident that the Mobile network has to be written down. The facts speak for themselves: "sixty of the 340 towers were damaged" and "the whole mobile telephone network was disabled." Most students will find the situation self-evident.
However, one should recollect the definition of "recoverable amount," which is the higher of an asset's or cash-generating unit's fair value less costs to sell and its value in use. Any student who does not remember that it is necessary to retain the higher of two values will provide a shorter, and certainly incomplete, argument. One needs also to determine whether the calculation of this higher value must be applied to "an individual asset" or to "a cash-generating unit." Yet again, students forgetful of this concept will, naturally, fail to bring up this aspect in their response.

There is certainly no doubt that one's ability to resolve a case is directly related to one's understanding of the theoretical concepts at play. Of course, there are writing strategies that are success-oriented, and one can also call upon one's intuition or general knowledge to help save the day: but all this can only make up partially for a lack of knowledge *per se*. When students need to call upon one or other of the concepts previously presented in their program of study, without being able to anticipate which one it might be, they will find themselves in great uncertainty.

TIP: Encourage them to make direct use of theoretical texts from reference works (an accounting standard, for example) in order to bring out theoretical concepts from their source, and not simply to rely on their memory. It is essential that they learn to delve for relevant concepts in the reference books.

TIP: Emphasize those subjects that need to be reviewed following a case analysis. There are always some!

N.B.: Parts 10 and 11 deal with different ways of retaining theoretical concepts.

When writing their responses, the natural reflex of many students is to sum up the theory applicable to a given subject, for example, the accounting treatment of property, plant and equipment. Subsequently, often in the following paragraph, they will discuss the specifics of the case under consideration, focusing, for example, on the accounting policy to be used for the buildings mentioned in the case. This approach, however, results in a lack of precision and smoothness in the connection between the theoretical and practical aspects of the case. Indeed, the link between these two aspects is simply non-existent and the marker has to consider only what is explicit, and not what is implicit. Consequently, students need to learn to simultaneously integrate theory and case facts, in order to demonstrate their professional skills. My own experience confirms that they have a strong tendency to parade their knowledge, without stopping to ask whether doing so is useful for either employer or client.

TIP: Have them practice drafting sentences or paragraphs that integrate theoretical concepts and case facts.

TIP: Provide examples of over-theoretical writing. Use an interactive whiteboard (IWB) in order to add whatever is missing, so as to provide a full discussion.

TIP: Present examples where the link between theory and case facts has not been clearly brought out. Explain that the marker cannot presume the existence of a link that has not been pointed out by the student.

TIP: Explain to the students that using the names of the entities or of the people involved makes for better case integration.

The CASE B brings out the fact that each subsidiary's reporting document is expected to meet StarNova's "Management Discussion and Analysis" (MD&A) requirements so that StarNova's senior management can easily incorporate it into their annual report to shareholders. Although it might be tempting, it would not be appropriate in this case to present the list of analyses usually included in a "Financial review by management". On the one hand a theoretical summary is not useful; on the other—and this needs to be said—it simply was not asked for!

Through my experience I am also aware that students often put down over-general ideas, ideas that could be applied to any entity. Or sometimes they will pick up a sentence as is, straight from the solution to a previous case. As illustrated below, they need to learn to use the case facts as much as possible, when writing the response.

Idea lacking integration	Idea integrated to the case
Financial measures can most certainly be used to always motivate employees and improve their performance on an ongoing basis. (CASE A) N.B.: The words "most certainly" and "always," are unnecessary.	Financial measures may be used to motivate **store managers** and improve their decision-making as regards **optimal product mix**, the **demand for each product**, and the **price that can be charged**.
A "management discussion and analysis" should describe the major changes facing the entity. (CASE B)	The **SableTel** MD&A should describe the major changes to its environment, such as the **financial consequences of the Baylee Hurricane**, or some indication as to **when the Mobile network might be back up and running**.

Objective: Knowing how to take the case facts into account

As mentioned in Part I, reading a case requires that one determines its parameters (context, role, requirements) and furthermore that one identifies the facts that influence the content of the response. Unfortunately, too many students, though they correctly determine the parameters of the case, later forget them. For example, they note from the start that the employees expressed "concern" about the change in ownership, but offer no means to reassure them. (CASE A) Or again, they mention clearly that the company is looking to generate a 15% return on investment, but ignore this fact in the rest of their report. In such a case, the information could be applied usefully at several points, for example when discussing profitability ratios or the evaluation of the budgeted financial information. (CASE B)

TIP: Remind the students that they should not invent problems or issues when the case provides no facts to support their discussion.

TIP: Remind the students that the number of facts or hints relating to a given subject is one of the elements to be taken into account when determining its importance.

TIP: Explain to the students that any discussion that is not based on valid case facts or hints will remain general or theoretical.

One needs to stick to the case facts in order to remain focused on what is required, and not deviate. Too often, students trot down hypothetical alleyways without having first looked properly at the case information provided. This is when you find them using expressions such as, "Yes, but if..." "Maybe..." "If I tried this..." "If management were able to change this or that..." In other words, they modify the basic data with which they are supposed to be working, and thus move away from their assignment, thus making their responses less relevant.

CASE A

The Human Resources Department (HRD) has considered introducing three incentives to motivate staff, and the student is asked to make a decision as to which to offer. It would thus be inacceptable to come up with a discussion about other forms of incentive, such as offering employee share options, if this was not included in the incentives proposed by the HRD. Since there is no suggestion or hint that one needs to look for alternatives to the incentives already on paper, ideally, simply mentioning the new idea is quite sufficient.

CASE B

We are aware that the company's objective is to generate a return on investment of 15%. It would therefore be inappropriate to react by making the following statement: "Given the difficult economic conditions, a return of 15% seems too high to me. I would suggest 12%."

TIP: Look at a case and point out where one could easily move away from what is required by putting in ifs and maybes.

TIP: Make the students aware of situations where they started the discussion with a hypothetical question; point out that by doing so they move away from the immediate considerations.

The preceding remarks are particularly important when preparing calculations. Too often, students base their hypotheses on facts that are not mentioned or even hinted at in the case, so that any adjustments they may make become arbitrary. For example, they may argue that "Since SableTel's financial position is not very good, I will write down the tangible assets by 25%." Or again, they may devote a long argument to a sensitivity analysis in order to demonstrate what might happen should one or other of the case's basic premises change. Thus, they might decide to explore the following assumption: "If the company were in a position to earn a gross margin of 52.2%, in line with the industry, it would generate a net income of $XXX."

TIP: Explain to the students that they should not "modify the case facts," "invent figures when they are already provided with the case" or "invent hypothetical facts."

TIP: Remind students that a sensitivity analysis consists of "studying the impact on a result of change in a variable." This definition is applicable to ONE variable at a time.

And where necessary, the sensitivity analysis will be short, direct, and targeted (for example, use of a different discount factor when calculating net present value).

One should not only use the case facts as such, but also be on the lookout for hints that may influence the response. There are certain words or expressions that affect the type of argument required, and they may sometimes point the student to the "best" conclusion or the "best" recommendation. *A priori*, one may appreciate intuitively how the analysis of a problem or issue needs to be carried out. For example, the following information: "To meet targets, sales staff will be given higher quotas. Senior sales staff will be asked to lead by example, and hopefully when they are successful, there will be a trickledown effect," implies a doubt as to the likelihood of the budgeted level being achieved. (B19) Having such reservations makes more sense than believing that raising the quotas will certainly have a positive impact.

Objective: Ensuring that one's ideas are adequate

Apart from integrating one's ideas to the case and its context, one needs to ensure that the ideas presented are adequate, given what is asked to produce. The trick I pass on to my students is to constantly remind themselves that they are working for an employer or client. An adequate response means one that meets their needs. I also remind them to be constantly aware of the case parameters and to regularly revisit the Subject of their report. As they move further into writing their simulation, students often lose sight of the requirements.

TIP: Remind the students that the case response needs to be focused on current and future problems or issues, on "what is going wrong" and "what needs to be changed." The reply needs to include only relevant ideas regarding "unresolved" questions.

TIP: Bring in some sample responses and ask the students to imagine they are the employer or the client and to ask themselves the following questions: "Would I be prepared to pay for this idea? And for this report?"

Students often decide what is good for the employer or client without considering their role or what they are asked to do. Naturally, anything that is not part of the work required is irrelevant. It is better to write down four or five relevant ideas than ten that are completely out of context. The purpose of resolving a case is not to make a display of everything one knows about a particular subject, but simply to transmit the ideas that are appropriate to the situation. Remaining focused on what is essential will prevent one going off track.

CASE A: One should not "suggest a list of different incentives that could be offered to the employees" rather than "discuss the steps that can be taken to assist in the transition of the new employees."

CASE B: One should not "provide management advice" instead of "providing a critical analysis of the document from a reporting perspective."

CASE A

The President specifically requests your advice on the accounting treatment for the two buildings owned by CYOF. This does not automatically signify putting on the table the accounting treatment of all the other aspects of the case, such as the acquisition of the subsidiary, or the amount that the former controller may have misappropriated. As regards the latter question, the ongoing lawsuit is the only other accounting issue that requires discussions, given its potential impact on CYOF's activities.

CASE B

The case contains enough information for a student to consider presenting both a qualitative analysis (risks and opportunities) and a quantitative analysis (cost-benefit), followed by a recommendation concerning the validity of the investment project. One must realize, based on the parameters of the case, more especially the specifics of the role and of the various requirements, that the analysis of the Wireless Technology Project is a secondary issue.

The fact that this subject is easy to analyze does not mean that it is important. Indeed, this is not one of the concerns of the Committee, the request being "to drop everything to respond to the issues raised in the email." The analysis of the Project is simply not on the list of requirements in Exhibit I.

Rather than bringing out the problems or issues that need to be discussed, and then structuring the response accordingly, some students put their efforts into anticipating how the case will be marked. For example, a student who thinks—or hopes—that an "integration" section will be part of the evaluation guide may offer such a section in his response. Another student will automatically anticipate a "taxation" section or a "governance" section in every case he simulates. I make it clear again and again that one needs to fully understand the specifics of the case and, above all, to provide what is asked for. The later assessment of the response can only reward such behavior.

The first stage in resolving a problem or issue is to identify its nature clearly and briefly. Subsequently, in order to come up with relevant ideas, I would suggest that students ask themselves the following essential questions throughout their analyses:

- **Why?**

  One needs to justify the ideas put forward by providing an appropriate explanation. The conjunction BECAUSE... is very useful, as is "since..." "due to" "given that..." "in order to...". Also, one needs to explain "why" one or other problem or deficiency exists, "why" such and such idea is valid or not, and "why" one has opted for this or that solution.

TIP: Make the students understand that the justification of an idea ("BECAUSE...") generally relates to relevant theoretical concepts or to the case facts.

TIP: Provide examples of student's responses and stress the lack of justification; show that the questions raised by the use of BECAUSE... may improve the quality of their analysis.

CASE B

In the response it is necessary to justify the opinion that the budgeted sales level is over-optimistic. One needs to state "why," making use of the case facts. For example, it could be mentioned that industry analysts expect revenue to grow by only 1.5% in 2011. Noting that the revenue figure has been overvalued is good, but the key fact here is the quality of the arguments put forward.

What is the impact?

One needs to take into consideration the consequences of what is suggested to the employer or client. The conjunction THEREFORE… will come in very handy, as will words and expressions such as "So," "Thus," "I recommend…," "You should...," "I conclude that…".

TIP: Present examples of responses from students who have not taken into account the consequences of the problems or issues; point out that the questions raised by the word THEREFORE may improve the quality of their analysis.

TIP: Explain which question requires an answer (Why?, What is the impact?, How?, Who?, When?, etc.) in order to ensure a full response as regards a problem, issue or given subject.

CASE A

We know that GFI receives higher prices for its products because they are biological and grown locally. It is therefore important to pick up on the impact or consequences of not living up to their commitment to the consumers. This could involve, for example, new lawsuits, a problem of public relations, a negative impact on the brand name, or a drop in sales. One must THEREFORE seek out solutions, such as the implementation of a vendor approval process.

How?

Resolving a case sometimes requires going into more depth as to how to implement the proposed measures. The important questions become: "What needs to be done?" and "How should it be done?" or even "How can we handle this?" Thus, an implementation plan generally includes the following elements: "Who?" "What?" "When?" "How much?"

CASE A

The validation process to be set up to ensure that suppliers meet the criteria laid down, answers the question "How?" (or "What needs to be done?")

The fact of "hiring specialists to conduct surprise visits in order to test supplier facilities and their ability to meet the standards" constitutes an action to implement. (A8)

In order to respond to the question "How?" the student needs to be able to visualize what takes place empirically and express in words the action he suggests. We should also note that the recommended action includes identification of "who" will carry out the task and "when."

CASE B

The procedures to be performed in order to ensure that the CRTC Fee is correctly calculated are a direct response to the question "How?" (or "What needs to be done?"). The fact of "selecting a sample of invoices from the billing system and tracing them through to the general ledger in order to ensure they are recorded properly" constitutes an action to implement. (B29)

In order to respond to the question "How?" the student needs to be able to visualize what takes place empirically and express in words the action he suggests. In the present example, it would be very useful to indicate the risk area that needs to be covered prior to drafting the procedure describing what needs to be done.

Finally, it is important to remember that resolving the case essentially comes down to resolving the problems or issues. Therefore, one should not be surprised to see more attention being paid to "what doesn't work." For example:

CASE A: One needs to analyze those problems that have to be dealt with on a timely basis. This is no place to list CYOF's strong points.

CASE B: One needs to identify the deficiencies within the executive reporting document, and also those in the strategic plan. This is no place to discuss "what is going well"!

Part 4
Writing new ideas

Do not finish a section, subject, analysis, calculation, etc. without providing a conclusion or a recommendation.

Accounting for Success, 2010, p. 101

Part 4
Writing new ideas

"The challenge is to understand the difference between MAKING PROPER USE of the case facts and REPEATING or SUMMING THEM UP unnecessarily."

This section is designed to assist students in writing new ideas and, to this end, provides three objectives: avoiding unnecessary repetition of case facts; diversifying the ideas contained in a response; being able to present conclusions and recommendations.

Objective: Avoiding unnecessary repetition of case facts

A case response should essentially include new ideas, i.e. elements of which the employer or client was unaware up to now. An idea is new if it did not appear earlier in the case in question or in the previous pages of the response. One has, therefore, to suppose that the recipient of the report (in this context the marker) is fully aware of the case data. In other word, students should not waste their time repeating or summing up the content of the case, since only the new ideas will be taken into consideration when the case response is assessed.

I have learned through experience that students tend to summarize the information provided in the case before moving on to resolving a problem or issue. Indeed, they sometimes repeat parts of the case word for word.

CASE B

The student might simply have repeated the following paragraph before settling down to the discussion concerning the accounting issue regarding the grant:

"During the year, SableTel received $2,750,000 from Industry Canada (IC) to assist with the development of its Wireless Technology Project. Once the project is complete, SableTel must share its technology with IC. IC will then formally approve the technology and will use it to support its own wireless initiatives." (B9)

This paragraph does not contain a single new idea. Of course, the fact that "the grant was received" and that "SableTel must share its technology with IC after the latter has formally approved it," are two pieces of information that the accounting analysis will need to take into consideration. Nevertheless, as far as the presentation of the subject is concerned, a heading such as "IC Grant" would be sufficient.

TIP: Present real examples of student responses where there are unnecessary case summaries.

TIP: Show how a short, clear title is enough to properly position a subject.

CASE B

Let us now look at the following extract:

"The Customer service Department plans to visit all customers (big and small) once every five years. Sales staff will visit those customers that are close to SableTel's office first in order to keep travel costs down.

While this may be a great way to enhance customer service, it is not clear that the benefits will exceed the costs. For example, visiting customers with annual revenues of $1,000 may not be worth the costs associated with the visit." (B55)

Since the whole of the first paragraph is merely a summing up of the case, a simple heading like "Customer Visits" is sufficiently self-explanatory.

The second paragraph has relevance, since it explains the way in which the planning of these customer visits constitutes a deficiency of the strategic plan. The theoretical "cost-benefit" aspect is incorporated well with the specific problem of low-level ($1,000) sales.

The last example shows clearly that there is a difference between "summing up the case" and "confirming the existence of a problem or deficiency." Students often confuse the two approaches and consequently waste a great deal of their writing time. In fact, they need to identify the problem or issue to be discussed, explaining it where necessary, but not indulging in a complete summary of the subject in question. In other words, there is a great difference between repeating or summarizing a case (as in the 1st paragraph of CASE B above) and making use of it (as in the 2nd paragraph). While the first approach makes for more fluid writing, the second is essential to a successful case response. To sum up: the various case facts must be used to justify, explain, assess the idea put forward. This process is an integral part of the resolution of problems or issues.

When dealing with calculations, it also happens that students waste a lot of time repeating the same ideas, or summing up the case. For example:

Students...	**Examples** (CASE B)
– spend too much time discussing the sources of the figures provided in the case.	There is no point in explaining that the calculation of the CRTC Fees does not include Internet and data service revenues and costs, since this information is already clear and evident. What matters is to look more directly at each of the items necessary to make the calculation.
– over-explain simple or obvious calculations.	There is no point in explaining how one calculates a gross margin. One simply needs to present the calculation *per se* without going into unnecessary details. The simple mention "gross margin of 45.8%" is preferable to "gross margin percentage = gross margin/revenue = $28,546,382/$62,322,224 = 45.8%."

Students...	Examples (CASE B)
– write out what is clearly demonstrated in figures.	There would be no point in explaining in the response itself that: "The calculation of the Fees payable to the CRTC will be made by taking 100% of net Canadian telecommunications revenue from long-distance, local access and mobile services while excluding related party revenue, less the qualifying costs corresponding to the cost of sales associated with long-distance, local access, and mobile services. Costs paid to non-Canadian entities and related parties are excluded from this calculation." Since it is fairly obvious what elements go into the calculation, the above qualitative summary is unnecessary.
– repeat the data as is and without any analysis.	It is unnecessary to repeat the financial information from the two columns of Exhibit VII (Actual 2010 and Actual 2009) in the response. It's quite possible to work from the case and remind the reader of the figures analyzed only when appropriate.

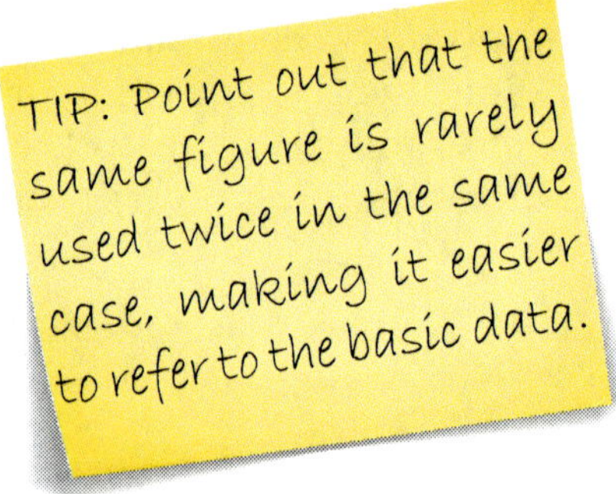

TIP: Point out that the
same figure is rarely
used twice in the same
case, making it easier
to refer to the basic data.

Objective: Diversifying the ideas contained in a response

So far I have indicated that the ideas presented in the case response should be relevant and new. I would now add another criterion: that the response should also show diversity, i.e. it should deal with a range of problems or issues. As mentioned earlier in Part 2, one must cover all the important problems and issues, along with the majority of the lesser ones. In fact, the time allocated in the response plan as regards the different subjects should take into account the objective of providing a diversified response.

> CASE A
>
> The President requests your advice on the accounting treatment for two buildings that are owned by CYOF. It would be preferable to deal with each building in a reasonable manner rather than focus in depth on just one of the two. Indeed, even if the analysis of the one were to be of exceptional quality, this would not compensate for the lack of discussion as concerns the second.

CASE B

When analyzing the SableTel strategic plan, one can pick out more than thirteen subjects for discussion. That is a large number. Of course, one does not expect the student to handle all thirteen, but it is essential that the depth and breadth of the response have a proper balance.

One needs, first of all, to determine whether certain aspects are more important than others. Personally, I believe that there are five subjects whose importance is dominant: Customers losses, Customers visits, Executive bonus plan, Hiring of sales staff and Compensation policies. All five themes should be properly discussed. I could next eliminate one or more subjects that appear to be of little importance, such as the cross-selling program. There would remain from five to seven subjects of lesser importance—providing they have all been identified!—and most of them, say three, maybe four, should be discussed.

To conclude, it would be quite unwise to deal in detail with only three of the thirteen subjects. Even if their analysis were to be of an exceptional quality, this would not make up for the lack of diversity.

The time allotted to resolve a case is limited, and we all know, by experience, that most students find that time too short. This is why I constantly remind them to write down as many new, relevant, and different ideas as possible. One must write efficiently, in order to best use the time available. Consequently,

Students must avoid...	**Examples**
– repeating the same idea more than once in the same response.	CASE B: There would be no point in repeating the same procedure three times when discussing the three different categories of revenue, i.e. from the long distance, local access, and mobile services. It is true that in Exhibit III the information breaks the revenue down into its three components, but that doesn't mean the same approach is applicable to the whole analysis. When the same idea applies to several items, these must be grouped efficiently.
– presenting the idea both as an option and as an argument, and then restating it in the recommendation.	CASE A: It is clear that the cost of replacing the roof can be treated as an addition to the asset and should be amortized separately as a significant component. Since there is only one way of dealing with this, there is no point in first discussing it and then repeating the same ideas in the form of a recommendation. Of course, the recommended accounting treatment needs to be justified, but repeating the same arguments twice is not useful.

Students must avoid...	Examples
– presenting the same arguments from different and apparently contradictory angles.	E.g.: "Inventory obsolescence has been entered under Cost of sales. I take this loss into account, since the amount is large and SableTel's inventory has a short life. However, I do not take this adjustment into account as regards the Cost of sales variance analysis." (CASE B)

TIP: Explain to the students that when there is only one possible solution, they may move directly to a recommendation. This approach is particularly useful when the time available to cover a subject is limited.

TIP: Suggest to the students that they use a comparative approach when analyzing two mutually exclusive options. For example, one does not need to first explain the advantage enjoyed by Bank A's offer of a rate lower by 0.5%, and then restate the same argument in its obverse form, i.e. that it would be disadvantageous to select Bank B.

TIP: Provide real-life examples of responses containing unnecessary repetition of the same ideas.

As concerns the actual writing of the response, it is often said that "the most workable ideas are those that come to mind in the first minutes devoted to the subject." Indeed, we know that the student has rarely time to hesitate or to indulge in lengthy contemplation when resolving a case. Consequently, it is usually those first minutes spent in drafting that are the most rewarding. In other words, if one is to respect the response plan, there is rarely much point in spending all one's time on the finishing touches. It's not worthwhile, since it means taking precious time away from the subsequent subjects. Those last minutes devoted to rounding out a subject are generally less productive than the first minutes devoted to the following one.

TIP: Encourage the students to put all their ideas into their responses. Some of them don't write down all their ideas because they are afraid of making mistakes or looking stupid. Sometimes one needs to take a shot!

TIP: Calculate the number of new--and different--ideas contained in a student's response. Point out, for example, that 16 new ideas, only 12 of which are relevant, are not enough to successfully pull off a 100-minute case (i.e. 42 marks)!

TIP: Suggest to the students that, over time, they compare the number of relevant and new ideas they bring out in their responses. This is another way of assessing progress.

I have noticed, over my years as a teacher, that students often have difficulty in properly structuring their responses. For example, they combine two (or more) subjects for discussion purposes, either because some case facts are relevant to more than one subject, or because they fall into a similar area of competence. Thus, a student may decide to pool the discussion of operating performance (ratios) and variance in results, instead of treating the two subjects separately.

I am not saying that this approach is necessarily bad. When subjects are combined, the ideas presented may be just as relevant, new and integrated as when each requirement is treated separately. However, students should be made aware that this will make it more difficult for them to determine the depth of treatment (the number of ideas) they have afforded each subject.

Personally, I prefer to resolve a case by taking each part separately. This is because an important aspect of case resolution is knowing how to take the context of each requirement into account. When the subjects are clearly separated, it is easier to remain focused on the specific context of each requirement. Obviously, as mentioned in Part 1, interrelationships between subjects do exist and students need to demonstrate their integrative ability. They will sometimes have to go back over a subject they have already discussed in order to do this.

TIP: Offer examples where the response covers more than one subject; count the number of ideas in order to determine to what depth each subject has been treated.

Objective: Being able to present conclusions and recommendations

Presenting a conclusion or recommendation is an integral part of a structured approach to resolving problems or issues. This end result of any analysis or discussion is essential, since it allows students to demonstrate their professional judgment. This means that the analysis of each problem or issue should end with a conclusion <u>or</u> a recommendation—sometimes the one, sometimes the other, and sometimes both. "This is where "Therefore..." comes into play.

I suggest that the students determine right at the start, i.e. at the response planning-out stage discussed in Part 2, the final aim of the analysis. This will help them stay focused on what is relevant. For example, the student must be aware of the need to draw a conclusion as to "the likelihood of the desired result being achieved." Or, again, he has to recommend "steps that can be taken to assist in the transition of the new employees."

I am aware, from experience, that students often find it very difficult to sound absolutely sure of themselves when writing a conclusion or a recommendation. Some of them are so afraid of making mistakes that they dare not take up a position and even go to great lengths in their writing to make their recommendations "look good," whatever happens. We need to remind them that they must strive to be accurate and trust in their conclusions and recommendations.

CASE B

Since it is necessary to obtain reliable financial information to carry out the analysis, one obviously should adopt a clear position as concerns the accounting treatment of the inventory, for example. One needs to conclude that an obsolescence provision must be established.

One should not hesitate or refrain from presenting a conclusion or recommendation on the grounds that the information is not complete. One can, of course, indicate that more details about the items in question will be necessary in order to determine more accurately the amount of the obsolescence provision. Nevertheless, this does not remove the need to draw a conclusion or make a recommendation by determining an estimated obsolescence provision now.

TIP: Show the students that the resolution of a case requires that they draw a conclusion or make a recommendation based on the information provided. Cases rarely come with all the information necessary for a full and perfect analysis!

TIP: Point out situations where a commentary merely underlines the evidence. Explain, for example, that no purpose is served in mentioning that the working capital ratio is 1.0, when that figure is already clearly indicated. Rather, one needs to interpret this ratio.

TIP: List the words or expressions that unnecessarily temper a conclusion or recommendation, for example, "It would appear that" "One might..." "Perhaps it would be possible to contemplate..." "I believe that arguably..." etc.

TIP: Bring together examples of sentences written is such a way that they do not indicate any clear position, the reason being that the writer is attempting to cover every possibility and avoid making mistakes.

TIP: Suggest to the students that they use the infinitive or imperative form to start off their recommendations (TO...). This obliges them to be sure of themselves when determining what actions have to be taken.

Recommendations need to be realistic and practical, and to take into account the specifics of the case. I am constantly reminding my students that they must play out their role by putting themselves in the place of the employer or of the client. Thus, if dealing with a 55-year old client who is wondering whether or not he should purchase such and such business, I ask the following question: "Would you recommend this purchase to your own father?" Obviously, it's not always easy for students with little or no work experience to come up with realistic and matter-of-fact recommendations. Nevertheless, there is nothing to prevent them from always taking into account the specifics of the case, such as the size of the entity, the number of employees, the business segment, production capacity, etc.

CASE A: We all know that accurate, speedy payroll processing is vital to the efficient working of a business enterprise. A simple and practical way of ensuring this would be to "Recommend the purchase of payroll software" or to "Suggest the installation of the same software that the parent company uses." (A11)

CASE B: Thus, looking at the size of SableTel, it would be normal to wonder if there was any point in visiting customers representing annual sales of $1,000. It would be more realistic to recommend a simpler, less costly approach, such as having customers complete a satisfaction survey or phoning them. (B56)

TIP: Warn students who prematurely jump to a conclusion or recommendation, more especially when dealing with an important problem or issue. They may find themselves dismissing rather too speedily some elements or options that are indispensable to a full analysis.

TIP: Make sure the students are aware that accurate detail is vital to a recommendation. They need to say WHAT to do or HOW to do it, and sometimes WHEN it must be done, and by WHOM.

TIP: Tell your students that it is better to suggest solutions clearly, even if they are mistaken ones, rather than to remain vague and to refuse to take any risks at all.

I personally believe that when drafting a conclusion or a recommendation, there are two aspects that need considering. On the one hand, as pointed out above, one needs to properly complete the analysis that leads up to them. On the other hand, one must seize every opportunity to identify interrelationships—more especially when resolving a long case. If this has not been done in the body of the subject analysis, it would be a good idea to take the time to check whether or not there exist any links with previous sections. For example, the earlier recommendation to stop doing business with suppliers further away than 250 km will need to be taken into consideration later when establishing the supplier validation process. (CASE A)

I also make it my regular task to urge my students to use their intuitive skills when drafting their conclusions or recommendations. Indeed, most evaluation guides reward conclusions or recommendations that stem logically and coherently from the analysis, whatever direction they take. Nevertheless, when reading a case, one must pay attention to facts or hints, even the most subtle, that point in a specific direction. For example, when asked for advice on the accounting treatment applicable to two different buildings, one should expect that the treatment to be recommended will not be the same for both. (CASE A) Or again, the fact that the Committee is "concerned about" the 2011 strategic plan and is asking for "suggestions for improvement" indicates that there must be some deficiencies to uncover. (CASE B)

TIP: Point out to the students situations where the evaluation guide requires a specific direction for the conclusion or recommendation.

TIP: Mention case facts that suggest a specific direction to the conclusion or recommendation.

It goes without saying that a case response will include a number of conclusions and recommendations regarding various subjects taken individually. It is sometimes a good idea to "take a step backwards" and to draw up a conclusion or recommendation that covers a number of the items analyzed.

CASE A

It would be appropriate to comment on each of the case facts indicating that the previous controller did not do a proper job: approval of suppliers whose rates were 20% higher than those of others; approval of suppliers located over 250 km away despite the agreement; cheques made out to him personally; staff unable to use the spreadsheets. Once all these ideas have been discussed, it would be appropriate to stand back and then draft a conclusion with regard to the ethical problems besetting the former controller.

In CASE B, one needs first to comment on the result obtained for each individual ratio, and subsequently present a conclusion that covers all the observations as a whole. This, for example, allows us to stand back and determine that "SableTel is not performing as well as its peers, both from an operational (income statement) point of view and from a financial condition (balance sheet) point of view." (B47) This conclusion is a good way of completing the section "Evaluation of SableTel's operating performance."

Under certain circumstances, more especially when dealing with a long case, one needs to contemplate the appropriateness of providing a synthesis-type commentary, usually to be found on the last page of the response. Thus, after having distanced themselves, students may decide to provide an overall or general conclusion, consequent on their analysis of a series of specific facts. Or else, they might decide to provide an overall integrative comment on the interrelationship between the various problems or issues analyzed.

The CASE B includes a large number of facts that lead us to an "overall" (or "general") conclusion.
Thus, the inexact calculation of the CRTC Fee, the significant errors in the financial statements, the deterioration of the company's financial condition, the deficiencies inherent in the activities report and in the strategic plan, and 2011 budget targets that cannot be met, are all signs which suggest, amongst other things, that SableTel will not meet the 15% return target in the future. (B69)

CASE B
We note a large number of links between the various subjects in this case. In fact, it often happens that discussing a problem or issue can impact on the resolution of another: for example, those items in the strategic plan that will need to be integrated with the budget. Of course, these links can be discussed while dealing with the subjects, but they can also be mentioned in an "overall" commentary presented on a separate page.

TIP: Before teaching a case simulation, carry out a Doodle survey, asking a few questions such as: "Have you presented an overall conclusion regarding the competency of the SableTel executive group?" (CASE B) or "Have you recommended the introduction of a suppliers' validation process?" (CASE A)

You could also make use of an in-class interactive survey tool, such as Turning Point.

TIP: Stress the usefulness of a conclusion or of an "overall" commentary; explain that a simple summing up of the various conclusions and recommendations is not what is aimed at.

To sum up, in order to ensure that the recommendations are correctly drafted, it is preferable to:

- Use a positive and constructive style to present the solutions or the actions that need to be taken. Mentioning "what doesn't work" is relevant when determining, for example, what the deficiencies are. However, indicating what must not be done is not the same as indicating what must be done.

CASE B

The following comment: "I do not recommend that you record the cost of replacing the roof as an expense," is not the equivalent of "I recommend that you record the cost of replacing the roof as an asset."

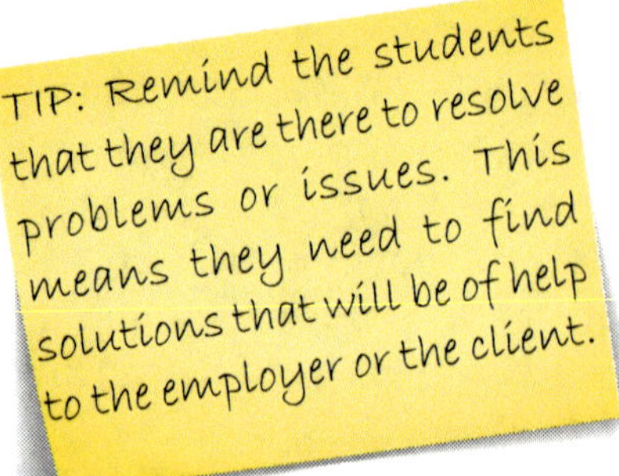

TIP: Remind the students that they are there to resolve problems or issues. This means they need to find solutions that will be of help to the employer or the client.

- Avoid the interrogative mode. Ending a sentence with a "?" is certainly not a good approach. One does not answer one case question by asking another. If the sentence ends in a question, the reader will not know whether it is supposed to be an argument, a conclusion, or a recommendation.

CASE B

"Would it really be appropriate to increase the sellers' basic salary on an industry base salary?"

An interrogative sentence may, of course, be used as the title for the subject under discussion. But the simple phrase "Sellers' salaries" is quite sufficient to alert the reader to the subject.

- Avoid conclusions and/or recommendations that are too vague or too general. If the sentence has no practical resonance, it will not be of much use to the employer or to the client.

CASE A

A sentence such as: "I recommend that measures be taken to ensure that the documents containing financial information are recovered," without further explanation, is not sufficiently practical. One needs to discuss the measures in question.

- Present conclusions or recommendations clearly by indenting it and identifying it for what it is.

Part 5
Presenting ideas efficiently

A simple writing style makes expressing one's idea easier.

Accounting for Success, 2010, p. 130

Part 5
Presenting ideas efficiently

"The challenge is to use concise and complete sentences."

This section is designed to assist students in presenting their ideas efficiently and, to this end, provides three objectives: giving priority to substance over form; using the right style; and adopting the right attitude.

Objective: Giving priority to substance over form

When discussing how a response should be presented, I turn to a well-known accounting concept—that of substance over form. My own experience has taught me that students waste time focusing on the look of their answer. They need to understand that a very well written paper that is lacking in ideas will not receive a better assessment than a less well structured paper containing several relevant and new ideas. We need, therefore, to ensure that our students do not waste any of the valuable but limited time they are allocated.

TIP: Explain to the students that they do not need to try and attract attention by writing in large or capital letters, nor use different colors, nor yet highlight, underline or encircle words. The marker or assessor is able to recognize a relevant idea, whatever its size or color!

TIP: Remind students to leave plenty of space, so that they have room to add ideas or figures where needed.

TIP: Remind students that ideas that have been crossed out will not be marked. Consequently, they should avoid erasing or crossing out text that might include valid ideas. They can simply put the discarded text between parentheses and write "draft" next to it.

TIP: Explain to your students that writing a text with perfect grammar and spelling is not an absolute must. The ideas need to be clear and accurate, but they do not necessarily need to be expressed in faultless English.

Students quite naturally—and in accountancy, quite understandably—want to make perfectly accurate calculations. When they are writing their answers, they often spend too much time on the quantitative approach to the detriment of the qualitative aspects. As was discussed in Part 2, one should not forget how important it is to stick to the response plan. Students need to understand that forgetting one element or dealing with it badly does not mean that the rest of their calculation is invalidated. It's not an "all or nothing" situation. For example, calculating the CRTC Fee is not a complete waste of time even if one has forgotten to include the adjustment regarding "costs paid to non-Canadian entities." (B27)

TIP: Explain to students that forgetting to include some less significant components of a calculation does not mean they have to start the whole calculation over again. Should this happen, they can simply insert a new figure without recalculating the end result. This is an especially useful strategy if the qualitative analysis contiguous to the calculation has already been completed.

TIP: Provide examples of time wasted in presenting a calculation. Thus, "Revenue from long-distance, local access and mobile services" could well be abbreviated to "Rev--long-d/local/mobile" while "Fee" would be sufficient when referring to the "CRTC Fee rate."

TIP: When using a computer to write a case response, students need to be reminded of the following:

- Not to overdo the various options offered (e.g.: bold print, italics, colors, display attributes).
- Not to waste time attempting to prettify their work by browsing through the various tools available on a word processor (dictionary, synonyms).
- To use the "cut/paste" function so as to transfer discarded texts to the very end of the response as a work sheet or draft.
- Not to include too much text within the same calculation software cell, such as Excel.
- Not to forget that the cell shows only the formula-generated result, and not the formula itself.
- To take into account the page layout, more especially when calculations are involved. Landscape format is to be preferred, so as to keep calculations on one page, wherever possible.

Objective: Using the right style

Clearly, I wish students to write their case responses in the most efficient possible manner. This is why I recommend that they opt for a direct, no-nonsense, and clear writing style. They need to get to the point and to convey their ideas without using unduly long expressions or sentences. They should also avoid meaningless sentences that do not contribute to solving the problems or issues. My ongoing objective is to provide students with tips that allow them to add more relevant and original ideas in their responses, while minimizing the number of unnecessary ones.

When drafting a response, one of the challenges is to use the right style. From experience, I am aware that students' sentences are either too short or too long. It is sad to realize that the meaning of the ideas put forward is often lost due to an inappropriate style—over-telegraphic or overelaborate. Personally, I believe that normally one should write full sentences, i.e. containing a subject, a verb and a complement. However, such sentences must express ideas simply, without unnecessary verbiage.

CASE A

Here is an example of efficient writing that integrates theory to the case, and demonstrates the usefulness of limiting oneself to:

one idea → one sentence → one paragraph

Replacement of the roof:

The $32,000 cost of replacement of the roof must be capitalized, since the amount spent extends the life of the building and CYOF will derive benefit from it over several years.
Under IFRS, the roof is a distinct component because its dollar value is significant, i.e. $32,000, compared with the value of the building, which is $196,000.

REC.: Amortize separately since its useful life will certainly be less than that of the building itself.
REC.: Ascertain the useful life of the roof.

TIP: Have your students draft a subject spontaneously while in the classroom, for example about accounting for the buildings, and ask them to make up sentences appropriate to the process. Then copy these sentences--unchanged--on the blackboard, or using an interactive whiteboard (IWB), where available. The latter will allow for various groups of students to subsequently access what others have written.

It sometimes happens that complete sentences (subject, verb, complement) are not necessary, for example when listing items that have one common thread. In such instances, one can omit the subject or the verb without jeopardizing the meaning of the idea. This situation occurs when the resolving of a problem or issue requires that one presents a "list" of items.

> CASE A: List of steps to be taken to assist in the transition of the new employees.
>
> CASE B: List of indications that SableTel is not performing up to expectations.

Additionally, as was mentioned in Part 4, when a series of actions need to be implemented, it is a very good idea to list them using verbs in the infinitive or imperative form.

> CASE A: List of steps to be taken when dealing with a colleague who has breached the Code of ethics.
>
> CASE B: List of procedures to be performed so as to ensure that the fees are correctly calculated.

It also happens that part of the response to a case may be presented as a table. When this is possible, I strongly advise the students not to hesitate, since a table both helps to better structure one's ideas, to facilitate identification of significant items, and to speed up the drawing up of the response.

> CASE A
>
> The determining of performance measures—whether financial or non-financial—lends itself to table presentation, as below:

Strategic objectives	**Suggested measures**

> CASE B

Specific risks	**Procedures**

> The two columns of the above table correspond to what was specifically required in the case in question. For a more complete analysis, it is useful to include two more columns: "Risk areas" and "Assertions."

From experience, I am aware that students need drafting guides in order not to forget all the aspects they have to deal with. Proceeding in stages is a way of ensuring a full and relevant response. As we saw in the examples above, knowing that the suggested measures must ensue from an evaluation objective, or that the procedures to be performed must cover specific risks will promote the drafting of relevant ideas.

TIP: Identify examples of situations where the presentation of a list of items or of a table would be an efficient drafting strategy (e.g. a list of risks and opportunities regarding the Wireless Technology Project).

CASE A

As requested, the resolving of problems that have to be dealt with on a timely basis should be undertaken in line with the following structure: Identification (of Problem P) – Analysis (or Impact I) – Recommendation (REC).

N.B.: The evaluation of the strategic plan required in CASE B may be carried out using the same structure.

CASE B

One may notice that the evaluation of operating performance (ratios) uses the following structure: 1- Calculation of the ratio, 2- Inter-year comparison/ Comparison with industry and 3- Analysis and interpretation (explanations, suggestions).

Of course, it is not necessary—though many students go down this path—to write, for example, the letters "P – I – R" on the case response itself. What matters is to remember each segment that needs to be dealt with, in order to hand in a complete response. In the heat of the moment, one may easily forget to compare ratios with the industry!

N.B.: Part 11 is more concerned with response structures.

Over the years I have drawn up a list of suggestions for students as to how to draft their responses. These are simple, but effective, the objective being to assist them express their ideas in a straightforward manner. Naturally, I put the emphasis on ideas of quality, while seeking ways to increase their number. Thus, I suggest:

- Removing introductory or presentation sentences that do not contain any ideas for resolving problems or issues. Relevant ideas need to be introduced as early as possible.
- Using easily recognizable abbreviations that are either common to business language or well known in everyday speech. The number of abbreviations in one sentence or paragraph should not be excessive.
- Sticking to a simple verb structure, so as to be able to focus on the substance rather than the form of the text.
- Writing clearly and accurately, making use as much as possible of the appropriate terminology so as to do full justice to the ideas set out. Vague or general terminology is to be avoided.

- Structuring one's sentences so as to transmit the essence of one's ideas while wasting no words. One should avoid encumbering oneself with unnecessary words.
- Cutting down as far as possible on link phrases, such as "However," "Based on the previous analysis," "Despite this," "I wished to tell you that…" and "Based on what I discussed in the previous paragraph, as requested by the President of GFI…"
- Making frequent use of titles and subtitles that precisely encapsulate the problems or issues. This orients the reader quickly and focuses the response on what is essential.

TIP: Offer examples where the use of parentheses can be especially useful to reduce writing time, such as by adding a clarification (for example indicating that the duration is counted "in weeks" [A10]), or giving the source of a brief calculation (e.g. calculation of the benefits of the investment project [B74]).

TIP: Ask the students what drafting problems they came up against when resolving a case. You can also carry out a Doodle poll and share the results. Finally, with respect to certain cases you might consider setting up a discussion forum.

TIP: Alert those students who use an over-telegraphic style, where too many words are skipped or shortened. The marker will not be adding those missing words on their behalf and the students will not be able to meet up with him and explain what they had meant to say!

TIP: Present real examples of writing that illustrate the following situations:

- "Empty" sentences that offer no relevant or new ideas.
- Over-lengthy sentences that make the text impossible to understand.
- Sentences so badly written that the reader can make neither head nor tail of the ideas being put forward.
- Generalities applicable to any entity without discrimination.
- Over-telegraphic sentences that make it impossible to understand the ideas contained.

Objective: Adopting the right attitude

When drawing up a case response, there are certain basic attitudes that need to be adopted. Indeed, when resolving problems or issues, the student must follow certain rules (implicit or explicit) that affect the writing of his ideas

Making use of professional language

The response must always be drafted using professional or business language. This means avoiding chatty expressions, as found in conversational English, that add little to the meaning of a sentence. If the language is inappropriate, the ideas expressed will not be sufficiently clear for them to be taken into account when assessing the response.

I also stress that the students' responses must be strictly focused on what is required. For example, one should avoid something like: "I did not take the 2% inflation into account in my calculations, since it was not my intention to make an in-depth analysis." The reason offered must be relevant and, where possible, related to the case facts. Thus, there would be no point in a comment on the difficulty of the case, such as "I know there is something special to do when it's a question of investment property, but I don't remember what!"

Playing the lead role

Whatever the case, it is the student who is best placed to resolve the problem or issue. He is central to everything, he is the only one to notice what is going wrong, what has changed; the only one who understands, evaluates, and resolves everything. Of course, there are other players in the case, but they do not have the skills or the objective approach needed to meet the various requirements. They are merely secondary players. For example, there would be no point in saying: "There has to be a chief accountant who knows how to account for the period's new operations."

On the other hand, the student does not have expertise in every field. An accountant is neither a lawyer nor an environmental expert, nor yet an IT specialist. He cannot, for example, juggle with the possibility that they will lose the lawsuit against a sick client, or decide that the previous controller is guilty of fraud. (CASE A) One needs to be prudent when making judgments and stick to our own profession's skills. It should also be noted that these cases never require the student to calculate the ongoing fee level. Of course, one can point out that a situation will have a negative or positive impact on fee levels, but the total amount is never mentioned.

Keeping in mind that the response is intended for an executant

The person who reads the report needs to understand its content and put the matter into execution without the need for any further clarifications. The language used must be directed to the resolution of the problems or issues (what has to be done and why) and to the implementation of the recommendations (how to carry them out), no matter who the addressee is. In other words, the recipient of the report needs to be informed in concrete terms and with precision of what has to be done (who, what, when). Nevertheless, one should also take into account the skills or knowledge levels of the recipient of the report when determining how much explanation will be necessary.

TIP: Identify examples where one is addressing a non-initiate and describe how this impacts on the resolving of the problems or issues. For example, if a legal counsel is the intended recipient, one may need to define some of the terms used.

Respecting the management practices of an employer or client

Knowing how to meet the needs of the employer or client is a fundamental rule, and it has to be taken into account at every stage of the drafting. Management objectives (e.g. a 15% return on investment), entity policies (e.g. all producers must be located within 250 km), risk tolerance, the biases and preferences of the stakeholders, etc. will all color the response. One needs, therefore, to take into account what the intended recipient hopes for, and not brashly overturn or dismiss elements that the recipient of the report holds dear. For example, it is not up to the student to query the 250-km policy. It would not be a good idea just to suggest eliminating this restriction in order to get round the current problems.

I believe it is important that the students remain objective—detached, even—whatever the situation they are analyzing. It is not their personal points of view that matter, but the point of view privileged by the employer or client. The students' personal, social, political or humanist opinions must not impinge on their analyses.

TIP: Mention to the students that it is rare to find occasions when a qualitative argument is a key aspect. It can happen, for example, when two supply options come to roughly the same cost; when the net present value is almost nil; or when the difference between the price offered by outside purchasers and local business people is low. It may also be possible when the risks attached to the issue are very high or the data used to make the calculations is very unsure or extremely hypothetical.

TIP: Get the students to understand that, whoever the intended recipient, one must suppose that he has some basic knowledge. For example, there would be no point in explaining to the StarNova Executive Committee how ratios are calculated. (CASE B)

Or, to take another example, to explain a performance measure to the President of GFI. (CASE A)

TIP: Show how the various management practices of an employer or client affect the response to a case.

Considering the monetary side of events

One of the intrinsic characteristics of case resolution is the importance of the monetary side of events. When a choice has to be made or a decision taken, the predominant aspect is usually monetary. Of course, there are places where the human or social aspects need to be discussed, but normally these are not major elements in the structuring of the conclusion or of the final recommendation. For example, there will be a recommendation to pursue the Wireless Technology Project only if the projected benefits (an estimated 5% margin) justify the risks involved.

Demonstrating one's honesty

When resolving a case, one needs to be honest and to comply with legal requirements, to behave ethically and to demonstrate one's moral rectitude. It is essential to ensure that GFI does indeed offer local, biological products, as announced to consumers. (A3) One also needs to comply with the CRTC Fee calculation method. (B12) It would not be appropriate to make a comment such as the following: "It's almost impossible for the CRTC to work out that the moneys paid to related parties were not excluded from the calculation." Of course, a professional accountant cannot allow himself to be associated with fraudulent, illegal or shady operations, such as money laundering or bribes! Finally, when one does detect a lack of ethical behavior in a colleague, one must immediately comply with our profession's Code of ethics. (CASE A)

TIP: Point out that it is not dishonest to attempt to meet the client's objectives. For example, a student working for a charity that is looking to obtain a government grant will try for the maximum possible amount. The student, then, will make an honest analysis in which he should ensure that he identifies all the relevant costs and suggest ways of allocating those costs so as to favor his client's position.

Being considerate

Students need to show consideration for individuals, more especially for their colleagues. Personal, direct or aggressive criticism should be avoided, particularly when it places blame on the person who will be receiving the report! One needs to be very careful and diplomatic when assessing the skills of another person and, from my own experience, I know that some students are rather too quick to recommend that an employee be sacked. As an example, I would suggest referring to the "report" presented by the Chief Executive Officer rather than directly discussing the person himself. And one should be even more careful if a "fraud" is suspected—it is not the accountant's job to pass judgments.

CASE B

One needs to understand that there are many indications that lead the student to doubt the level of competence of SableTel senior management, more especially as concerns the Chief Executive Officer. In such a situation, one would be well advised to temper down the analysis as follows: "There are numerous indications that suggest…" "It would also seem that…" "It is possible that…." As for the conclusion, which needs to be more specific, one more usually refers to the work carried out by the person in question, or to the relationship he established, rather than discussing the person as such. (B68)

Part 6
Making the right calculations

The assumptions included in your response are the result of a choice.

Accounting for Success, 2010, p. 96

Part 6
Making the right calculations

"The challenge is to properly determine the extent of the quantitative analysis that accompanies the qualitative analysis."

This section is designed to assist students in properly managing their calculations, and, to this end, provides three objectives: determining what calculations are needed; knowing what to do with calculation results; and presenting calculations efficiently.

pages 90-95

Objective: Determining what calculations are needed

I know, from experience, that students have trouble identifying the calculation required, more especially when they reach the point where they need to determine how far they must go. I would suggest the following actions as a guide to the proper handling of their calculations.

Clearly stating the objective of a calculation

I believe it to be important, right from the start, to determine what is to be analyzed or assessed. The fact of knowing what the aim is, i.e. being aware of the final outcome of the required calculation, focuses one's efforts on what is essential. Situations where a case requirement is closed-ended or clearly indicated create no difficulties. However, cases often include various data scattered here and there—not necessarily in an orderly fashion—and sometimes having no common basis. It is in such situations that the student is liable to waste time on unnecessarily long, over-complicated, or simply unsuitable calculations.

TIP: Tell students that the exact determination of the objective to be met finds its expression in the action to be undertaken. In other words, if the objective of the calculation is "To determine a preliminary estimate of the error in the CRTC Fee calculation," this allows a clear identification of its end result. The student will not only be calculating the 2010 fees payable, but he will also calculate the difference between that and the amount established in the Draft CRTC Submission in Exhibit VI. (B27)

Once the objective of the calculation has been determined, I would suggest that students take a step back and ask themselves how they are going to achieve it. In other words, they need to determine, as accurately as possible, the means they will use to implement their objective. Over the years I have come to realize that students tend to rush to the calculator every time they see something that looks as if it can be added up, divided, or turned into a ratio. However, when it is difficult to decide what to do with the figures, a simpler and speedier solution should be sought. It is easier to make later adjustments where necessary than to make up for time lost carrying out over-complicated or too detailed calculations.

TIP: Make students aware that a simple, short calculation is better than none at all! Often, because they lack time, or because they know they will not be able to complete their calculation, students will simply pass up on making one. This is a bad strategy because most business decisions presented in a case need to be underpinned, at least partially, by calculations.

TIP: Present real examples or discuss situations where calculations are not worthwhile. For example, when they see Document 1 of CASE A, some students will systematically calculate all the differences between this year and last year. Or they will recalculate the profit (loss) consequent on each of the suggested adjustments, rather than bringing them all together in one overall calculation. (B39)

Establishing one's working assumptions

The important calculations that lead to the solution often require clear working assumptions from the very beginning. This is often a problem for students who do not know how to go about it. Hence the following reminders:

Elements to remember	**Examples** (CASE B)
Assumptions included in the response are the result of a necessary choice.	– We could assume that items representing sales greater that one year require a writedown. One needs to justify the amount of the provision to be recorded, since it is based on an analysis of the situation, an analysis that may vary from one student to another. – As regards the $2,750,000 received as a grant, this is the amount indicated in the case. It is not necessary to explain where it comes from in the list of assumptions.

Elements to remember	Examples (CASE B)
Assumptions must be both realistic and reasonable.	For example, it would be inappropriate to assume that the complete inventory of routers and modems needs to be covered by an obsolescence provision. Not all items on hand are obsolete!
Assumptions adopted need to be easy to work with.	Assuming that a student wishes to make a quantitative approximation of the extent to which the Mobile network is impaired, he needs to make a simple calculation. Given the case data, a write-off of 60 or of 340 towers may be envisaged. The following comment would not be appropriate: "I am writing off 60 towers plus 45% of the other 340." Why 45%?
Assumptions must be based on case facts.	There would be no point in involving oneself in complicated calculations in order to approximate, say, revenue from related parties by establishing pro rata costs. This would be a very arbitrary action, since no case fact supports the existence of such revenues.

TIP: Take another look at case working assumptions and explain their usefulness and source. For example, it would be pointless to assume an inflation rate of 1% if there is no such mention in the case.

TIP: Provide students with examples of calculations made without taking case facts into account or prepared on the basis of arbitrary or unrealistic assumptions.

TIP: Show some genuine responses where students spent too much time explaining their assumptions; demonstrate how these can be reformulated clearly and concisely.

Planning how to make the required calculation

Apart from identifying the objective and means by which it can be realized, one must also plan out the structure of the calculation. In other words, one needs to know ahead of time the elements or stages of the calculation, and then determine 1- the important components, 2- the components of lesser importance, and 3- the components of little (or secondary) importance. Students too often integrate into their calculations all the data they have in hand without asking themselves what is important and what is not. This is not the best way of going about things, when one takes into account the fact that calculations take up a lot of the limited time allotted to resolve a case. Sometimes one has to deliberately set aside some components.

CASE B

It is obvious that an important objective here is to obtain an adjusted profit (loss), in part because the return on the investment is an evaluation criterion for the parent company. In addition, there are a number of accounting errors and SableTel went from a loss in 2009 to a profit in 2010, a result that "confused" the Executive Committee.

This calculation must include three important adjustments: R&D expenses, government grant, and inventory obsolescence. It is absolutely essential that these three adjustments be taken into consideration in the quantitative analysis. As concerns the impairment of the Mobile network, the uncertainty as to what the writedown amount should be makes it a toss-up as to how much should be assigned.

Finally, the other items (CRTC Fee and Deferred revenue) are much less important and can therefore be ignored.

TIP: Remind students that it is not necessary to present a perfect calculation. For example, it is not indispensable that the statement of financial position (balance sheet) balance out to the nearest dollar!

TIP: Help students work out the time needed for a calculation for each case under discussion; provide them with guidelines for the planning out of the minimum and maximum time required.

TIP: Bring out the major segments of a calculation. For example, for a fuller interpretation of the results, it would be useful to differentiate fixed costs from variable costs.

Being ready to update calculations

It often happens, particularly when dealing with a long case, that a calculation may be dependent on the discussion of other problems or issues. For example, an accounting discussion with respect to the inventory obsolescence provision will affect the calculation of the CRTC Fee via Cost of goods sold, along with the calculation of the current ratio via Inventory and Payable Fee (CASE B).

Though it is not always clear, one nevertheless needs, right from the beginning, to identify those situations which have an impact on the sequencing of subjects in order to plan out an adequate response. Ideally, taking the above example, one would start off by analyzing the accounting issues. On the other hand, a student might decide, of his own free will, to start off his response by correcting the CRTC Fee, simply because this is a key element. But he must be ready to go back on that calculation later in order to finalize and then interpret it. Since it is not always easy, *a priori*, to identify interrelationships between subjects, it often happens that students make calculations that prove to be incomplete a little while later. When this happens and if the missing component is important, one needs to be prepared to update one's calculation and, consequently, the resulting interpretation.

TIP: Explain to the students how they should handle situations when later information (whether important or not) modifies a calculation that has already been completed and interpreted.

TIP: Point out to the students that, under certain circumstances, some value will be given by the marker to a "tentative" calculation. This happens when the calculation is relatively complex or when few other students have considered making one. In this type of situation, presenting a simple, short, even incomplete calculation is generally enough.

TIP: Explain to the students who use computers to write their responses that it is possible to insert an adjustment of lesser importance into a calculation, while excluding it from the overall result.

pages 96-99

Objective: Knowing what to do with calculation results

In most cases, the calculation is part of the analysis but not an end in itself. In other words, the calculation is required because it allows for a more complete analysis of a problem or issue.

I regularly remind my students to check out the plausibility of their calculations before using them. Unfortunately, they too often juggle with figures mechanically without really thinking about what they are doing. For example, I find dropping from a profit of 1.2 million to a loss of 75 million very hard to believe. Maybe there was a calculation error; maybe over-adjustments, such as writing down the whole of the $62.5 million property, plant and equipment just because the entire Mobile network is disabled. (CASE B) In such circumstances, the student should lay down his pen, take a step back, and, where necessary, correct the enormous error that will otherwise totally wreck his interpretation. Without obtaining formal proof that the calculation is correct, it should be possible to determine a plausible range, or to establish some validating reference.

TIP: Explain to the students how to validate their calculations by using the case facts along with some common sense. For example, using "$275,000" instead of "$2,750,000" will certainly change the calculation result enough to attract their attention.

TIP: Point out to the students that it is not enough merely to refer to calculations. They need to interpret and explain them, or at least offer an opinion!

I also try and make my students aware of the need to take into account those case facts which impact the sense of future results. For example, as concerns CASE B:

Taking into account the following facts:	**It is to be expected that:**
– The Committee is confused by the results for 2010. (B3) – The Committee is concerned about the 2011 strategic plan. (B3) – The Committee is not sure that the initial CRTC Fee calculations are accurate. (B5) – SableTel turned the corner from a loss in 2009 to profitable operations in 2010 despite difficult economic conditions. (B6) – Hurricane Baylee hit SableTel in August 2010. (B10)	• The 2010 adjusted profit (loss) will be lower than the unadjusted profit. (B39) • The operating performance analysis indicates a lower performance than that of the competitors. (B47) • Variance analysis indicates a number of deficiencies. (B42 to B45) • The 2011 adjusted budget indicates a less favorable situation than does the unadjusted budget. (B62)

Too often I find myself noticing that a calculation presented in the student's response contributes nothing or at most stimulates a brief remark. For example, there is little point in writing: "SableTel's adjusted current ratio for 2010 is 0.7x." The student is simply putting into words what the figures show clearly, and from that point of view he is adding no new idea. In fact, every calculation should be interpreted and used according to the problems or issues that have to be resolved. The calculation needs to be integrated with the case facts or other elements of the response. It is within the interpretative framework that the student will apply his professional judgment and show his ability to use a calculation for specific purposes. The following list of items can improve the interpretation of a calculation:

Comparison	The results obtained may be compared against standards, against results from other years, or compared with the industry, in order to identify trends. For example, "SableTel's interest coverage ratio is worse than the industry average and has deteriorated further in 2010." (B48)
Usefulness of the calculation	One needs to remember the reasons behind the preparation of a calculation. Thus, when the objective is "To determine a preliminary estimate of the error in the CRTC Fee calculation," one can indicate that "the Fee as calculated is materially misstated." (B27)
Specifics of the case	When resolving a case, the objectives, the entity's policies, risk tolerance, restrictions, along with the biases and preferences of the stakeholders must all be taken into account. Thus: "SableTel's performance is much lower than the 15% return target." (B69)

One should never provide a calculation without an accompanying comment, interpretation, conclusion or recommendation. A calculation bereft of any accompanying text is not really useful. What makes the difference is not so much making appropriate and accurate calculations—all the students eventually master this art—as actually knowing what to do with them. One must therefore plan out a qualitative analysis, even when the result of the calculations does not correspond to one's expectations. Consequently, one will assess the risks and opportunities of an investment project even if the net present value turns out to be negative.

TIP: Point out to the students that most evaluation guides consider a conclusion or recommendation to be acceptable when it is based both on a qualitative analysis AND on a quantitative analysis.

TIP: Suggest that qualitative and quantitative analyses should be drafted side by side so as to provide a conclusion or recommendation that is complete.

pages 87-90 150-164

Objective: Presenting calculations efficiently

Calculations should be well spaced and easy to follow. I suggest leaving a blank line between each line of the calculation itself; even leave two lines, if the calculation is complex or temporarily incomplete. The extra space will provide for inserting a bracketed explanation, a new item or a working assumption. Each calculation should be presented on a separate page, in an exhibit, with the objective of the calculation clearly stated at the top of the page. However, very short calculations can be put between parentheses, or indented inside the text of the response. Finally, where the data permits, it is recommended to round out the figures to the nearest thousand or even million dollars. This does not vitiate the usefulness of the calculation and allows one to save some precious time.

TIP: Teach students to express their working assumptions in a clear and concise manner. Generally, there is no need for elaborate explanations of one's choices.

TIP: Point out to the students that they are not required to overdo the presentation of their calculations. There is no need to spend time prettifying the lay-out. For example, if the response is handwritten, perfect column to column alignment of the figures is not essential.

TIP: Tell the students that they would also do well to space out their figures, and to round them out even when using a computer. A well-spaced calculation is easier to understand.

I have learned through experience that it is better to list the basic assumptions that underlie the calculations in an exhibit, so that the reader may find in one place all the information necessary to understand the figures. This also makes it easier to write the response. My preference goes to presenting the working assumptions on the same page as the calculations. However, I suggest to my students that, when a calculation takes up more than one page, they should avoid interspersing it with working assumptions. Naturally, short assumptions (e.g. assume = $0) can be included directly in the body of the calculation itself. If they are bracketed, they are unlikely to affect the professional appearance of the response.

With a view to presenting calculations efficiently, making use of tables is one very useful approach. For example, efficiency is obtained by presenting side by side the financial ratios for each year. Doing it this way ensures that the name of each ratio calculated is written out just once. The references or explanations are applicable to each column. Additionally, when the same figures are repeated from one column to the next, it is faster—and visually better—to calculate a subtotal that will be brought forward.

When the case requires the adjusting of financial information, one should be aware from the start that doing so will take up a great deal of time. The student must first make certain this is absolutely essential to the resolution of the problems or issues. Next, he will need to clearly identify the items or groups of items that need adjusting. One is not always required to completely redo the statement when only one figure needs to be adjusted. What matters is not the presentation of a complete financial statement, but the impact the adjusted figure will have on the analysis. The calculation may, thus, contain fewer details and be structured differently from the usual financial statements. One should remember to give priority to substance over form.

In CASE B, for example, one can either completely start over a comprehensive income statement (integral approach), as in the official solution, or simply go straight into adjusting the profit (loss) (marginal approach). Thus, starting off with the actual profit, the necessary adjustments will be taken into account, and the adjusted result will be established, as follows:

SableTel
Adjusted profit (loss) (B39)

	2010
Actual (unadjusted) profit	$ 1,178,000
Adjustments:	
– Grant – classification [a]	–
– Inventory writedown [b]	(2,539,572)
– CRTC Fee [c]	(521,401)
– R&D expenses [d]	(9,160,250)
– Impairment of network [e]	(2,100,000)
Adjusted loss	$ (13,143,223)

a There has been no impact on the profit (loss) since the grant has to be debited from the revenue and credited to Administration expenses.

b The obsolescence provision needs to be recorded under Cost of sales so that inventory can be measured at the lower of cost and net realizable value.

...

Looking at the above example, we notice that:

- Figures could be rounded out to the nearest thousand dollars.
- There is no dollar sign. (N.B.: Measures other than $ need to be indicated.)
- The headings accompanying the figures are clear and concise; abbreviated more than they would be in a full text.
- References *"a"* to *"e"* explain the adjustments made to the calculations. Such explanations should be short and may accompany the calculation or be placed within the body of the text itself along with the analysis of the accounting issues. There would be no point in repeating them in both places.
- When income tax expenses need to be taken into account, it is preferable to start off the calculation with the Earnings before tax figures, to then present the list of adjustments, and finally make an overall calculation of the tax on the restated balance. I believe that such a procedure would minimize the danger of errors or omissions.

TIP: Point out to the students that writing "XXX" instead of the amount of an adjustment, explaining in words what should have been put into figures, or simply mentioning that such and such figure was forgotten when making the calculation, does not replace that calculation–which is not there anyway!

TIP: Check that the adjustments made to the financial information were fully understood by showing the students that one needs to end up with the same result, whether one entirely redoes the financial statement or whether one simply adjusts the figure in question. In other words, one proves the first result via the second approach... and vice versa.

TIP: Point out to the students that a $0 adjustment sometimes requires explaining, as in the case of the grant issue, for example. Although its impact on the profit (loss) is nil, one still needs to indicate the change as it affects its presentation in the financial statement. If nothing is mentioned, the reader will not be able to know whether or not the student has understood the notion.

TIP: Present real examples of over-detailed explanations of one or other of the calculation components. There is no point in using the exhibit to sum up what was explained in the qualitative part of the response, and vice versa.

Of course, when it is a matter of adjusting a financial statement, one needs to take the specific situation into account and choose the most efficient path. When there are many adjustments to be made or when the statement that requires adjustments contains few items, it will be faster to start the whole statement over again. You also need to take into account the later use of the adjusted figures. In CASE B, since the objective is to obtain reliable and accurate information with respect, amongst other things, to the analysis of ratios and variances, redoing a complete comprehensive income statement would be the preferred choice.

CASE B

The question of knowing whether it is better to adjust certain items or to redo a complete financial statement is a particularly prickly one when it comes to the statement of financial position (balance sheet). On the one hand, it seems to me highly possible that the student really won't have enough time to adjust such statement—or it simply won't occur to him to do so! A student who decides to make such a calculation needs to have realized the usefulness of obtaining exact figures in order to be able to calculate the ratios. That too is not certain.

On the other hand, a student might decide to adjust only certain specific items, those he deems to be the most useful and most important. In the present case, only two items will be used for the calculation of the ratios: Inventory in the current ratio, and Shareholders' equity in the profitability ratio. Consequently I see no point in redoing, in due form, the whole statement of financial position.

TIP: Remind the student that what matters in the assessment is not the obtaining of a precise figure, but rather the quality of the calculation components. In fact, mathematical mistakes are not usually penalized.

TIP: Stress the fact that things go faster when one determines all the necessary adjustments or calculation components prior to calculating the taxes or discounting the figures.

When it is necessary to adjust both the comprehensive income statement and the statement of financial position (balance sheet), I would suggest adjusting both statements simultaneously, as follows:

1- *Present any new statement on a separate page.* I would suggest preparing both statements side by side, as a single activity.

2- *Establish a framework for the statement to be adjusted.* I would suggest entering all the significant headings and items.

3- *Enter adjustments in both statements simultaneously.* I would suggest thinking in terms of "debit-credit" so as not to forget a significant offsetting amount and to ensure that the adjusted "journal entry" balances out. It will be more efficient to draft explanations that apply to both statements as you go along.

4- *Add up all the totals at the same time.* I would suggest only adding up totals required for the interpretation. Therefore, there is no need to check that the statement of financial position (or, as the case may be, the statement of cash flows) balances out!

TIP: Remind the students that it is only very rarely that journal entries per se are included in a case evaluation guide. It is the determination of the adjustment and the use one puts it to that matters, not the journal entry itself.

TIP: Remind the students that it is the adjustments or corrections they make to the financial information that matter. Consequently, they should minimize the time spend recopying data from the case (even though indispensable to some extent).

TIP: Take a given calculation and differentiate those figures that originated with the case itself from the new figures generated by the student; point out more especially those that derive from integration with other problems or issues.

TIP: Ask the students, as an exercise, to adjust the two statements in CASE B simultaneously.

Part 7
Analysis of the proposed solution and of the evaluation guide

Why?
That is the question you constantly need to answer when analyzing a case.

Accounting for Success, 2010, p. 170

Part 7

Analysis of the proposed solution and of the evaluation guide

"The challenge is, starting from the official solution, to determine what would be a realistic response."

This section is designed to assist students in analyzing the suggested solution and the case evaluation guide and, to this end, provides three objectives: going back over the case parameters; carefully studying the suggested solution; and bringing out the key elements of the evaluation guide.[1]

pages 168-172

Objective: Going back over the case parameters

The detailed analysis of the suggested (or "official") case solution, along with that of the evaluation guide, is an integral part of the case learning process. Despite this, I have very often noticed that students either do not know how to handle this, or simply skip reading the suggested solution and only take into account the evaluation guide. On the one hand, reading the suggested solution provides an excellent source of relevant ideas that also allow one to review a number of subjects. On the other hand, it is the cornerstone of any later assessment of a response.

TIP: Insist on the fact that learning requires a positive attitude. The suggested solution and the evaluation guide need to be studied, not criticized. Unfortunately, some students will say: "If the guide had been any good, I would have done okay with this case." In my opinion, they should rather be focusing their efforts on constructively analyzing and understanding their content, so as to perform better in future simulations.

One of the tasks the student needs to carry out when he is dealing with the suggested solution is to pick out the specifics of the case under study. This allows him to revise or add to the case parameters, and thus come to a better understanding of the content and structure of the suggested solution. In Part 1, I indicated the importance of properly identifying the elements presented below (context, role, requirements) so as to contribute to the success of a case. Here, at the time of the post-simulation analysis, one needs to fully understand what it implies.

1 Exhibits A and B contain many comments stemming from a thorough analysis of the suggested solution and of the evaluation guide for the short case (A7 to A24) and for the long case (B25 to B76).

TIP: Encourage students to analyze all the simulated cases, preferably within hours of the simulation, however well or not they performed. It's not only the result that matters!

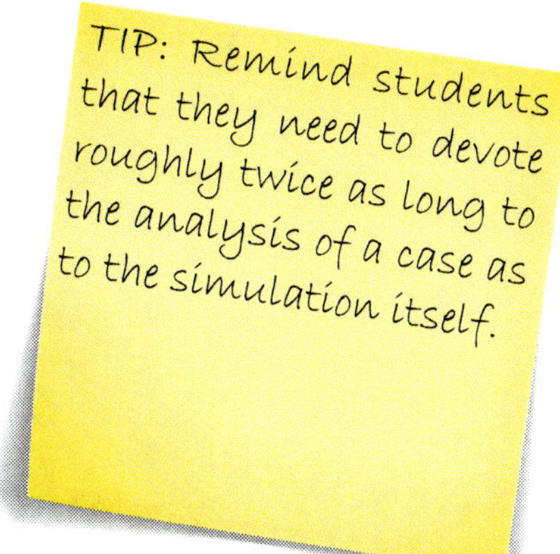

Objectives	**Examples** (CASE A)
Bring out those aspects of the CONTEXT that will affect the response.	The fact that CYOF clients are willing to pay a premium price for local, biological products affects the solution. This point is referred to on a number of occasions, including during the discussion regarding the suppliers' adherence to the terms of the agreement, when establishing a vendor's validation process, and when discussing performance measures.
Be aware of the impact of the ROLE, since this is what determines the angle from which problems or issues will be examined.	As a controller, it is normal that one should recommend the use of the balanced scorecard approach to assess the non-financial performance of the entity.
Understand the work to be done or the various REQUIREMENTS so as to provide a relevant discussion.	In *a)*, the President requests identification of recent issues that should be dealt with on a timely basis. This requires an evaluation both of the operational risk and of the urgency level of the various problems or issues so that they may be appropriately classified. It is thus not surprising that, amongst other issues, the implications of the lawsuit and of the former controller's behavior should be discussed prior to accounting for buildings. In like manner, the discussion regarding supplier adherence to terms of agreement (short term) will precede that concerning the setting up of a vendor validation process (medium term).

Throughout this reading of the suggested solution, I suggest that students examine the structure of the presentation, and this for three reasons. First, it highlights the analytic process used. Secondly, according to the importance of each subject, it helps determine the depth of each discussion. And thirdly, it permits the identification of the interrelationships between the subjects. By examining the structure of the suggested solution, taking into account amongst other elements the headings and subheadings, the student will be able, at least *a posteriori*, to identify the "ideal" structure of the solution. Thus, he will notice the following elements:

To be observed	Examples
Sequencing of subjects	A number of the comments made in the analysis of variances, of ratios and of the reporting document help complete the analysis of the strategic plan and of the budget. Understanding first what is happening at the present time will contribute significantly to the evaluation of what may happen in the future. (CASE B)
Stages covered when resolving a problem or issue	The analytic structure of the issue "Suggested incentives" is as follows: (CASE A) Employees' point of view: Qualitative analysis – perceived value Quantitative analysis – taxable – net value Employer's point of view: Qualitative analysis – cost-benefit Quantitative analysis – deductible – net cost Conclusion
Manner of presenting the subjects	CASE B asks for "an evaluation of the 2011 budgeted financial information and of the likelihood of the result being achieved." When one examines the suggested solution, one identifies the following analytical structure: 1- An adjusted budget is presented and includes three important categories: Revenue, Cost of sales and gross margin, Expenses. 2- Each important budget item is subject to a discussion that takes into account those previously discussed in the solution, to wit: – SableTel's performance from 2009 to 2010; – Industry past and expected performance; – Comments from the analysis of the reporting document and of the strategic plan. The discussion culminates with the drawing up of a working assumption that will determine the budget adjustment. 3- An overall conclusion on the "likelihood" of the result being achieved is presented.

TIP: Look at various sections of the suggested solutions and, as an exercise with the students, examine their structure in order to bring out the main elements of the response plan.

Objective: Carefully studying the suggested solution

The study of the suggested solution calls for active reading, where one is constantly questioning and thinking over the relevance of each component of the solution. "Why?" is indeed one of the questions the student will be asking very often.

It is important to be able to explain the presence and significance of each problem or issue that enters into the solution, taking into account the case parameters. This means that one's work consists in interacting with the case itself so as to be able to track down, *a posteriori*, the relevant facts. For example, one needs to target those facts that allow one to explain the ratios, variances or other deficiencies. Additionally, one needs to understand why the tax issues are only a secondary issue as regards the requirements. (CASE B)

Understanding the ideas in the solution

I believe it is absolutely essential that the student take the time to understand each idea, each argument and each calculation put forward in the suggested solution. Apart from understanding the case in question, he needs to take the opportunity to improve his knowledge of the various subjects dealt with. He also needs to bring out the links between the various problems and issues; interrelationships that may become apparent throughout the solution but which are more often evident in a conclusion or recommendation.

TIP: Insist on the fact that the suggested solution needs careful reading. Skirting a subject on the grounds that it is not very important, or that it is too complex, is not a valid reason. One can always learn something!

TIP: While reading the suggested solution, suggest to the students that they note down the subjects that need reviewing: those that were forgotten or not dealt with adequately.

Linking the solution to the case facts

Since integrating one's response to the case and to its specific characteristics is a basic condition for success, one needs to focus on those case facts that allow one to explain the content of the suggested solution. This analysis will help the students to understand how the response must be integrated into the case, as discussed in Part 3, with a view to their better reading of the next case.

TIP: Repeat the following exercise regularly with your students: take ideas from the suggested solution and look for one or more facts that explain the inclusion of these ideas.

Elements of the suggested solution	Case facts
"In order to determine optimal product mix, it is important to identify the demand for each product and the price that can be charged." (A10)	Exhibit 1 provides information by product category, including, amongst other things, the percentage of total sales, the number of units sold, and the average unit selling price. (A6)
"Therefore, Dan's explanation that this variance is a result of cost containment in the marketing area is likely not accurate." (B44) Comment: The two case facts cited are contradictory.	– Selling and marketing expenses presented in the draft financial statements have increased by $291,588 from 2009 to 2010. (B8) – "I understand from our Marketing department that the reduction is the result of their cost containment." (B17)
"Therefore, it seems unlikely that SableTel will increase sales by 15.9% over the next year." (B63) Comment: The number of facts and their meaning can only persuade the student that the sales forecast is doomed.	Several sales facts are to be found at various points in the case: a long-time employee of the Sales Department who will be retiring (B6), high turnover in the sales team (B16), loss of two major customers (B16), industry analysts expecting revenue to grow by 1.5% in 2011 (B11), etc.

TIP: Demonstrate to the students that the suggested solution and the evaluation guide derive directly and essentially from the case facts.

Making use of core concepts

I would suggest that the students, while reading the suggested solution, pick out the theoretical concepts—standards, rules, regulations, laws, principles, etc.—that are referred to therein, and observe how they are applied to the specific context of the case. In the examples below, we can see how theory (highlighted in green) and case facts (highlighted in yellow) are intermingled in the same sentence or paragraph.

TIP: Using examples, show the students how concepts used in the suggested solution are directly linked to the case facts. Theoretical discussions not linked to the case are rarely useful.

N.B.: Part 11 deals with subject info-cards.

CASE A

"Prior to this, however, legal advice should be sought as the controller appears to be acting in a criminal capacity as well, and is in effect stealing from the company. If he is in fact stealing, this would be serious enough to contact the association directly without speaking to him first." (A8)

CASE B

"The internal audit team will need to determine if there are any transactions with non-Canadian entities. First, they will need to determine the definition of non-resident entities for regulatory purposes." (B29)

"Given that both revenue and costs are decreasing in this category, we would expect that part of this variance would be the result of lost customer volumes (volume variances). However, the sales within this category decreased by 15.2% while costs decreased by only 4.9%, lending support to the assertion that the margin is shrinking as well (pricing variance)." (B43)

TIP: Indicate to the students that not dealing adequately with every problem or issue is quite normal, more especially during their initial simulations. When they first read the suggested solution, some students are discouraged and are convinced they'll never get through. In such situations we need to help them identify the basics for success.

Pinpointing the relevant ideas

The student needs to bring out the relevant and new ideas contained in the suggested solution. Since the solution is written as a continuous text, and presented as a professional report, one may expect to find a rather more elaborate, stretched out style. One needs therefore to be able to see past the style and pinpoint the ideas that the marker will take into account. The following page contains two examples where relevant ideas from the suggested solution have been underlined. Subsequently, you will see my suggested example of efficient writing, a potential student drafting exercise.

I would suggest that while students are reading the suggested solution, they should examine the way in which the solution is built up. To this end, I suggest that, amongst other things, they highlight those words that lead in to the ideas put forward ("because", "since", "due to", "given that", "in order to", etc.), those that introduce consequences or actions to be undertaken ("therefore", "so", "thus", "I recommend…", "You should…", "I conclude that…", etc.) and those that explain what needs to be done ("How can we handle this?", "Who?", "What?", " When?", "How much?", etc.).

TIP: From time to time get your students to rewrite some part of the suggested solution so as to bring out the ideas that are relevant to the case resolution, while practicing to write a greater number of ideas in the same lapse of time.

Relevant ideas taken from the suggested solution (CASE B)	**Efficient drafting of relevant ideas from the suggested solution**
Profitability ratios – "SableTel's return on equity ratio is below the industry average, and after adjustments it is negative. This indicates that SableTel is not earning an adequate return for its shareholder (StarNova). StarNova has indicated that it typically expects all of its investments to earn a return of at least 15%. SableTel is not earning a return that is anywhere close to this percentage. As well, after the 2010 adjustments, SableTel's ratios have deteriorated significantly from 2009 due to the large loss in 2010." (B47)	**Return on equity** – is below industry before adjustments and negative after adjustments. – is much lower than the 15% return required by StarNova CONC: negative return after adjustments VERY insufficient. – significant deterioration compared with 2009 (after adjustments), due to imp. loss in 2010.
Compensation policies "Salespeople at SableTel are paid a base salary of $45,000, while comparable positions in the industry pay a base salary of $65,000. Dan has indicated that this is done to encourage the sales staff to make sales in order to increase their commissions. There seems to be a large difference between the compensation offered to SableTel sales employees and the market. This may not be appropriate, and may account for the high turnover of SableTel sales staff and contribute to the lack of achievement of the sales targets. This policy should be reviewed to ensure that SableTel's compensation is achieving its desired results. If necessary, the base sales amount should be increased to ensure it is competitive with the industry. In conjunction with this, the sales compensation program should be reviewed to ensure that it is meeting its stated goals (in other words, increasing sales) while still maintaining its cost effectiveness." (B58)	**Salespeople compensation** There seems to be a large difference between SableTel salespeople base salary ($45,000) and industry base salary ($65,000). This may explain the high sales staff turnover and the lack of achievement of sales targets. REC: – Review compensation policy in order to achieve desired results, i.e. increase sales. – Increase base salary to compete with industry. – Review compensation program to ensure achievement of sales goals (quotas), as Dan wishes.

Note: The ideas in the right-hand column are expressed in the present tense and are practical, clear, concise and direct. The sentences are complete, the number of abbreviations is reasonable, there is no unnecessary verbiage, conclusions or recommendations stand out, and the use of parentheses is useful. Case facts are highlighted in yellow.

Understanding the quantitative analysis of the suggested solution

As mentioned above with reference to the qualitative analysis of the suggested solution, I believe that students need to make the effort required to understand the full quantitative analysis. Amongst other things, they need to consider the usefulness of the calculation when it comes to resolving problems or issues, the choice of means to meet the sought-after objectives, the choice of working assumptions, the source of the financial information used, and the link between the qualitative analysis and the quantitative analysis.

Looking at the suggested solutions, one notes that the quantitative analyses are often lengthy, detailed and laid down without worrying about how long it may take to do so. This means we need to identify which components are the most important, thus enabling us to determine what will be a realistic and adequate response. For example, looking at the CASE B "Variance analysis" we may notice the following, amongst other things:

Level of importance	**Elements to be discussed in the variance analysis** (B42 to B44)
important	– "Long-distance" category. These are the most important revenues as concerns SableTel and they dropped sharply between 2009 and 2010. One may also note that the cost of sales did not drop proportionately. – "Internet and data services" category. Revenues in this category had the highest percentage increase. – Selling and marketing expenses. There is an inconsistency between what the Chief Executive Officer said and the information obtained. This situation absolutely needs clearing up. – Administration expenses. There is a wide gap between 2009 and 2010 once research and development costs are excluded.
of lesser importance	– "Local access" category. Revenues are high, but the variance between 2009 and 2010 is reasonable and the cost of sales follows the same rhythm. – "Mobile" and "Internet and data services – routers and modems" categories. Amounts of lesser importance and nothing unusual as regards Cost of sales/Revenue.
of little (or secondary) importance	– Since SableTel has no control over the CRTC Fee, I don't see the need to discuss this aspect. – The negative variance of $90,000 made up of many "smaller expense items" is of little importance. – Although $2,750,000 is a high amount, one does not need to calculate the grant variance, simply because it is not recurrent.

TIP: Take a calculation from an official solution and identify the minimum basic components that should constitute an adequate solution, taking into account the time allotted. As an exercise, work out how much time is necessary to prepare an adequate calculation.

TIP: Draw up a "model" calculation in order to guide the students with respect to the content and presentation of a quantitative analysis.

TIP: Start off the discussion of a simulated case by analyzing the evaluation guide. The tendency is to re-read the case in class and then to discuss the solution. Why not do the opposite? In other words, simply take the evaluation guide and go back over the case to check out the facts that justify the presence of such or such evaluation criteria.

Objective: Bringing out the key elements of the evaluation guide

From experience I am aware that a thorough analysis of the suggested solution is an indispensable prerequisite to the application of the evaluation guide (assessment key). Each evaluation guide includes a list of the competencies (or indicators) subject to assessment according to the case specifics. For each evaluation competency, the guide indicates the criteria that must be met in order to pass each established performance level. The achievement of any given level generally means that all the criteria required for lower levels have also been met. I believe it is essential to provide a very detailed analysis of the content of the evaluation guide.

When one lays his hand on the evaluation guide, the first thing to do is to study its structure. This involves looking at the organization of the guide by identifying the various competencies evaluated. For example, the controller's potential breach of the code of ethics is serious enough to be treated as a distinct competency in the guide. (A15)

One then needs to establish a link between the suggested solution and the evaluation guide in order to understand the whys and wherefores of each criterion. Just as when analyzing the suggested solution, I think it is absolutely essential to find a justification for each component of the evaluation guide. One should not skip any of these elements, even if they appear to be too complex, or not relevant or important for the time being. One should be able to identify reasonably well the ideas required to deal successfully with each competency of the guide. For this reason, and also because the evaluation guide contains only the major evaluation criteria, or provides only a very concise text, it is essential to constantly establish the links with the suggested solution.

When carrying out a detailed examination of an evaluation guide, I suggest one should pay particular attention to anything that may make the difference between a successful or an unsuccessful case resolution. This means one needs to take the time to fully understand the criteria that govern the achievement of a passing standard, for each competency. For example, in the section "Management Decision-Making" (variance analysis) of CASE B, one may notice the following:

Objectives of the analysis	**Indicator: Management Decision-Making** (B42 to B45)
Establish the link between the structure of the suggested solution and the evaluation guide.	The suggested solution covers three main sections: Sales, Cost of sales/Gross margins and Expenses. The first two provide a breakdown by product category and there is a more extensive discussion of the major variances. As indicated in the previous table, there are four important elements. One can therefore expect that the analysis required in order to achieve the "Competent" level, will need to deal with the variances attached to three or four of these elements.
Spend some time on the words used to explain each criteria of the guide.	For the information to be "relevant to the Executive Committee," one must, using the case facts, explain the possible causes of the variances calculated. This is a requisite for the "Competent" level. In other words, simply mentioning that the variance is good or bad is not enough to meet the passing standard. At best, it will make one eligible for the "Reaching competence" level.
Identify the interrelationships between sections.	– Given the importance of Research and development costs, one needs to take into account the reclassification of these costs (B40) so as to make an adequate analysis of the Administration expenses variance. – Since the obsolescence provision for the router and modem inventory is a non-recurrent feature, it does not need to be taken into account when analyzing the Cost of sales variance. However, for integration purposes, explaining why this is the case would be a good idea.
Notice how "**and**" and "**or**" are used in different places.	The criterion "…**and** recognizes that a comparison with the approved budget would provide additional meaningful information" is the extra element required to reach the "Highly competent" level. In fact, the basic analysis of these variances should be carried out using the adjusted 2010 figures and the adjusted and approved 2011 budget. However, given the limited time allowed for this simulation, this would be an excessive requirement at the passing standard.
Identify the presence of an evaluation criterion that is determining, indispensable or unusual.	An "attempt" to analyze is rarely sufficient for the "Reaching competence" level. This is probably justified by the fact that few candidates (less than 40%) even attempted to analyze the types of variance. Here, "attempt to analyze" is a criterion that allows one to separate out those who did nothing! N.B.: This will probably not be repeated in the next case where a "variance analysis" will be required. In other words, an "attempt to analyze" is not going to become a requisite standard.

Objectives of the analysis	**Indicator: Management Decision-Making** (B42 to B45)
Examine the sliding scale that allows one to move from one performance level to the next.	Simply "attempting to analyze" variances is sufficient for the "Reaching competence" level. However, one needs a meaningful variance "analysis" at the success threshold of the "Competent" level. Its qualifying requirements are much higher than those imposed at the preceding level. N.B.: The difference between the "Reaching competence" level and the "Competent" level is usually less pronounced.
Take into consideration comments on the candidates' performance or markers' observations.	– "…for candidates to use the product line detail as well as other information provided in the case to make some insightful comments about SableTel's results year over year." – "To demonstrate competence, candidates were required to identify some of the significant variances between the two years and provide some insight into the variance, such as why it occurred, why it was important, and how it could be addressed." These extracts—with essential parts underlined—simply confirm the analysis presented above with respect to the interpretation of the suggested solution and the evaluation guide.

TIP: Identify as clearly as possible what are the "basic passing standard requirements" for each competency of an evaluation guide. Some students mistakenly believe that an evaluation based on competencies, known as an "overall" approach, means that there are no marking guidelines. This is not true. The way in which the criteria are applied is fairly precise.

TIP: Suggest to students that they make a note of every observation that stems from the analysis of the suggested solution and the evaluation guide. The specifics of the case under study should be brought out, along with those elements that may have something in common with previous cases.

N.B.: Part 10 is more concerned with case reference notes.

Part 8
Assessment of a response

A new and relevant idea is a successful idea.

Accounting for Success, 2010, p. 196

Part 8
Assessment of a response

"The challenge is to correctly assess a case response, without under-evaluating or over-evaluating it."

This section is designed to assist students in evaluating their response to a case, and, to this end, provides three objectives: identifying the appropriate ideas; determining the performance level reached; and evaluating the effectiveness of a response.

Objective: Identifying the appropriate ideas

It seems to me primordial that students take the time to mark each case simulation. Experience has shown me that they do not in fact pay enough attention to this activity, although it is highly beneficial. Most of them wish simply to obtain the evaluation results and learn whether or not they have been successful. Students should however recognize this activity as a constructive objective where the analysis of how they resolved the case is an essential part of their learning process.

TIP: Suggest that students keep a copy (or make of photocopy) of their response before handing it in to the marker, in order that they may analyze a case as soon as possible after the simulation.

TIP: Suggest that students identify the appropriate ideas in their responses, by providing reference to the criterion or competency of the evaluation guide to which each idea is related.

For purposes of evaluation one needs to identify those ideas that are appropriate, i.e. relevant and new, because they are the ones that are taken into account in the assessment. It is not always easy for a student to know when a written idea can be considered suitable, particularly when the evaluation is competency-based. Indeed, a sentence written in the context of a simulation is rarely identical to that found in the official solution of the case. The question to ask oneself is whether the idea written in the response means the same as the idea set out in the suggested solution (or in the evaluation guide), even though the words used are not the same. And the answer is that the use of synonyms is acceptable, providing the main idea is in the text.

Before recognizing an idea as being fully adequate, one needs to ensure that it is presented in the appropriate context. Therefore, one must not forget that the relevance of an idea is fundamentally dependent on its usefulness taking into account one or other of the case requirements. For example, "obtaining a legal opinion" is a good idea within the context of the analysis of those CYOF issues that need to be dealt with on a timely basis. (A5) On the other hand, expressing the same idea from the point of view of an external auditor, when that was not the role assigned, is quite irrelevant. Thus, when assessing the ideas put forward, one must pay attention to the context in which they are presented.

Idea proposed in the official solution	Idea not retained by marker	Idea retained by marker
"Moreover, bad publicity will have a negative impact on the brand and could result in a loss in sales if customers lose trust in us. (A7) The major idea is about the impact of the lawsuit on the "Organic Foods" brand AND on CYOF's business continuity. More specifically, reference is made to the impact on the company's financial performance.	"A customer became very ill after eating some of the vegetables purchased from one of the stores and filed a lawsuit looking for damages, something that could damage the company's reputation." The impact of the lawsuit is introduced via the expression "damage the company's reputation," but only generally. One needs to further discuss the "financial consequences" as such.	"The situation could impact the company brand, bringing down the number of customers, because they are worried about the environment and so are willing to pay more for CYOF products." The negative impact on the brand image, and its possible financial consequences, introduced via "bringing down the number of customers," are defined in concrete terms. So the important idea is there.
"Further indications that sales may be lower in 2011 are ... that its Mobile network is currently disabled and likely not earning any revenues." (B63) The major idea concerns the fact that the budget is likely not to be met because of the losses that will be incurred during the period when the tower network is disabled.	The Mobile network is no longer working. The company is contemplating bringing in a faster system. That will certainly have an impact on the 2011 budget. The "impact" resulting from the fact of the Mobile network being disabled is not explained. The idea that the 2011 budget will be compromised is valid, but vague.	"The budget does not take into account revenue losses in Nova Scotia and the expenses linked to the restoration of the Mobile network." (B84) The practical impact on the budget data is specified. The "revenue losses" and the "expenses linked to the restoration" result in a reduction of income. The response is acceptable, even though no direct reference is made to revenues.
"We need to implement a method of testing produce regularly for contaminants to ensure suppliers are adhering to the terms of the agreement." (A7) The main idea revolves round the need to carry out regular inspections on top of the initial inspection. It is also necessary to explain what may be inspected and why.	"I therefore recommend ongoing inspections and having this requirement written directly into the suppliers' contract." There is no description of how the inspection will be carried out. The text does not answer the question "What needs to be done?" The idea of having regular inspections is introduced, but not in enough detail to cover the specifics of the case.	"I would also recommend product quality controls after the initial inspection, for example sampling products when they come in. There should be employees assigned to this task." (A25) The idea of a control after the initial inspection is presented clearly. The example of the procedure to be implemented is sufficiently justified. The procedure is valid, even if it is not laid out in exactly the same terms as in the suggested solution.

Of course, it does happen that a relevant and new idea, one that meets the requirements within the context of the role to be played, is not mentioned in the suggested solution. For example, I believe the suggestion that "for now, a financial institution could look after payroll processing" would be as valid as a suggestion to "invest in appropriate software for payroll." (A11) In fact, we know that most evaluation guides are flexible enough to allow any relevant idea to be taken into consideration. However, we need to remember that a student cannot hope to meet the passing standard if he does not discuss what really matters and if he fails to consider every important aspect of a problem or issue. And, on this account, a suggested (or "official") solution generally contains everything that is important.

Many students find it very difficult to determine whether their idea corresponds to what is expected, particularly if its wording differs from that of the suggested solution. My own experience leads me to suggest that as long as an idea conveys the main sense, as illustrated in the above examples, it should be accepted. When in doubt, it would be more prudent not to retain the idea when assessing the response, but rather to inscribe "+/–" next to it. When uncertain, I think it is preferable to underestimate rather than overestimate the performance level achieved, more especially when meeting the passing standard is at stake.

TIP: Make the students realize that they need to differentiate between "what they know," "what they thought at the time," and "what they have written." All that matters is what is written in their response!

Many students wonder whether the concept of negative marking is used in the assessment of a case response. Not really. However, when one idea is contradicted further on in the text, it is not generally retained as part of the evaluation since the argument has become confused or imprecise. In other words, the student needs, as much as possible, to avoid self-contradiction or the uttering of incoherencies.

We are also often asked whether the fact of writing an "inexact" idea will negatively affect the assessment of the response. For example, a student may write something like: "The incentives suggested are not employee taxable, but they are employer deductible." This idea is incorrect. However, one needs to realize everyone—including students who have reached the highest levels—can come up with somewhat "bizarre" ideas. On the other hand, experienced markers and assessors have seen plenty of oddities, and their marking is usually not seriously affected by one or two untoward ideas. However, if a number of ideas indicate that the student is lacking in knowledge or professional judgment, this will probably affect the assessment of the competency in question.

TIP: While marking student responses, note down any ideas that are contradictory, imprecise, mistaken, badly expressed or incomplete. Draw up a list of examples per case.

As part of the learning process, I strongly encourage students to annotate their own responses as they mark them. They can thus comment on the content and underline their good and their weak points. For this purpose, they might use short annotations such as "because?", "CONC" (for conclusion), "REC" (for recommendation), "cont" (for contradictory), "INC" (for incomplete), "+/–", "W" (for weak), "dump", "R" (for repetition) or any other abbreviation they like.

pages 200-210

Objective: Determining the performance level reached

It is certainly not easy for a student to make an assessment of his own case response using a guide that only offers a broad outline of the evaluation features. This means that we have to provide them with guidelines, because case simulations are not all assessed by an outside marker. And even if the exercise is particularly difficult for the student tackling his first case simulations, he must nevertheless evaluate his current performance so as to improve his future performance. It should also be remembered that published solutions are made to look more formal and professional, and consequently are written in a more elaborate and elegant manner than is necessary. One must also keep in mind that the time allotted to resolve a case is limited.

It is true that evaluation criteria are not always described as precisely as one would wish. When the evaluation guide is of a very summary nature, it becomes more difficult to work out a *modus operandi*. For example, phrases such as "… discussed some of the risks," (A22) or "… discusses some of the relevant accounting issues" (B41) do not provide many marking guidelines. One then needs to find some way of defining the evaluation criteria in greater detail. In such situations, it is clear that a full understanding of the suggested solution is a trump card. Normally, this "official" solution easily meets the passing standard. All the important elements have been mentioned, in a context where time restrictions seem to have been less felt. For example, the variance analysis takes into account all the main sections of the statement of comprehensive income as well as each product category (B42 to B44). This is an "almost perfect" solution.

TIP: Get the students to understand that they cannot expect to meet the passing standard if they fail to discuss the important matters, although subjects of lesser importance will probably be taken into account at lower evaluation levels. However, such subjects of lesser importance do not usually make any difference when it comes to the passing standard. THE SUCCESS OF A CASE DEPENDS ESSENTIALLY ON HOW WELL IMPORTANT PROBLEMS OR ISSUES ARE RESOLVED.

In Part 7, I presented an exercise on how to identify the relevant ideas in a suggested case solution (page 76). It will certainly come in useful here. Generally, to meet the passing standard, the student's response should contain most of—though not all—the important ideas found in the suggested solution. It helps realize how deeply one has to go into the subject. Once the student has brought out the relevant ideas, he has to identify the approach or the analytical structure adopted in the suggested solution. The objective is to bring into the open every required aspect. For example, prior to calculating the necessary adjustment to the financial statements, one must have recommended an appropriate accounting treatment. Identifying the approach or the analytical structure is very useful since, to meet the pass standard, one normally needs to ensure that each important aspect has been taken into account.

On the following page, I present two examples of how to match the evaluation guide with the suggested solution.

TIP: As an exercise, identify the main ideas in the suggested solution with respect to a given subject. For example, it is essential to recognize that the risk associated with this engagement is high "because the CRTC license is required in order for SableTel to continue operations." (B26). No matter how good the other ideas put forward by the student, if he has not picked up on this aspect he cannot consider that his risk analysis is complete or sufficient. Of course, evaluation guides are "flexible," but this flexibility does not extend to the key elements.

Extract from the evaluation guide. The candidate...	In the suggested solution, one notices that...	To meet passing standard one will probably need to...
"Recommended internal controls that meet the expectations of the customer and that are consistent with the company's branding." (A14)	– This is a key aspect for CYOF, because there is a clear policy, known to clients, with regard to the source of the products (less than 250 km). – A number of justified procedures have been listed. – The procedures listed are precise, practical, and realistic. Reference is made to specialists, to CYOF officers, and to the purchasing department employees (Who?).	– Mention that the objective of the internal controls recommended is to ensure that suppliers adhere to CYOF standards. – List a number of procedures, no less than three and indicate "why" they are necessary. – Suggest procedures that are as practical as possible by explaining "how" things will be done, "who" must do them, and, where appropriate, "when" they are to be done.
"Calculates relevant financial ratios for SableTel and performs a meaningful analysis, comparing SableTel to the industry." (B49)	– Six categories of ratios are analyzed; profitability ratios and margin analysis ratios are important categories. – Each of these ratios is compared with those of last year, then with the industry ratios. – The solution contains properly thought-out explanations regarding the deficiencies picked out, along with justified recommendations. – The use of adjusted financial information brings out more clearly the fact that SableTel is not performing as well as its peers. – The solution does not offer other ratios than those presented in Exhibit IV of the case.	– Calculate a certain number of ratios—say, four or five—from amongst the two important ratio categories. Apart from calculating the ratio itself, one needs to make a comparison from one year to the other, and then with the industry. – Carry out a meaningful analysis of the ratios calculated, in other words an analysis that goes further than simply stating how SableTel is positioned in comparison with its peers. Using the case facts, one needs to explain SableTel's trends and position with regard to the industry, interpret the situation and then, where appropriate, make suggestions. It seems to me that such an analysis should cover no less than three ratios.

Apart from the foregoing, other elements such as those presented below may have an impact on the response assessment. They are well worth taking into consideration, especially when the evaluation criteria are over general or when one has the impression of being too severe or too generous in the application of the evaluation guide.

It is useful to...	Examples
– Take into account the competency objectives–expectations.	– "Did the candidate identify possible "fraud" and analyze the facts of the case and suggest further investigation?" (A15) Here, the three elements required to meet the passing standard are clearly established. The candidate who does not realize that he is dealing with a potential case of fraud, even if he analyzes the former controller's "actions," cannot hope to master this competency ("Assurance").
– Take into account the target level of evaluation.	I believe it is essential to act with somewhat greater severity when applying passing standard criteria, since this is a critical level. One can allow oneself to be a little more generous when dealing with lower levels, but not when the successful mastery of a competency is at stake.
– Read the marker's or assessors' observations.	– "There were a number of accounting issues associated with SableTel that candidates could have discussed, ranging from the need for an obsolescence provision for inventory to how costs incurred for the Wireless Technology Project (WTP) and the related grant received from Industry Canada should be recorded.)" (B41) This presumably means that these three accounting issues should have been reasonably well discussed by the candidate who achieves the "Competent" level.
– Take into account the performance of all the candidates.	– Assurance results showed that 41.5% of the candidates achieved the "Reaching Competence" level and 51.5% passed the "Competent" level. (B31) Experience has shown that audit planning and recalculation of the Fee are not subjects that the candidates find very difficult. So it is probably the description of the audit procedures that makes the difference. Looking at the candidates' performance one can see that, on the one hand, they did not find this subject easy and, on the other hand, the markers' expectations were precise. In fact, only those procedures which are specifically applicable to the engagement in question (CRTC submission correctly calculated) should be considered in the assessment.

TIP: Make your students aware that passing from one level to the next will depend on a number of variables, including the level in question. For example, it is usually easier to move up from "Nominal competence" to "Reaching competence" than from "Reaching competence" to "Competent." Similarly, it is generally easier to move up from "Substantially below expectations" to "Below expectations" than to go up from "Below expectations" to "Meets expectations."

Obviously, any response to a case must be marked according to the evaluation criteria. Additionally, one needs to be careful not to skew the process, unintentionally or not. My experience leads me to offer students the following list of warnings and to strongly suggest they keep them in the forefront of their minds throughout marking.

They must not...

– suppose that a very good theoretical essay will replace one that is properly integrated into the case.	Unless specifically requested, a theoretical essay is not useful in itself, even if complete and well structured. A student who demonstrates his knowledge without applying it to the case itself will not meet the passing standard and, in all likelihood, not even achieve the level immediately below.
– discuss ideas without being concerned with their quality or importance.	A student will not meet the passing standard if the only elements he offers are of little importance or relevance, no matter how many there are! The quantity of ideas cannot make up for their lack of quality.
– compensate for one element that is lacking with another.	A very good discussion on a subject of lesser importance will not compensate for the absence of any of the main subjects required to meet the passing standard. Likewise, a perfect calculation will not compensate for a weak qualitative analysis. For example, a remarkable discussion of financial performance measures will not offset an incomplete discussion concerning non-financial ones. (CASE A)

They must not...

– imagine that success in one competency will positively influence evaluation of the others, or *vice versa*.	Each competency is evaluated individually and objectively. In other words, the results obtained with respect to one given competency will not have a spill-over effect on the results of others. The student must show what he is capable of each time. N.B.: This comment does not obviate the need to point out interrelationships between problems or issues.
– presume on the facility of evaluation criteria.	When there is no specification or explanation as regards the application of a criterion, this does not mean that mastering a competency becomes automatically easier. One generally expects to find some mention of the consequences of a problem or deficiency. The fact that there is no explicit reference in the evaluation guide does not necessarily mean that this is not a passing standard requirement. I would be inclined to suggest quite the opposite!

Personally, I would suggest that students take notes on the evaluation guide itself at each step in the marking of their case response. For each competency, it is useful to enter a brief comment on each of the criteria, with their reference page numbers. It would be faster, for example, to assess the competency on "The need for ongoing communications with employees to alleviate their apprehension" (A19) if every segment of the response that deals with it has been identified and if comments such as VG ("Very Good") have been put in.

If a student wishes to check out his performance with respect to a competency, his first reflex should be to assess whether or not he has met the passing standard. If not—and that happens very often—he should take a look at each of the criteria for the next level below, and so on. This is the way to proceed when starting one's evaluation based on the passing standard. I know, however, that some students prefer to start their evaluation by examining the criteria for the lower levels. It is less discouraging! Whatever they decide, students should always make sure they have understood the basic requirements of the passing standard, because it is this level that makes all the difference.

TIP: Encourage the students to familiarize themselves with the criteria of the next upward level ("Highly competent", "Exceeds expectations". Most of them do not do so on the grounds that they are inaccessible or too complex. This is perhaps true as concerns the current case, but ideas at that level may be useful to meet the passing standard for the next case.

TIP: Point out that there is no such thing as a "single solution," which means that an evaluation guide is sufficiently "broadminded" to accept the fact that a relevant and new idea may be taken into consideration even when it is not explicitly mentioned in the suggested solution.

TIP: Encourage the students to mark each one of the evaluation guide competencies, even when they know in advance that they have not been very successful. They need at least to properly understand the criteria necessary for the passing standard, whatever their performance or the complexity of a given competency. For example, it is necessary to study the "Management Decision-Making" indicator, even if only 13.9% of the students have passed the "Competent" level. (B45)

TIP: Encourage students to validate their assessment upwards and downwards. Let us suppose, for example, that the "Meets expectations" level has been achieved. On the one hand, it is necessary to meet all the criteria applicable to the next level down ("Below expectations"). On the other hand, one needs to check that the response does not meet the overall criteria for the next upward level ("Exceeds expectations"). Doing this will confirm the evaluation.

I suggest strongly to the students that they mark their response to each case, but also that they make a habit of exchanging their simulations with their peers. Having their responses evaluated by other students allows them to:

– become acquainted with someone else's way of writing by observing the efficiency of their drafting or of the analytical strategy of a response that received higher marks;
- obtain a more objective evaluation. The other student marks what he reads, not what the writer of the response knows or wanted to say;
- bring some variety to the learning process, which is relatively long and too often lonely.

TIP: Suggest to the students that they evaluate their response to a case in order to be able to compare their own evaluation to that of the outside marker. One can also ask for the results obtained for a given competency using an interactive survey tool such as Turning Point, or via Doodle, which allows one to find out about results distribution by competency and by student group.

TIP: Put the students into groups where, for example, two students mark each other's response; or set up groups of 4 or 5 students and ask each one in turn to mark the same case for the benefit of the rest of the group.

TIP: Present a real example of a response and ask the students to proceed with its evaluation individually or in a group.

TIP: When a student marks another's response, remind him to be objective, constructive, coherent, encouraging, efficient and creative!

pages 210-213

Objective: Evaluating the effectiveness of a response

Quite correctly, a student's first reflex is to evaluate whether or not he has written a successful case simulation. Naturally, the fact that he has met all the basic passing standard requirements of each of the guide's competencies is the first indication of the quality of his performance. Nevertheless, one needs to be able to relativize the result obtained. When one of the competencies in the case is difficult to define or to deal with, the fact that one reaches a level just below the passing standard may be a good result in itself. Thus, when over 60% of the students have not even attempted to analyze the variance in results between 2010 and 2009, the simple fact of having turned in an analysis, even if one has not met the passing standard, is in itself excellent. (CASE B) Moreover, having noted the need for a disaster recovery plan, something most of the other students had not even contemplated, would be encouraging. (CASE A) When the information is available, one needs to take into account the comments of the markers or assessors, along with the strengths and weaknesses of the mass of students who simulated the same case.

Some students attach too much importance to writing or not a successful case. This is, of course, a natural and understandable reaction, but one should not forget that drafting a case is an ongoing learning process. Performance improvement is not necessarily something that follows an unbroken rising line. It has its ups and downs! One may very well write a successful case today and run into great difficulties tomorrow. Each case is separate and each individual has his own strengths and weaknesses.

TIP: Remind students that there is always room to improve their case drafting skills. It is a process that can be constantly added to, even when the results are already good.

TIP: Suggest the following exercise to the students: take their own response and add what is missing to meet the basic passing standard requirements.

Part 9
Report on assessment

Bringing out the strong and weak points is an integral part of the case learning process.

Accounting for Success, 2010, p. 218

Part 9
Report on assessment

"The challenge is to encourage students to persevere while at the same time underlining the weaknesses in their responses."

This section is designed to assist case markers or assessors to deliver a summary of their assessment and, to this end, provides three objectives: supervising the marking of a case; improving the way a response is assessed; and establishing realistic learning objectives.

Objective: Supervising the marking of a case

It happens regularly that a teacher or an instructor has to supervise the marking of simulated cases. Given the requirements attached to case teaching, it is often necessary to call on markers. Also, since the ongoing preparation of candidates for professional examinations involves a considerable amount of marking, this task is entrusted to a range of people for practical reasons. In the course of my years of experience, I have identified certain essential qualities of which I regularly remind the markers I supervise.

The marker or assessor must be objective.

The marker marks what he reads, without adding or removing any words. He cannot make presumptions as to what the student knows or wished to say. For example, one might be inclined to believe that a student understands that the additional CRTC Fee is a current liability in the statement of financial position (balance sheet), since this is a basic notion. (CASE B) However if this is not clearly written down, the marker cannot assume that it was simply overlooked or that the student was certainly aware of this concept, as a reason for taking it into account in his assessment.

From experience, I know that it is easy to allow oneself to be influenced by previous responses. For example, after reading three weak responses, the marker must not suddenly become generous in the fourth response because the performance has improved, or *vice versa*. Indeed, a student who has performed very badly with respect to the first two competencies in an evaluation guide may complete the third one very successfully. It is necessary to be impartial from one competency to the next, from one response to the next, and from one student to the other—especially when the marker recognizes who wrote the simulation.

Finally, one must look beyond bad handwriting or poor drafting in order to assess the quality of the ideas put forward.

TIP: Take the time to clarify the requirements for each level, more especially when the passing standard is involved. One needs to clearly establish what elements are indispensable to the mastering of a competency.

TIP: Keep your marking anonymous, more especially as concerns official examinations. This ensures that no one can say that the best student in the group was favored!

The marker or assessor must be consistent.

The way in which the marker applies the evaluation criteria over time must be even and steady, in order to be fair and so that each student can reliably compare his performance with that of the group. In real life, some markers are naturally a little more severe or a little more generous than others. Up to a certain point, this doesn't really matter, providing they are even-handed from one simulation to the next. It is especially important to maintain the steady nature of the passing standard requirements.

Of course, if more than one marker is involved with the same simulation, they need to come to an agreement as to how they will apply the evaluation guide. Personally, I would suggest that markers always read a few student responses—without lifting the red pen—before starting their marking *per se.*

TIP: Ask markers to simulate the case before they start marking it. This helps set more realistic expectations as to what an "average" student can achieve in the time allotted. As we all tend to ask the best students to act as "markers," we also need to be aware that they may be more demanding than necessary.

TIP: Ask the markers to pass on the results of their own simulation, via a Doodle survey, for example, to allow for comparison of the results obtained by the members of the marking team. A marker who has handed in his result may then have access to the group results as a whole, and to the assessment wished for by the teacher.

The marker or assessor must be flexible.

The objective of an assessment is to properly reward the ideas expressed by the students. With this in mind, the marker must be sufficiently flexible to adjust his evaluation so that it reflects the group's performance. Without making any drastic changes, one can adjust one's way of marking so as to single out those students who have done better than the others.

If all the students are at the "Substantially below expectations" or "Nominal competence" levels, this won't be very useful.

Personally, after marking some ten percent of the group simulations, I sometimes review the evaluation guide. For example, if only a few students have discussed the usefulness of the balanced scorecard for determining performance measures, I may slightly adjust the evaluation criteria accordingly. Thus, I could possibly attribute the "Below expectations" level to students who have picked out two to three factors (instead of three or four). (A18) The idea here would be to bring up the performance level of those students who have at least worked on this aspect. For example, an "attempt" to analyze areas of variance may be sufficient to achieve the "Reaching competence" level. (B45)

TIP: Use a sliding scale within the same level, more especially for those close to the passing standard. For example, one might add a classification such as "strong", "average" or "weak" to a "Reaching competence" result. This helps the student to better situate his evaluation and measure his progress.

Objective: Improving the way a response is assessed

For most students, case learning is not something easy, partly because the results of the first simulations are generally low. In fact, students should expect to wait a fair time before meeting "passing standard" requirements. They do so occasionally, but only as concerns a few competencies. With some students, it only happens once they get to the official examination! It should also be pointed out that the results obtained orbit round the passing standard and are basically somewhere between the "Below expectations" and "Meeting expectations" levels, or between the "Reaching competence" and "Competent" levels. For certain responses, there is not really much difference between one or the other. One must admit that it is not always easy for a student to remain motivated in such circumstances.

Based on my own experience in case teaching and marking, I believe it is important to provide students with information other than the result they have achieved for each competency contained in the evaluation guide. In order to guide a student as he goes through the learning process, I offer a considerable number of comments on the responses I mark. This I do in two stages. First, as I read the response, I use key words or short expressions—often in question form—so that the student is immediately aware of his performance, whether positive or negative. I find short sentences such as, "How should it be done?" or "What theoretical concept?" very effective.[1] My objective is to let him know concisely how I feel about the content—or lack of content—of the response. Here are a few examples of useful remarks that can be written on the students' responses.[2]

- "Your recommendation is good, but not justified!"
- "Mentioning the objective of the procedure is not the same as mentioning the procedure itself."
- "What does your idea mean? An advantage/disadvantage?"
- "You've listed the deficiencies… no suggestion for improvements?"
- "A three-page response with a whole page for the introduction? Whoa!!!"

---

1 Other examples: "impact?", "why?", "therefore?", "conc? (for conclusion), "REC" (for recommendation), "cont" (for contradictory), "INC" (for incomplete), "+/–", "W" (for weak), "dump", "R" (for repetition), "who?", "what?", "when?", "how?", "N/A", "vague", "general", "not clear", "off-mandate", "outstanding", "VG" (for very good), "OK", etc.

2 Pages A25 to A32 and pages B77 to B94 contain many examples of comments that could be found in a student's response.

- "The idea was not to provide management advice but rather to critically analyze the document prepared by the Chief Executive Officer," (CASE B)
- "Only two audit procedures: at least 5-7 were needed."
- "Your quantitative analysis is overdone: didn't leave enough time for the qualitative analysis."
- "Don't mix up internal control and internal management! Your ideas may be valid, but they are irrelevant to what was required."
- "You're not obliged to agree with everything stakeholders say. The Director of Operations is wrong and you should say so." (CASE A)

Next, I step back and examine the complete response so that I can sum up my comments and emphasize what matters. For example, the repeated presence of the word "general" clearly indicates that the student found it difficult to integrate the case facts into his response. I therefore try to analyze the performance from different angles, so as to be able to identify the major strengths and weaknesses in the response. With this objective in mind, one might ask the following questions:

- Where do we find the ideas that were taken into account in the assessment? In what section(s)?
- Were the important subjects discussed first?
- Was the quantitative analysis useful and adequate?
- Are there aspects of the evaluation guide that have been neglected?
- How many ideas are there that qualify as "CONC" or "REC"?
- Is the number of ideas with respect to certain subjects too high (or too low)?
- Where in the sentence or paragraph is the idea that was taken into account?
- Have the easier ideas been neglected?
- How many arguments are presented as part of the analysis?
- Have a sufficient number of problems or issues been dealt with?
- How many annotations "+/–" or "W" ("weak") are there?
- What specific elements of the case were left out?
- How many ideas are repeated ("R")?
- Does the response take into account all the important aspects required?

Of course, weak points must be picked out during the assessment, but possible solutions also have to be offered to the student. This is not always an easy task, but when possible, it might prove useful to use one or more of the following strategies:

- Strike out any excess paragraphs, sentences or words in the text, or in some part of the text, in order to show the student that there are shorter ways of writing what really matters.
- Place square brackets next to each relevant and new idea to make the student realize how few he has included or, on the other hand, how unnecessarily long his text is.

- Point out where the style is too telegraphic or the words too abbreviated for a marker to be able to understand the ideas put forward.
- Add a figure or two to the quantitative analysis in order to indicate to the student what is lacking for him to meet the "passing standard."
- Underline all those items that bring out a weakness that is recurrent throughout the response, for example preceding the analysis with a summary of the case, or introducing too many secondary ideas.
- Rewrite part of the text in order to demonstrate how ideas should be presented.
- Bring out the weaknesses of the response plan as regards time distribution between the various problems or issues.
- Suggest rewriting a part of the response—text or calculation—that was especially weak.

Since commenting on student responses is an important part of the case learning process, I remind the markers I supervise of the following:

The comments of the marker or assessor must be relevant.

I would start off by saying that any marker writing comments on a student response would certainly want to prove useful to him. I have no doubt about this. However, it does happen that markers write in comments—even though perfectly accurate in themselves—that are of little value to the student. Since the annotated marking of a response requires both time and patience, one must ensure that it adds something positive to the assessment *per se*.

One should not forget that the student has the case and can access the suggested solution as well as the evaluation guide. He can also access a large number of references, such as accounting standards and tax rules. Consequently, there would be no point in providing the student with a summary of the theory of accounting for investment property, or of accounting for government grants. The mention "Revise!" in the margin is quite sufficient. Likewise, I see no point in telling a student who achieved only the "Nominal competence" level for the Management Decision-Making indicator (CASE B) something such as "You got the variance analysis completely wrong!"

In a way, looking in from the outside, the marker or assessor should generally rather be making students aware of what they are not seeing or don't know.

TIP: Provide markers with a list of examples of comments on a specific case. Show examples of student responses with appropriate comments.

The comments of the marker or assessor must be constructive.

Generally, one can say that a marker's comments focus on one of the following three aspects:

1- the results obtained for each of the following evaluation guide competencies (more especially when the passing standard has not been achieved);

2- the content of the response (its coverage, depth, integration, relevance, recommendations, quantitative analysis, etc.);

3- the presentation of the ideas put forward.

Indeed, as was mentioned above, it is important to bring out the weaknesses of a response. Nevertheless, one needs to be constructive and to suggest solutions as soon as it is possible to do so. In other words, writing, for example, that "the discussion is not complete," does not greatly help the student understand why he has not achieved the "Meets expectations" level. One needs rather to write something such as, "The consequences of the supplier's failing to comply with the terms of the signed contract are not mentioned." (CASE A)

Nor is it very useful to write, "Your response is very confused." One needs to be more explicit and say, for example, "The response would have been easier to follow if the suggested improvements to the reporting document had been presented separately from the suggested improvements to the strategic plan." (CASE B)

N.B.: The marker's or assessor's comments could be shortened.

TIP: Revise the marking of at least a few responses in order to show where comments made to students are incomplete.

The comments of the marker or assessor must be encouraging.

In most situations, it is possible to bring out the strong points. Of course, there are often very many weak points, but I would suggest that one also take the time to mention the good ones. Usually, a simple mention such as "outstanding", "excellent", "good", "close" or "better than last time" will do.

One should also remind the markers to show consideration in the way they draft their comments. Remarks such as, "You don't have a clue about the balanced scorecard approach!" or "I have never before seen anyone mess up something as straightforward as a ratio analysis" serve no useful purpose.

TIP: Don't give up hope! One needs to explain, sum up, develop, encourage, comment, set objectives, and then start over again! The case-teaching indispensable qualities include patience and a strong sense of humor!

Objective: Establishing realistic learning objectives

When I am almost through with marking a student response, I always take the time to prepare a short summary of the strong AND the weak points. This overall report can later be used by the student for comparison from one case to the next. Personally, I start with the strong points because they are motivating. There are always some, but too often one forgets to take them into account, especially when the simulation result is weak. Another good idea is to pick out those elements that have improved since the previous simulation in order to stress what has been added. These are the points TO REMEMBER. I try to find at least three!

I also list the main weaknesses identified when analyzing the response, especially those that prevent students from achieving the various passing standards. Normally, there are more weak points than strong ones, especially in the early simulations. I suggest drafting a list of weak points in the form of things to be done or not to be forgotten the next time round. Personally, I always identify the three most important objectives that need to be worked on with a view to the next simulation. These are the points TO IMPROVE, which I draft as actions to be taken.

TIP: Suggest to the students not to write new simulations in the days before official exams. This is often counterproductive, and bad both for the motivation and for the level of nervousness.

TIP: Suggest to your students different strategies that will help them keep their learning objectives in mind. Some students make sure these objectives are where they can see them on their work table.

In fact, whether their simulation is assessed by an outside marker or not, I encourage my students to set their learning objectives after each simulation. Since it is not possible to progress on every front at the same time—especially during the early simulations—I suggest that they identify what it was that most damaged their case performance. For example, it is more important to understand exactly what such and such requirement implies than to be able to write short sentences. One will have to work on the latter at some point, but everything in its time! Ideally, as indicated earlier, one should not go beyond a maximum of three objectives at a time. This helps concentrate one's efforts.

TIP: Provide students with an objective to be met or some drafting advice at the beginning of each new case; and make sure it is apparent throughout the simulation. For example: "Today I will be dealing with all the required problems or issues."

TIP: Regularly remind students that case learning is a process that will never be completely over. A student may, for example, integrate theory and case very well over two simulations, and then have problems when he comes to the third one. One generally notices improvements over time, as simulations accumulate; but the absolute certainty that one will deal successfully with a subsequent case from every aspect is rather rare. In fact one can always find elements that can be improved, even in the best responses.

Finally, before signing off on this list of the attitudes necessary to a marker or evaluator, I would like to add the following remarks:

Marking must be efficient.

We know that a student likes to receive the result of his simulation assessment quickly, so as to be able to finalize his analysis as early as possible. In order to speed up marking and have enough time left to make written comments, the marker may use a range of signs and annotations. It is easy, for example, to encircle an "if" or to put a "?" beside an incomprehensible abbreviation.

One can also refer to a list of pre-set comments. Indeed, since some comments are applicable to several students, the marker may simply draw up a pre-numbered list that is handed out to the group. If, for example, comment number 3 reads: "... failed to take the risk areas into account when providing audit procedures" (CASE B), the student will simply find a reference to "#3" at the appropriate place in his response.

The aim is to make marking more efficient, without losing sight of the fact that the objective of a commented assessment is to provide each student with customized assistance. One should therefore make discerning and limited use of comments applicable to students at large.

TIP: Draw up a shortened marking guide that can be directly "copied" in after a computer-drafted response.

Marking must be creative.

There are a number of ways to help a student, and it is interesting to devise new ones. For example, one may assess the simulation response in the presence of the student, thus allowing for interaction. In this way he can comment verbally on his understanding of the student's simulation, and explain how he applies the evaluation criteria. This gives the student the opportunity of asking interesting questions about the process; it may also help him understand why his personal evaluation is different from that of the marker.

One can, naturally, mark a computer-drafted response directly on-screen. This way, the student will have access to the marked-up version more rapidly, and the marker's comments will automatically be easier to read. Amongst other functions, the use of "track changes", "new comment", "cut and paste" and "highlight text" facilitates marking.

Marking must be followed by a summary.

It is my belief that once a marker has completed his assessment, he should step back and present a brief summary of his comments to the students as a whole. Personally, as I move along with my assessment, I take down notes with the intention of later providing an overall summary. Markers or assessors all have their own ways of doing things, but I suggest below some examples of elements that can be included in such summary.

- The percentage of students who have reached every competence level in the evaluation guide, when such information is deemed useful.
- The list of the main strengths and weaknesses of the responses as a whole.
- The presentation of examples that can illustrate one or other concept presented in the present volume.
- The identification of the subjects where a review of the theory is necessary.
- The presentation of the analysis of a problem or issue that was particularly successful, thus qualifying as a "model."

TIP: Draw up a shortened marking guide[1] that can be directly "copied" in after a computer-drafted response.

TIP: Prepare a short questionnaire that the markers have to fill in once the marking is completed. This helps obtain a standard, useful and complete summary.

TIP: Provide an example of a response deemed to be a "successful attempt." This can be used to demonstrate, amongst other things, what can be accomplished within the time allotted.

1 The exhibits contain two examples of shortened marking guides to be used to summarize the assessment of the short case (A30 to A32) and of the long case (B90 to B94).

Part 10
Usefulness of one or more simulated cases

The comparative approach
is very useful for learning through cases.

Accounting for Success, 2010, p. 239

Part 10
Usefulness of one or more simulated cases

"The challenge is to find a balance between individual and group work."

This section is designed to assist students in getting the most out of case learning, and, to this end, provides three objectives: determining what should be retained subsequent to a simulated case; making an objective evaluation of the student's learning progress; and encouraging comparative analysis of cases.

Objective: Determining what should be retained subsequent to a simulated case

Since case simulation is an activity that can stretch over a long period, years even, I find it necessary to make a synthesis of the information. The objective is to bring out the specific and decisive elements of a case so as to be able to return to them if necessary or to carry out a comparative analysis of several simulations.

It therefore seems to me a good idea for students to prepare reference notes when concluding a case analysis. These notes—which may vary in length, as needed—should be clear, precise, and take into account the essential or key elements that need to be retained from the simulated case. Finding a practical way of grouping one's notes together and keeping them in a separate file, makes it easier to later find the information quickly. These reference notes could be separated into two parts, one called "Case Information," the other, "Case Simulation Performance."

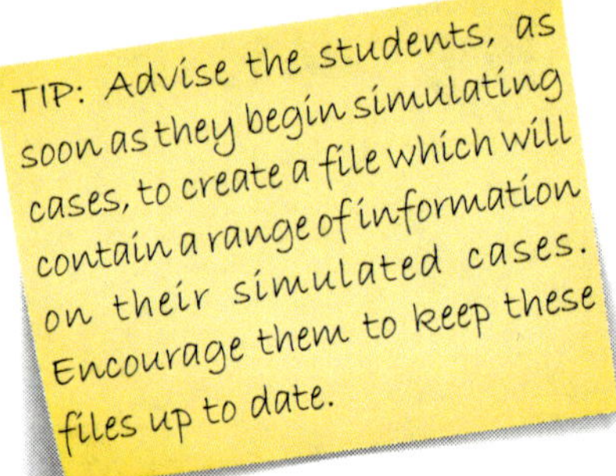

TIP: Advise the students, as soon as they begin simulating cases, to create a file which will contain a range of information on their simulated cases. Encourage them to keep these files up to date.

Case information

The "Case Information" card, on which the case parameters ("Context", "Role" and "Work required or Requirements") are repeated, makes it easier to later track down the essential elements of a case. Apart from these three parameters it would be a good idea to note down the "Structure of the solution" for the important subjects and to indicate any interrelationships between them, where applicable. Of course, any "Other observations" deemed useful can be added, for example a reminder about a criterion that must be met in order to achieve the passing standard.

CASE A:	Apart from stating the possibility of fraud by the previous controller, one needs to suggest further investigation of the matter.
CASE B:	Apart from mentioning deficiencies, one needs to recommend improvements OR explain why the reporting document presented is not useful.

Extract[1] from a "Case Information" card (CASE A)

Simulation date: 06/14/X2 **Case:** CYOF (100 minutes)

My evaluation: (A30 to A32) **Other candidates:** N/A

Context:

Publicly accountable company: IFRS (1st time for CYOF).

The controller gave his notice at the time GFI purchased CYOF, one month ago.

Role:

Accountant from the Head Office Finance Department, asked to replace the controller for CYOF until a new one has been hired.

Requirements:

a) Issues to be dealt with on a timely basis:

Lawsuit; Supplier adherence to terms of agreement; Ethical issues regarding former controller; Accounting for buildings; Vendor-appointment process.

b) Steps to be taken to assist in the transition of the new employees:

Training/Compliance with IFRS; Payroll processing; Disaster recovery; and Business continuity planning; Performance measures congruent with corporate objectives; Balanced scorecard; Suggested incentives and tax implications.

Structure of the solution:

Immediate risks: Identification of the problem ("P"); Discussion of Impact ("I"); Several recommendations for each subject ("R").

Introduction of future improvements: clear objectives followed by justified recommendations. (validation process, post-disaster recovery, performance measures)

Other observations:

One needs to pick up on the incorrect comment made by the Director of Operations, who said that he was not worried about a lawsuit initiated before CYOF was purchased. Comments made by stakeholders are not always correct!

One needs to be careful and not recommend that all the suppliers be replaced! It is important to make the difference between 1) a supplier who does not adhere to the terms of the agreement, but whom one can henceforth supervise and 2) a supplier lacking ethics (kickbacks involved) and who is located more than 250 km away. It is still possible to do business with the first one, but not with the second!

...

The above information can be completed with notes regarding how some of the case specifics may influence the solution. For example, the fact that customers are willing to pay a premium price for local, biological products (CASE A) or the fact that the Wireless Technology Project is the key to strategic growth for StarNova (CASE B) are elements that come up regularly throughout the suggested solution.

Thanks to this case classification card, it becomes easier to later inventory all the cases that deal, for example, with performance measurement (CASE A), or, another example, to highlight those contexts where the entity operates in a strictly regulated industry. (CASE B)

1 This is an extract. A number of additional observations with respect to CASE A, which can be found throughout this volume, could be added.

TIP: Suggest to your students that their "Case Information" should be concentrated in no more than two pages in order to allow a rapid review of the essential points. It is better to keep it brief!

Case simulation performance

The "Case Simulation Performance" card includes a concise summary of performance obtained, thus allowing the student to make a synthesis of the assessment of his response, to keep track of his progress over time and to set his learning objectives with respect to the upcoming simulations. This card includes the following headings: "Concepts to be revised", "Simple ideas that were forgotten", "Difficulties experienced", "Questions pending", "Points TO REMEMBER", "Points TO IMPROVE", and "Other observations" deemed useful.

TIP: Mention to your students that "Case Simulation Performance" cards are classified chronologically so as to evaluate the learning curve, and their content may vary from one student to the next. As for the "Case Information" cards, they are more likely to be classified by category and contain information of a more neutral nature, since its stems directly from the case.

TIP: Provide students with a classification system for simulated cases. A summary table indicating the duration, context, role, important problems or issues, the major competencies of the evaluation guide, along with the simulation date for each case will come in very handy for all future references.

TIP: Suggest that the students prepare a general framework for completion of their notes for each simulated case.

Extract[1] from a "Case Simulation Performance" card (CASE B)

Simulation date: September 23, X2 **Case:** StarNova (5 hours)

My evaluation: (B90 to B94) **Other candidates:** (B90 to B94)

Concepts to be revised:

Impairment of assets! Mentioning the necessity of a write-down is not sufficient in itself. Other concepts must be discussed: individual asset/cash-generating unit, recoverable amount.

Simple ideas that were forgotten:

Interpreting ratios! Not so hard, if you think about it!

Difficulties experienced:

Dividing time between subjects. Not enough time given to budget evaluation.

Not that easy to use some case facts more than once in my response. Didn't expect to have to do that.

Questions pending:

Why is the tax issue secondary? $500,000 in tax losses; that's not peanuts.

Points TO REMEMBER: (B94)

– All analyses end with a conclusion or a recommendation.

– Adequate calculations.

– Good use of the case facts. Good integration.

Points TO IMPROVE: (B94)

– Review priorities and give more time to the most important subjects.

– Make more use of calculation results. Make less calculations and analyze them better.

– Better identify the problem to be discussed before plunging into its analysis.

Other observations:

It is important to use the right accounting concepts when analyzing accounting issues. It is not necessary to sum up the standards, but it is important to refer to the key concepts in the discussion.

Audit procedures have to be tied in with the specific risks. They mustn't be so general they could work with any audit engagement.

REMINDER: Take enough time to plan out the response and to sequence the subjects so as to deal with all the requirements and make sure the interrelationships between the various problems or issues are taken into account.

...

1 This is an extract. A number of additional observations with respect to CASE B, which can be found throughout this volume, could be added.

Objective: Making an objective evaluation of the student's learning progress

We do of course understand that students attach importance—indeed a great deal—to whether they write a successful case or not. My reaction to this might seem somewhat peculiar, but I would say that they take it much too personally. Mastering a competency or writing a simulation successfully does not mean they have fully understood everything nor that they have no further need to write simulations. An excess of optimism is not a good idea. On the other hand, one bad result does not mean that they are ignorant nor that they will never manage to write a successful case. That would be a swing to an excess of pessimism. One needs to constantly step back in order to evaluate the learning process from the right perspective.

Once a student has handled a few simulations, it is normal that he should wish to determine whether he is making progress. For starters, he should realize that determining whether or not he is improving is not a straightforward activity. Competency-based evaluation makes this task difficult, since it may take a considerable time before one achieves the passing standard. Additionally, each case is unique in itself. The next case may come as an utter surprise to the student, because of its contextualization, or the way in which the problems or issues are brought in. So there is nothing astonishing in seeing progress over the course of a number of simulations, followed by a period of stagnation or even sometimes counter-performance.

I suggest to my students that they monitor their performances not only to assess their progress but to detect any recurring weakness. It is here that the comparison of reference notes may allow a student to have a better overall idea of his work. For example, a student may discover that he is having difficulty with all cases involving a not-for-profit organization. At that point, he should take the time needed to identify all the characteristics, implications, type of problems or issues, etc. specific to such organizations. One needs to confront each of the weaknesses identified so as to be able to neutralize them.

TIP: Regularly remind the students of the importance of their Accounting for success! One has to be able to appreciate every improvement in performance, whatever it may be.

One self-encouragement ploy used by students is to draw up a graph illustrating the chronological progress of their performance. Thus, in a given case ("x" axis), they might calculate the following ratio ("y" axis):

$$\frac{\text{Number of competencies at passing standard}}{\text{Total number of competencies in the case}}$$

Or again, when dealing with a specific competency—one that gives them greater difficulty—some students will put together everything concerning the competency in question in a table that they will fill in from one simulation to the next. This makes it easier to follow up on performance over time and allows the student to focus on specific competencies.

Extract from the table "Competency: Performance Measurement and Reporting/ Financial Accounting and Reporting"

Case	My evaluation	My observations	My work objectives
CYOF 06/14/X2 (A16, A17)	– Buildings: "Meets expectations" – Replacement of roof: "Below expectations" (A27, A28, A30)	+ Theory application OK for both case buildings. - Discussion about roof too vague and not smooth enough.	– Review theory about treatment as separate component. – Better highlight my recommendations.
StarNova 09/23/X2 (B41)	– "Reaching competence" (B78, B79, B90)	+ Recommendations clear and precise! Impact mentioned. ± Only one subject really successful (inventory). The rest are incomplete! - 2010 R&D costs not analyzed, though subject easy! - Accounting aspects not determined precisely enough.	– Do things in the right order: discuss R&D costs before grant! – Read case carefully… look out for analysis-relevant facts. – Better identify the problem to be discussed before plunging into its analysis.

Finally, some students design a table, sometimes of quite imposing dimensions, where the first column lists a number of questions that need answering, or else a series of learning objectives. Each of the subsequent columns corresponds to a simulated case, in its chronological order. As can be seen in the example below, as he moves from one simulation to the next, the student simply comments on the achievement of each objective listed.

TIP: Provide, as examples, a range of tables or graphs drawn up by students with a view to monitoring their case-learning process.

TIP: Where possible, invite a former student to come and talk about his experience in case learning, especially when success was a long time in coming.

Extract from the table "Follow-up of my learning objectives"

Learning objectives	CYOF 06/14/X2 (A25 to A32)	StarNova 09/23/X2 (B77 to B94)
To identify all important problems or issues.	Yes!	Yes!
To correctly establish a subject sequencing.	well done	OK, except in accounting
To make an appropriate time budget for the different aspects or subjects.	Not enough time for last two subjects (measures and incentives)	Too much time given over to calculations; Last subject unfinished (budget evaluation).
To provide a fair balance between the qualitative and the quantitative analyses.	N/A	Calculations: insufficient interpretation
To mention the consequences deriving from the problems or deficiencies identified.	Yes	Almost perfect!
To present more specific recommendations in the form of actions to be undertaken.	+/– sometimes too general	Better!
To avoid unnecessary summaries or repetitions of the case.	GOOD	OK

For each learning objective that the student sets himself, he needs to determine how he can achieve it. Obviously a first step would be to recognize that the main objective of his work will be, for example, "to better integrate theory into the case." However, before starting to write the next simulation, he either needs to carry out some exercises, or pick up some tricks that will help him to improve. For example, one good idea would be to redraft the discussion about the roof replacement cost (CASE A), or the one about the impairment of the Mobile network (CASE B).

It happens regularly that students tell me they are simply lost when they have to deal with some type or other of requirement, calculation or subject. Let us suppose, for example, that a student never knows how to react when faced with situations of unethical behavior. I would suggest preparing a table in two columns containing: 1) a reminder of the case facts; 2) ways of solving the problem. By filling in this table each time he comes up against a case that includes an ethical issue, the student will end up with a wide range of situations that have been resolved. This can only help him minimize his weak points and face up to the next case better.

Objective: Encouraging comparative analysis of cases

When students have a few cases under their belts, they can begin to make a comparative analysis of simulated cases. Using an analytical approach, they can step back and discover what they can learn from the simultaneous analysis of several cases. The objective is to specify the characteristics, the key elements or rules of conduct, often implicit, that they need to absorb. One needs to remember that the ultimate objective of every analytical exercise is to allow students to better come to grips with what is expected of them when they draft their next case. This means they need to have dealt with the same role, context, requirement, problem or issue more than once. With time, the observations that result from any comparative analysis should be written down in order to facilitate the learning process.

N.B.: Part 11 is more concerned with info-cards.

TIP: Provide students with guidance when it comes to post-simulation exercises, pointing out the usefulness of comparing their current case with previous simulations.

TIP: Take a case and simply change the role in order to stimulate discussion as to the implications of such change for the solution. For example, how would one look at the "lawsuit for damages" (CASE A) or the "CRTC Fee" (CASE B) aspects when planning out the audit of the financial statements by the external auditor?

Comparative analysis of different roles

First of all, one has to look at the way in which the role to be played impinges on the attitudes that need to be adopted when writing the response. As mentioned in Part 1, the angle from which a case fact is examined or a problem or issue is dealt with varies from one role to the next. Thus, one needs to look at the way in which the role to be played affects the solution by, amongst other things, comparing cases. The objective here is to bring out the similarities and to explain the differences, in order to better understand the various situations one comes across.

TIP: Remind the students that a comparative analysis of simulated cases is an exercise in understanding material that is already available, but that there is no way of predicting what the next case will look like.

In CASE A and CASE B, at first sight the role is the same, since the accountant works in the Head Office Financial Service. However, for the purposes of CASE A, the accountant is asked to temporarily take over from the controller who has left the company.

Similarities in the attitudes to be adopted:

- The resolution of the problems or issues is effected from an insider's point of view, keeping in mind the objectives and preferences of the company for which one is working. These include motivating the managers to focus on performance measures that are critical to the success of the company (A5) or to generating a 15% return on investment. (B3)
- The report is addressed to insiders, i.e. the President of GFI (A3) or the Executive Committee (B3). Since these people have management experience, it is not necessary to explain to them, for example, what international accounting standards are, nor do they need to be reminded of the definition of a financial ratio.
- In both cases, the role calls for making suggestions with a view to improving information presented to senior management, such as the implementation of the balanced scorecard approach (A11), and the improvement of the reporting document content (B50 to B54).

Difference in the attitudes to be adopted:

- Although the difference might be subtle, the controller does not play quite the same role. The task of a controller is usually to carry out control activities, as shown in CASE A, since the accountant, amongst other things, must set up a vendor-appointment process and discuss what performance measures need to be taken into account.
- As a participant in the internal audit group (CASE B), the accountant is required to prepare an audit plan that includes a risk analysis and procedures that will need to be performed. This is not a task that generally falls to a controller. (CASE A)
- In CASE A, the student is required to set up testing or supplier validating procedures. These must ensue from the targeted objective, i.e. ensuring that the suppliers respect the criteria of the agreement. In such a situation, it is not necessary to refer to audit assertions. As for CASE B, the requirement is for audit procedures regarding the CRTC Fee. The objective is not the same since one needs to fully check on the assertions of "accuracy" and "classification."

By and large, the objective of the exercise is to examine and compare the different roles as one accumulates simulations, in order to adopt the attitudes required to properly resolve each problem or issue raised. Every case has its own distinctive parameters and, of course, one needs to "play the game" and adjust to the different circumstances each time.

Comparative analysis of the various requirements

One also needs to look at the links between the case facts and the relevant ideas in the suggested solution (or in the evaluation guide). The objective is to perform an overall analysis in which several cases—limited to two in the present volume—are examined simultaneously. This exercise demands from the student a very high level of understanding of the solutions to previously simulated cases. It also requires concentration and reflection.

When I wish to underline the similarities between one case and another, I express the cause and effect links as follows: "When there is/are… you should consider…" Recognizing this type of relationship will help identify aspects that come back often and to take them into account in future simulations. This also facilitates the integration of case facts into the response and the drafting of relevant ideas.[1]

When there is/are…,	**you should consider…**
– an accounting issue to discuss (CASES A and B)	– making a direct reference to the theoretical concepts of the standards in question. – offering a clear and precise recommendation as to the accounting treatment that should be used.
– a performance evaluation to carry out CASE A: performance measures CASE B: ratio analysis	– dividing the discussion into separate parts: Sales, Costs of sales/Gross margin, Expenses.
– a threat with respect to the survival of the entity A4: lawsuit by a client who became ill B13: non-renewal of the CRTC license	– making it a response priority.
– a list of problems or deficiencies to analyze A5: analysis of operating problems B5: comments on the strategic plan	– discussing the impact or consequences prior to recommending improvements.
– enough facts regarding the unacceptable behavior of one of the stakeholders A8: possibility of fraud by the former controller B69: level of competence of senior management team	– clearly expressing one's opinion respecting the situation in question, while showing consideration.

The previous discussion dealt with how to bring out the similarities between one case and another. Moving on with it this exercise, one needs also to point out all the differences and explain their whys and wherefores. In other words, one needs to understand why such and such idea or discussion is relevant while others are not, taking into consideration the specifics of the cases presented. The first thing to do is to identify the difference, which is not always easy, and which supposes that one has previously simulated a certain number of cases with similar characteristics. Next, one needs to fully analyze the reasons for this difference and, again, it is not always easy to find the answer. Sometimes, everything may depend on a very slight nuance somewhere in the case itself, or even half hidden towards the end of an exhibit. Finally, the analysis must be made while constantly taking into account the relationship between the case and the suggested solution, and even the evaluation guide.

1 As suggested in Part 7, a student who, for example, highlights theoretical concepts in green and case facts in yellow when dealing with the suggested solution and the evaluation guide (A7 to A24, B25 to B76) will find it easier to carry out a comparative case analysis.

	Difference identified	Explanation
CASE A:	One needs to discuss the necessity of guiding and training employees, since CYOF has to change accounting resources and adopt those of the IFRS. (A10)	One month ago, GFI, a publicly accountable enterprise, purchased 100% of the shares of CYOF, a private enterprise. CYOF's accounting standards must therefore be changed over the current year.
CASE B:	There is no discussion of the need to guide and train the employees with regard to the adoption of the IFRS.	"Since 2008, the financial statements for SableTel have been prepared using International Financial Reporting Standards (IFRS) in order to consolidate with its parent company." The change in the accounting standards is part of the past.
CASE A:	It is not appropriate to explain or analyze the trends and variances between the previous year and the current one.	The trends and variances in Exhibit 1 are the measures considered for personnel performance evaluation. In this context, the performance of the entity itself is not an issue that needs to be discussed.
CASE B:	One needs to present a thorough analysis of the variance in results between 2010 and 2009.	The requirement is very clear on this point.
CASE A:	One needs to state the possibility of "fraud" by the previous controller. The competence of the controller in carrying out his functions is not questioned.	The former controller of CYOF made a quick departure from his job, received checks from suppliers made out in his name, and failed to respect the criteria established with regard to supplier validation. There are clear indications that his behavior was intentional.
CASE B:	One needs to question the competence or judgment of SableTel Chief Executive Officer or senior management team. One should not go as far as accusing someone of fraudulent behavior.	The Chief Executive Officer does not carry out his job adequately. He presented a reporting document that contained errors, failed to answer the questions put to him and came up with an "improbable" strategic plan. However, there are no hints that suggest any underlying intentional or deceitful action.

TIP: Suggest drawing up the list of "When you have... you should consider..." by subject, context, problem or issue. Also, the student may take advantage of this to work more on those aspects where he feel less comfortable.

TIP: Suggest to the students that they present their analyses in the form of tables, as exemplified above. To do so requires planned forethought resulting in a concise presentation of information whose form is more concise and that will be easier to revise later.

TIP: Suggest to the students that they meet in small groups in order to take stock of their comparative case analyses. Indeed, they could very well hold a discussion forum to exchange their ideas, or swap files via a drop site such as Dropbox.

Part 11
Creation of response structures and info-cards

Do not squeeze a subject into a response just because one usually finds it there.

Accounting for Success, 2010, p. 258

Part 11
Creation of response structures and info-cards

"The challenge is to differentiate between looking alike and being alike."

This section is designed to make case learning easier for students, and, to this end, provides three objectives: bringing out the response structures; creating context-based info-cards; and creating subject-based info-cards.

Objective: Bringing out the response structures

If a student has simulated cases with any frequency, he will have noticed some level of repetition in the way certain problems or issues are dealt with. Being able to bring out the response structure is important, because it allows one to determine more rapidly what steps should be taken in a given situation. More specifically, one looks for a way to highlight the main features or major sections **that are open to discussion**. By doing so, students feel more confident and do not waste precious time trying to work out how to begin their response. It is thus worth taking the time to examine the suggested solutions—and evaluation guides—in order to root out similar approaches.

The response structure presented below is very familiar, and any student who has simulated even only two or three audit cases will easily recognize it. It is the one required for "Planning an audit of financial statements," and it comes with observations as to its application. In CASE B, the audit plan requested is, on the one hand, prepared internally and, on the other, focused on a very specific topic. One needs, therefore, to know how to make use of the usual response structure **while adjusting it to the specifics of the case**—the fact, for example, that less people will be using the audit report. Additionally, the discussion as to the approach to be adopted must essentially take into account those systems that are specifically concerned with determining the CRTC Fee.

TIP: Remind students that the response structures are guides that do not apply automatically to all simulated cases. They should use them as start-off points, but they then need to take a step back and adjust to the specifics of the case.

TIP: Be aware of the fact that some students devise their own ways of doing things. This is sometimes good, sometimes bad. For example, I have seen students analyze accounting issues using the following series of code letters: P-O-B-T-I-I-R, which translate respectively as "Problem", "Objective", "Bias", "Theory", "Integration", "Impact" and "Recommendation." This type of multi-step structure--many elements of which are unnecessary--is more likely to slow down the resolution of the issue.

Example of a response structure[1]

Subject: Planning an audit of financial statements

Response structure: Risk assessment
Materiality
Audit approach
Specific risks and procedures

Observations:

→ The factors taken into account when assessing the risks stem directly from the case. Most of the time, such factors relate to new events that occurred during the year in question or that are specific to the entity.

Example: "The risk associated with this engagement is high because the CRTC licence is required in order for SableTel to continue operations". (B26)

→ The risk assessment must always end with a clear and precise conclusion as to the risk level of the audit engagement.

Note: The engagement risk is usually high, but not always...

→ The determination of materiality is influenced by the auditor's perception of the financial information needs of users of the financial statements.

Example: "Given the sensitive nature of this engagement, the overall high risk associated with the engagement, and the scrutiny that this engagement will receive from its key users (the CRTC and the EC), preliminary materiality should be set at a low level". (B26)

→ The discussion of the audit approach should always take into account the entity's internal control. One should attempt to link any discussion of the approach to be used to the case facts.

Example: "The approach to the assurance regarding the components of the CRTC Fee can be a combination of substantive and compliance procedures. The use of compliance testing will be tempered with the knowledge that there are discrepancies between the Finance and Marketing customer databases". (B26)

→ The relevant audit procedures must be related to the risk areas identified. They need to be practical and mention the taking of a specific action. The "how" and the "why" of each procedure is made clear. It often helps to refer to the assertion in question.

Example: Select a sample of invoices from the billing system and trace them through to the general ledger to ensure they are recorded properly." ("Accuracy") (B29)

› ...

1 As suggested in Part 7, the student who carefully studies the structure of the proposed solution and of the evaluation guide (A7 to A24, B25 to B76) for each of the simulated cases will be in a better position to determine the response structure.

In fact, generally, when it comes down to most problems or issues, one may *a priori* make use of the following basic structure, a structure that can be adjusted to the situations that occur. I believe it is absolutely essential, right from the start, to clearly determine what is the problem or issue that has to be resolved. Subsequently, one needs to decide how to discuss it, taking into account the various stages required, and then finally one should conclude any analysis by making a recommendation or coming to a conclusion.

Identification of Problem (or Deficiency)	"P"	"IDENT"
Analysis/Evaluation (qualitative or quantitative)	"A"	"ANAL/EVAL"
Recommendation or Conclusion	"R"	"REC"

When examining, for example, the discussion regarding the "Supplier adherence to terms of agreement", one can come up with a more precise response structure, as follows:

Example of a response structure (CASE A)

Subject: Supplier adherence to terms of agreement

Response structure:	Identification of problem (or Deficiency)	"P"	
	Analysis: Consequences of deficiency (or Impact)	"A"	("I")
	Recommendation supported by the analysis	"R"	

Observations:

→ Need to explain nature of deficiency--why there is one—using case facts for this purpose.

Example: Since there is no ongoing control by CYOF of supplier adherence to the signed agreements ("P"), there could be more breaches of agreement and consequent lawsuits ("I"). (A7)

→ Need to point out deficiency (and its consequences), and then indicate "How" to reduce or eliminate it, taking into account as often as possible the specifics of the case: names, vouchers, amounts.

→ Normally there is no competitive option to consider before making a recommendation, but there is more than one recommendation per subject.

One needs to indicate in practical and specific terms which improvement(s) should be implemented. Who? What? When?

Example: I recommend the hiring of specialists to conduct surprise visits to test supplier facilities. ("R") (A8)

→ ...

Comment: The response structure is pretty much the same whether one is commenting on the strategic plan. (B55 to B61)

TIP: Point out that a code such as "P-I-R" helps the student not to forget the different elements as he proceeds with his writing. But also point out that no code should lead him to simply repeat the same ideas. For example, there would be no point in stressing the impact of a deficiency and then justifying the ensuing recommendation by mentioning that it will serve to invalidate that very impact.

Objective: Creating context-based info-cards

As soon as a student acquires case simulation experience, he can begin to consider building up a stock of individual context-based info-cards. To do this, the student will bring together in one place, using one card, all his observations respecting a given context. The info-card, therefore, will be built up from an accumulation of simulations with a similar contextual background. It is important to understand that these info-cards will be used for a period of several months and not only over the time of a study session. In fact, one could say that info-cards are never outdated, because every new simulation may bring in new ideas.[1]

The info-cards include the following items:

- The list of simulated cases using the featured context;
- Any reference to theoretical concepts underlying the context under study;
- Any similarity or difference between simulated cases, as concerns the role or the requirements;
- The response structures used;
- Observations as to the content of the proposed solutions and of the evaluation guides, which can be formulated as follows: "When there is/are…, you should consider…";
- Concrete examples that can strengthen a discussion;
- A reminder of those items that are more difficult to deal with;
- Tips that might improve drafting efficiency;
- Any other useful observation.

"Existence of fraud" situations are dealt with on the next page, and relate to the observations made subsequent to the analysis of CASES A and B. This is not an exhaustive info-card; the student will certainly be able to add to it once he simulates another case that presents the same context.

TIP: Select one or two contexts that come up on a regular basis, and then help the students complete their info-cards as they do more case simulations. For example: "Specifics of a not-for-profit organization" or "Preparation of a reporting document for the creditor" are recurring contexts. Likewise, what are the characteristics of regulated entities?

TIP: When the time is right, suggest to the students that they meet in small groups in order to compare their context info-cards. They could have brainstorming sessions to work out together the specifics of various contexts. This very useful activity can be planned out as part of their preparation for a professional exam.

1 Observations stemming from the comparative analysis of the different roles and requirements, as mentioned in Part 10, are included in the info-cards.

Extract from a Context Info-Card

Context: Existence of Fraud

Observations:

→ One needs to be prudent when offering an opinion regarding illegal or fraudulent activities. It is not up to the accountant to make accusations or to pass judgment as to the guilt of the person concerned.

Example: "Given the circumstances, identified that sign-off of vendor appointment criteria exceptions by former controller and higher rates charged by such vendors could mean possible fraud." (A15)

→ It is a good idea to recommend a full investigation of the situation in order to determine how extensive the problems are.

→ When a colleague is suspected of ethical lapses, one needs to take the appropriate steps while respecting our profession's Code of ethics.

1- Attempt to make contact with him.

2- Inform the Institute.

3- Seek advice from legal counsel, where necessary.

→ Case facts must be interpreted correctly. Lacking competence or making errors when exercising one's functions does not necessarily signify fraud. One needs to show good judgment. (CASE B) However, when there are several facts to confirm the possibility of fraud, one should take a step back and be prepared to consider this possibility. (CASE A)

→ The key factor here is to assess the intentional or unintentional nature of the actions that underly the irregularity. (CAS 240 par. 2)

N.B.: One needs to distinguish between "lack of competence" and "fraudulent behavior."

→ Examples of facts that <u>may be</u> fraud risk factors: (A4)

- The controller gave his notice hastily when GFI purchased CYOF.
- A check was found to be made out to the controller rather than to CYOF.
- The suppliers on the controller's list levied rates that were 20% higher than the rates charged by the other vendors.
- The controller gave his approval to suppliers (five in all) who failed to conform to the established criteria.

→ Examples of facts that <u>are not</u>, *a priori*, fraud risk factors:

- The Chief Executive Officer does not understand the details of the business. (B68)
- "The executive reporting document prepared by Dan is not informative and may in fact be misleading". (B50)
- The Director did not have the answers or was making up answers as he went, to relatively simple questions. (B68)
- With this new bonus plan, senior executives are adding a perk to their current compensation packages. (B58)

Based on all my experience in case learning, I am in a position to say that every new case can carry its own surprises. In other words, despite all his good intentions and the fact that he has practiced many simulations and built up very good Context Info-cards, a student may still find himself at quite a loss when his next case comes up. Indeed one never has a guarantee that the next case will be along the same lines as the earlier ones. Its context, and even a problem or issue, may appear to be similar or to have points in common, but nothing should be taken for granted. It is pretty rare that one can simply take information from one case and apply it without change to another.

I would like to stress that a student can create any info-card that he believes to be useful; and such cards do not need to be limited to contexts. In fact, the moment one runs into a difficulty, making a card is often the best way of getting round it. Of course, it is very tempting to simplify life by simply photocopying other students' info-cards, but although I do encourage idea sharing, I regularly insist on the fact that students need to build up their own notes and observations if they are to draw full benefit from the information acquired.

"Share knowledge? Yes! Copy someone else's knowledge? Absolutely not!"

TIP: Discuss some less usual contexts with the students with a view to making them feel more comfortable with any "situation that has not been encountered so far." "Just suppose that..." is an interesting exercise to do in class or in a student forum. Concocting unusual scenarios and trying to determine what they would involve can help the students realize that new cases can often be unsettling. However, they will learn that they can step back a little and use what they already know in order to find ways of resolving new problems.

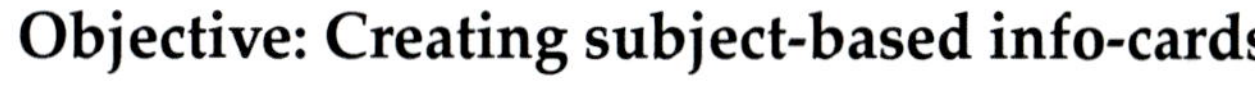

Objective: Creating subject-based info-cards

One needs to remember that cases remain essentially an academic tool and serve, amongst other things, as a way of assessing knowledge. Of course, the case provides a context that demands an integrated and multidisciplinary resolution of problems or issues, but this does not dispense the student from ensuring that he has acquired that necessary basic knowledge. As mentioned in Part 3, no drafting technique, however sophisticated it may be, can offset a weakness at this level. Given the range of knowledge required from a professional accountant, I believe it to be important to guide students as to how they may best store up the ideas and concepts they have studied.

I suggest that students create info-cards, one per subject, covering those that appear in cases regularly, that are complex, that are "in fashion," for which there is little current literature, or that they find especially difficult. For example, if a student has problems mastering the subject of "Contingent liabilities," he will certainly benefit from a summing up of its relevant notions.

One info-card per subject simply provides a summary of the notions and concepts proper to a given subject, whatever the field. It allows for a synthesis of the information available and for a grouping of observations sourced from texts and reference books that provide a wealth of explanations on that subject. The content of a subject-based info-card may be quite different from one student to the next. Some write in only short sentences without many explanations, which for them is sufficient. Others make long summaries, sometimes almost as long as the original reference texts. An info-card on the subject of the "Balanced scorecard approach," for example, may take up half a page for one student and three pages for another. What matters is that both do well out of it.

Extract from an info-card

CONTINGENT LIABILITIES (IAS 37)

DEF: (par. 10, 13)

POSSIBLE obligation arising from PAST events

AND existence confirmed only by one or more uncertain FUTURE events occurring (or not)

Not wholly within control of entity

OR

PRESENT obligation arising from PAST events but <u>not recognized</u> because:

1- not probable that an outflow of resources will be required

and/or

2- the amount cannot be measured with sufficient reliability

Examples:

- Part of the obligation to be carried out by others when the entity is jointly and severally liable (par. 29)
- Lawsuit by customer who was ill after eating vegetables (CASE A)

STANDARDS:

→ General rule: DO NOT RECOGNIZE CONTINGENT LIABILITY (par. 27)

If more likely than not – becomes a present obligation – must be recognized (par. 15)

→ Provide brief description of nature of contingent liability (par. 86)

- Estimate financial effect ($)
- Uncertainties (Amount/Timing of outflow)
- Possibility of reimbursement (third party)

N.B.: No note if possibility of outflow of resources remote. (par. 16, 28, 86)

N.B.: If serious prejudice expected, only general information. (par. 92) (CASE A)

TIP: Simply offer a practical example in class where perhaps the key concepts of a post-disaster recovery plan (A20) or of a financial review by management (B50 to B53) come out clearly.

Ideally, an info-card should contain the following items:

- a list of the theoretical concepts (standards, rules, laws, regulation, principles, etc.);
- a brief reference to texts and books that explain the relevant notions;
- an accurate summary of the theory underpinning the subject;
- pragmatic examples of the application of theoretical concepts to a case.

It is necessary to understand that the prime objective of the subject-based info-card is to sum up the "basic" concepts. There is no need to get lost in the details, or to make an in-depth study of all the exceptional situations. Taking an example: when evaluating operating performance, one is well aware that there are a number of known ratios with which it is essential to be familiar. However, it would not be important to know anything about, for example, the "defensive interval ratio," which is rarely used. In other words, the student needs to learn to focus on the essential elements of a subject.

TIP: Make your students aware that they need to work on their weak points. I have found that when they draft their cases, they spend too much time on subjects they know well, unfortunately to the detriment of those they know less well. It would seem to me even more important that they draw up info-cards the moment the analysis of their case performance reveals the necessity of so doing.

TIP: Tell the students that when they need to resolve a case, it is generally preferable to be aware of all the basic concepts regarding every subject in the program, rather than having an in-depth knowledge of only half of them.

Whatever the content of an info-card set up by a student, it seems to me that it is essential at least to bring out the theoretical concepts of the subject heading. One needs to be able to express these concepts in a concise and clear manner, using just a few words—rarely complete sentences—as the basis for a discussion. These theoretical concepts are an intrinsic part of the resolution of the case problems or issues. My feeling is that all Subject Info-cards should list basic theoretical concepts in a few separate lines, each preceded by a dash; I always mention them at the very beginning of the card, as in the "Contingent liability" example above.

TIP: Explain to the students the usefulness of bringing out theoretical concepts when it is time to resolve a case. This would be a very useful reference base more especially when one is wondering what would be the best angle from which to approach a subject. For example, when the student needs to discuss the implications of the CYOF client's lawsuit for damages, his task will be greatly facilitated if he remembers that "the probability that an outflow of resources will be required" and that "the capacity to measure the amount with sufficient reliability" are the two key criteria determining whether the "contingent liability" needs to be recognized. (CASE A)

From experience, I know that drawing up tables, diagrams or graphs as a way of summing up a subject is an excellent idea. It is certainly simpler to review a table than a text, especially one that runs on and on. Using a table obliges one to clearly indicate the links involved and to bring out more clearly the similarities and differences. Summarizing notions in the form of a list is also very useful. When it is possible to structure information in such a way as to facilitate understanding and comparison of ideas, as in the examples below, I strongly recommend that my students take this line without hesitation.

CASES A and B

International Financial Reporting Standards (publicly accountable)	**Accounting Standards for Private Enterprises**
...	...

N.B.: Other examples Part 5, page 51

TIP: Make a point of always providing examples of situations where creating tables is useful.

CASE A

Tax treatment for employer	**Tax treatment for employee**
...	...

Subject--based info-cards can be regularly added to during the simulated case analysis process, as illustrated below.[1] Amongst other things, one may identify those ideas that return to the same subject from one case to the next. For example, the concept regarding the "future economic benefits" within the framework of accounting for intangible assets often comes up. (IAS 38 par. 17) Which offers the serious advantage of being able to find practical examples of the application of the theory to the case facts.

1 In the analysis of the suggested solution and of the evaluation guide for cases A and B, which are presented as exhibits, the various theoretical concepts used to resolve problems or issues are highlighted in green. (A7 to A24, B25 to B76)

Extract from Info-card "Intangible Assets"

Theoretical concepts (IAS 38)	**Examples of application** (B33 and B34)
Technical feasibility	"Dan has indicated that SableTel is currently awaiting a third party feasibility study for this project. Therefore it is unlikely that this criterion has been met at year-end".
Intention to complete	"Management has indicated that they intend to complete the Wireless Technology Project, so this criterion is likely met".
Ability to use or sell	"We can assume that this criterion is met, and the Industry Canada grant may provide further evidence supporting this criterion since Industry Canada wants to use the technology (indicating that SableTel may be able to sell the technology as well)".
Generating probable future economic benefits	"Therefore, SableTel likely meets this criterion because the technology is supposed to increase margins by 5% across all of its product lines. This would provide substantial benefits (5% of $65 million is $3.25 million on an annual basis)".
Availability of technical, financial and other resources	"Dan has indicated that SableTel does not currently have the financial resources to finish this project and requires funding from StarNova to complete the project. Therefore, this criterion is likely not met currently since StarNova has not committed itself to the funding".
Ability to measure the expenditure reliably	"Dan has indicated that accounting came up with the $20 million necessary to complete the project, but he is not sure how they came up with this number. As well, SableTel would also need to demonstrate that it had the necessary systems in place to track the costs associated with this project reliably. Therefore, this criterion may be met, but more information is required".

Audit assertions	**Examples of audit procedures** (CASE B)
...	...

TIP: Suggest to the students that they regularly read the content of their info-cards. Myself, I suggest three 15-20 minute periods per week.

TIP: Suggest to students that they meet in small groups in order to discuss the identified theoretical concepts and to share some tables. Nevertheless, more especially with respect to subject-based info-cards, it is essential that the students have first put in an individual effort.

The cards and tables prepared by the students are excellent reference tools that are regularly updated, read and reread. The information gathered is completed as the student acquires more and more experience in case simulation. I cannot overstress the fact that the binder or computer file containing all these analyses constitutes a precious asset. This is especially so in the period before an official examination, when the context-based and subject-based info-cards are often the last documents that one will read. They provide a clear, succinct picture of the characteristics and implications of the whole range of situations the student has studied, for a given context or subject.

TIP: Collect info-cards and tables from former students in order to share with your current students samples of what can be done while, at the same time, stressing the wide ranges of approaches that are possible. For example, some students jot down theoretical concepts, using only a few key-words, on small cards (3" X 5") that they carry about so as to be able to reread them on a regular basis.

Dear reader,
Allow me to wish you every success
and to Thank you for appreciating my work.

EXHIBIT

A1

CASE A

Close to You Organic Foods

CASE A

Close to You Organic Foods

(100 minutes)

GFI ↓ 100% CYOF

Close to You Organic Foods (100 minutes)[a]

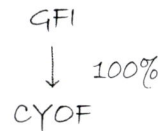

description

Close to You Organic Foods (CYOF), is a new division of Green Foods Inc. (GFI), a publicly accountable national Canadian food distributor. GFI purchased 100% of the shares of CYOF one month ago. GFI has retained all of the key executives in CYOF except for the controller, a CGA, who gave his notice at the same time GFI purchased CYOF.

IFRS — to date private

CYOF has several small stores that feature organic fruits and vegetables that are grown within a 250-kilometre[b] radius of the selling store. The company was originally created by a group of small business owners to take advantage of the growing market for locally grown organic foods. Organic fruits and vegetables are grown under strict conditions by suppliers who have to pass an inspection and sign a specific agreement about the foods they sell. Each supplier must be located within a 250-kilometre radius of the store that is selling the produce. This minimizes the impact on the environment from the pollution from travel times. This is one of the key brand differentiators for CYOF and is reflected in the choice of name for the company. The company has been able to obtain a higher price for its product based on this selling feature as there are many customers who are concerned about the environment and will pay a premium price.

conditions — IMP KSF

A3

ROLE

You, CGA, work in the Finance Department in the corporate office for GFI. You have been asked to take over the controller role for CYOF until a new controller has been hired. The President of GFI has asked you to look at the operations more closely and identify any issues that should be dealt with on a timely basis. *a)* The President noted that CYOF's accounting staff expressed concern about the change in ownership and the quick departure of the controller. He would like to know what steps can be taken to help them through the transition. *b)*

ACCT

The President has also requested your advice on the accounting treatment for two buildings that are owned by CYOF.

at purchase

prop #1

The first is where the office of CYOF is located. It was bought in 1998 for $100,000 and the current Net Book Value (NBV) is $48,200. Its Fair Value as of this date is $196,000. The roof of this building is to be replaced this year at a cost of $32,000. The President would like you to clarify whether the cost of replacement would be treated as repairs and maintenance or as an addition to the asset, and if so, how it would be depreciated.[c]

1- PROP; 2- roof → asset? → amort

prop #2

The second building was bought by CYOF three years ago for $100,000, and the current NBV is $88,000. It has been earning monthly rentals of $8,500 under an Operating lease. Its Fair Value as of this date is $120,000. Both buildings appear in CYOF's books at their respective NBVs. GFI uses the revaluation method under IFRS to record permanent assets.

INV PROP

A week has passed since you started to review the operations and you have obtained the following information.

---

a When reading, the relevant case facts were highlighted in yellow, whereas everything that concerned the requirements was highlighted in green. Comments that a candidate could write down on the case itself were written in the font used here.
N.B.: Since annotations are used by the candidate only, words are abbreviated. Thus, one will find "IFRS", "IMP" (important), "KSF" (key success factor), "ACCT" (accounting), "PROP" (property), "amort" (amortization), "INV" (investment), "FS" (financial statements), "ST" (short term), "MT" (medium term), "info" (information), "obj" (objective)", "tax" (taxation).

b 155 miles

c For the first building, a short plan is written down in the margin in order to identify and organize the various aspects to be discussed.

IMP RISK a)

Lawyer? FS?

One of the employees mentioned that a customer became very ill after eating some of the vegetables purchased from one of the stores. This customer filed a lawsuit looking for damages. You have talked to the CYOF Director of Operations who told you not to worry about the lawsuit because it was initiated before GFI purchased CYOF, so GFI would not be responsible for any of the legal implications.

wrong!

controls a)

≠ ORG

Later?

You have asked some additional questions about this customer and have found out that the vegetables purchased came from a major supplier who uses pesticides in growing produce, in violation of the agreement that has been signed. There is no ongoing testing in place to test the quality of the produce received from the suppliers because CYOF relies on the initial inspection procedures when the supplier is signed up and the integrity of the suppliers to comply with the terms of the signed contracts. [a]

A4

IMP RISK a)

verbal?

fishy! fraud?

rates + 20%
> 250 km

When you reviewed the mail in the former ✓ controller's in box, you found a cheque from one of the new suppliers. The cheque was made out ✓ in the name of the controller instead of Close to You Organic Foods. You inquired with the accounting department to determine if any of the previous cheques from this supplier had any improprieties. The Accounts Payable staff mentions that the rates this supplier charges are 20% higher than the full rates by other vendors of the same products. As you make further inquiries, you find out that this supplier is located more than 250 kilometres away and that the former controller ✓ has signed off on the acceptance of this supplier. Prompted by this sign-off by the former controller, you review the vendor files and find that there are 4 other suppliers who fall outside the 250- kilometre radius, who have all been ✓ approved by the controller. [b] You are left wondering what your course of action should be. [c]

b) transition

- info
- job loss

employees IMP

As you spend more time with the accounting staff, you observe that there is a general unease with the transition from being a separately operated company to being a division of GFI. Employees believe that the former controller had knowledge they were not privy to and several employees are concerned that they will lose their jobs shortly. You are surprised to hear this since all of the employees have good performance evaluations on file and have worked for CYOF for several years. The experience that these employees have is critical in ensuring that the suppliers are paid promptly and that key analytical reports are prepared on a timely basis for the Operations Department.

b) transition

ST: pay
MT: other

The payroll staff at CYOF, Kim, is concerned about how she is going to process payments in future. Kim says, "I was processing payroll based on a printout given to me by the former Controller. I know he maintained a spreadsheet,? which he updated, when required, and gave me a printout based on which I issued payroll cheques." You probe further and come to understand that there are several other such spreadsheets that were used by the former Controller, and the staff are now unable to process payments without the spreadsheets. [d]

check:
business continuity

a We note that, for the moment, only one supplier--major--is violating the condition regarding organic foods, which represents a short-term risk. There may be others and, in the medium term, an ongoing validation process will be necessary.

b The three facts suggesting the possibility of fraudulent behavior by the controller are clearly and appropriately signalled (✓).

c Five suppliers are in violation of the condition regarding the distance from the fruit store. It is mentioned that the first supplier charges 20% more than do others. However, we do not really know if the other four act in the same manner. There is nothing in writing about this.

d THE FACT THAT THE EMPLOYEES CANNOT UNDERSTAND THE SPREADSHEETS OF THE PREVIOUS CONTROLLER IS A PROBLEM THAT NEEDS TO BE SETTLED URGENTLY. It is important to stress the urgent need to do so in order to ensure business continuity, more especially as concerns payroll processing.

performance b)

The Human Resources Department of Green Foods has determined that a financial performance measure should be used in the annual performance evaluations for the CYOF store managers. They believe this will be an effective way to motivate the managers to focus on performance indicators that are critical to the success of the company. (Refer to Exhibit 1 for an extract from a list of financial performance measures that are being considered for inclusion in the annual performance evaluation.)

KSF obj

incentives b)

The Human Resources Department has decided to recommend the inclusion of an incentive to motivate staff to focus on these measures. This incentive would be based on the quarterly results (for each department as well as firm-wide) and would be awarded at each quarterly review meeting. Several incentives have been discussed and have been narrowed down to the following:

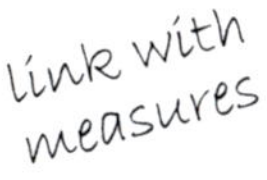

- A $100 cash bonus
- A fruit basket with a cost to the store of $100

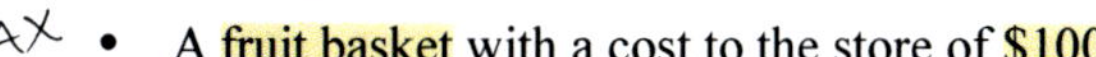

- A meal at an upscale restaurant the evening of the quarterly review, hosted by the President (estimated at $100)

A5

b) transition +/- imp

Once a decision has been made on the incentive that will be offered to the employees, you will be responsible for ensuring that this information is communicated to the employees as soon as possible.

Required

Draft a memo to the President of Green Foods addressing the integration of the new division. (2,300 to 2,500 words)

a) Identify and analyze recent issues that should be dealt with on a timely basis, providing recommendations where appropriate. ID - ANAL/EVAL - REC

RISKS

ROLE Controller

b) Discuss the steps that can be taken to assist in the transition of the new employees. As part of the transition plan, discuss potential performance measures that are congruent with corporate objectives for use in performance evaluations for CYOF employees, including possible non-financial measures.

financial + non-financial

CONTEXT: a

→ IFRS (1st time for CYOF)
→ clients pay more for organic and local food
→ RISK: lawsuit
→ controller's abrupt departure
  lack of ethics
→ lack of control of producers (agreement: organic + 250 km)
→ employees fear job loss
→ need for performance measures

a This list of case specific elements can be entered on a separate page. Alternatively, one might simply highlight them in a different color.

EXHIBIT 1 *a*

Extract from the weekly analysis for store #3:

performance measures b)

TREND and VARIANCE ANALYSIS *b*

Week 45

sales ↑ price ↓ margin ↓ (Organic Vegetables) — *minor* (Organic Flours)

A6

		Organic Fruit	Organic Vegetables	Organic Flours
✳ **Sales**				
	TY	$10,000 ↑	$8,000 ↑	$200
	LY	$9,500	$7,000	$150
✳ **% of total Sales**				
	TY	55% ↓	44% ↑	1%
	LY	57%	42%	1%
Unit Sales				
	TY	12,000	8,300	50
	LY	11,700	7,100	38
Average Unit Selling Price				
	TY	$0.83 ↑	$0.96 ↓	$4.00
	LY	$0.81	$0.99	$3.95
✳ **Gross Margin %**				
	TY	65% ↑	70% ↓	50%
	LY	62%	72%	51%
Inventory				
	TY	$20,000	$14,400	$1,000
	YL	$19,950	$11,200	$1,050
✳ **Weeks of Stock on Hand**				
	TY	2.0	1.8	5.0
	YL	2.1	1.6	7.0

At least one supplier whose prices are > 20%.

NOTE: TY = this year *(current)* and LY = last year *(past)*

industry?

---

a One needs to note that this is an "extract" and that it concerns "one store only" and a "weekly analysis."

b Since Exhibit 1 provides a number of financial performance measures, one needs to speedily determine what matters most (*). Thus, since "organic flours" are not a very important product, we may focus on the other two.
We can also split the measures considered into three categories: revenue mix, gross margin, and inventory. This can help with structuring the response.
The main changes are indicated, for example, the fact that the "organic vegetables" margin is dropping, while the sales figure increases.

Sample Solution [a]

MEMORANDUM

Date: January 29, 20X1
To: President, Green Foods Inc.
From: Controller, Close to You Organic Foods
Re: Integration of Close to You Organic Foods and Operational Concerns

I have reviewed the operations of Close To You Organic Foods (CYOF) and have identified several issues to be resolved in a timely manner.

Part a

A7

Structure: RISK - solutions

Lawsuit [P]

clear and exact conclusion

Green Foods Inc. (GFI) has purchased 100% of the shares of CYOF; therefore, GFI assumes all liabilities of CYOF. If the lawsuit against CYOF is successful, [I] GFI would be held accountable for the damages, despite the fact that this incident occurred prior to the sale of CYOF. We must [R] contact legal counsel and [R] determine our potential liability and [R] record the amount if it is estimable and if the lawsuit is likely to end unfavorably.

1- estimable amount
2- probability of loss

practical aspect: The publication of information regarding the lawsuit may seriously tarnish GFI's brand image, via CYOF.

impact on FS

At a minimum, we should [R] disclose this information in a note to the financial statements. Note that IFRS permits reduced disclosure if it would be severely prejudicial to an entity's position in a dispute with the other party to a contingent liability.

IAS 37 par. 86

third party

We must also [R] seek legal advice as to the recourse that we have against the supplier of pesticide-contaminated vegetables in violation of the agreement.

why

Supplier adherence to terms of agreement [P]

contractual liability + social responsibility

CYOF has stringent controls over the initial acceptance of the supplier but does [I] not monitor for compliance with the signed agreements [P]. This lack of control means there could be [I] more breaches of agreement and consequent lawsuits.

initial + ongoing

Customers pay a premium price in the belief that standards are met, so in addition to [I] possible lawsuits, we could [I] have a serious public relations concern if this information is leaked. It also involves a breach of trust with customers who we have assured are being sold local organic produce. [b]

1- ORG
2- local

Link to information to be disclosed in a note to FS.

Moreover, bad publicity will have [I] a negative impact on the brand and [I] could result in a loss in sales if customers lose trust in us. We [R] need to implement a method of testing produce regularly for contaminants to ensure suppliers are adhering to the terms of the agreement. [c]

$ impact sales

why

---

a In this sample solution, the case facts are highlighted in yellow, whereas the theoretical concepts are highlighted in green. Comments that a candidate could write down during the analysis of this suggested solution are written in the font used here. The following abbreviations: "P" (identification of problem), "I" (impact, consequences), and "R" or "REC" (recommendation) are used frequently. Assessor's observations are in italics

b There are two key aspects that need to be taken into account in this analysis: 1- selling organic foods, and 2- doing business with local suppliers. A candidate who has not brought out both aspects should reread the case and pick out the relevant facts.

c The annotations stress the fact that "compliance" with contractual requirements is an essential element if one is to resolve the problems or issues.

Ethical issue regarding former controller [a]

ONE NEEDS TO ACCUMULATE CASE FACTS IN ORDER TO EVALUATE THE SITUATION.

The former controller's inbox contained a cheque (made out to him personally) from one of the company's vendors. Research proved that this vendor is located more than 250 kilometres away and does not qualify as a vendor for CYOF. The former controller had signed off on this vendor's appointment. Also, the rates charged by this supplier are 20% higher than the rack rates charged by other vendors of the same products. The fact that the cheque is made out personally to the former controller raises concerns of possible illegal activities.

suspicion fraud

A8

A further review of the vendor files uncovered four suppliers who fall outside the 250-kilometre radius, all approved by the former controller. Upon reviewing the rates charged by these vendors, it has become evident that they all charge higher rates than those charged by vendors who fall within the 250-kilometre radius. This appears to be a clear case of kickbacks being given by these vendors to the former controller for having approved their vendor status for CYOF.

implications

The controller's abrupt departure on acquisition of CYOF may indicate that there could be other concerns, so a full investigation will be made to determine how extensive the problems are.

The conclusion stems from consideration of a number of case facts.

éthics controller

The controller is a fellow CGA so I will attempt to contact him to discuss this issue. If I am unsuccessful, then I will contact the CGA association for the next steps. The unethical nature of his activities has an impact on the organization, its customers and the public at large in a way that raises questions as to the credibility of the profession. Prior to this, however, legal advice should be sought as the controller appears to be acting in a criminal capacity as well, and is in effect stealing from the company. If he is in fact stealing, this would be serious enough to contact the association directly without speaking to him first. [b]

Steps:
1- Colleague
2- Association
3- Legal

éthics suppliers

ST

We must also cease doing business with these suppliers. The suppliers' ethics are questionable as the suppliers are knowingly shipping product over 250 kilometres, which is inconsistent with our brand promise and customers' expectations. [c] We need to begin our search for replacement vendors who meet our criteria and also inform our other approved vendors about possible volume increases in the size of orders placed with them.

conclusion

indirect impact

validation suppliers

MT WHO

Additionally, we need to set up a process of validating that the vendors meet our criteria (objective) and then monitor that they maintain the standards we set for providing organic fruits and vegetables grown within the 250-kilometre radius. This monitoring might involve hiring specialists to conduct surprise visits to test supplier facilities on their ability to meet the standards. A vendor approval process will need to be developed and implemented that will include documentation that they meet our criteria, and approval by two CYOF officers. At least one of the approving signatures should be independent of the purchasing department. The approval process should include an initial inspection of the vendor facilities.

→ initial
→ subsequent
documentation

The recommendations regarding the validation process are clear, precise, and practical. What to do? Who? When?

---

a This page of the proposed solution deals with several different problems or issues. Each one is indicated in the left-hand margin, in such a way as to clarify the structure of the analysis.

b Since the former controller is a colleague, one needs to consult the Code of ethics. One may note that each one of the actions to be undertaken is justified.

c The fact that the customers are willing to pay a premium price for CYOF products is one of the specifics of the case. This is referred to continually within the proposed solution.

Accounting for buildings

Note that the candidate will not be expected to quote standard numbers in his response. What is important is to correctly apply the appropriate theoretical concepts.

EXPLICIT DEMAND → EXPLICIT CONCLUSION

new accounting resources for CYOF

The accounting treatment for the two buildings, under IFRS, is as follows: [a]

Building 1 Use by CYOF → Property, Plant and Equipment

Building 1 is a self-owned and occupied property. As such it would be considered Property under "Property, Plant and Equipment" per IAS 16. This standard permits property to be held at fair value at the date of the revaluation less any subsequent accumulated depreciation and subsequent accumulated impairment losses (under the Revaluation model). Revaluations will be made with sufficient regularity to ensure that the carrying amount does not differ materially from that which would be determined using fair value at the end of the reporting period.

Reminder: No need to revalue every year. objective

Accordingly, Building 1 could be recorded at $196,000 and the depreciation would be calculated on the increased value. The difference between the NBV of $48,200 and fair value on revaluation date of $196,000 can be reported in either of the following two ways:

A9

Whatever the method used, the net carrying amount will be equal to the fair value of $196,000 and the revaluation surplus of $147,800 will be presented in the comprehensive income.

For the 1- elimination method, accumulated depreciation is eliminated first, then the balance in the Property accounting would be adjusted upward if required. The amount of the revaluation is recorded in Other Comprehensive Income (OCI) in a Revaluation Surplus account.

The 2- proportional method allocates the revaluation adjustment between the asset account and the accumulated depreciation account. The revaluation amount would be recorded in OCI.

One method can be recommended.

Building 2 rental income → investment property

By definition, under IAS 40 paragraph 8c), this building is an "Investment Property." IAS 40 permits valuing Investment Property at fair value, as long as the entity measures all of its investment property at fair value, unless the fair value of the asset cannot be reliably determined. Note that the fair value also reflects the rental income from current leases.

A gain or loss arising from a change in the fair value of investment property will be recognized in profit or loss for the period in which it arises.

Accordingly, $32,000 ($120,000 - $88,000) may be credited back to the Income Statement.

short calculation between parentheses

Accounting for cost of replacement of roof

Given the important amounts at stake, the discussion on the cost of replacement of the roof follows the one regarding the two buildings.

The $32,000 cost of replacement of the roof would be capitalized under Land and Building. The amount spent extends the life of the asset and the benefit from the newly replaced roof would be derived by CYOF over several years.

← because

IFRS requires that each significant component of an asset be depreciated separately. In this case, the roof may be considered as a significant component because it needs to be replaced more frequently than the building itself (it has a different useful life than the building as a whole) and its dollar value is significant when compared to the total value of the building. So, we should ascertain the useful life of the new roof and depreciate the cost over such useful life.

32/196

[a] Since it is indicated in the case that GFI uses the "revaluation model" to account for its property, plant and equipment, this model must be used for CYOF. It is not necessary to discuss the "cost model" that can also be used for the buildings.

Part b

Transition[P] *first application of IFRS → employee training*

Accounting - With GFI taking over CYOF, the financial accounting and reporting[R] would have to be in accordance with IFRS as applicable to publicly accountable enterprises. I recommend that the[R] employees in the Accounting department be oriented and trained in the changes in accounting standards, including the reasons for the change.

see beyond the immediate problem ✓

It is critical to ease the[R] employees' concerns about the transition. Continuity of accounting staff will facilitate the integration of the new controller into his/her role and will ensure that CYOF continues to operate without any serious impediments. We have to[R] instil a sense of confidence in employees about their job security so that they are willing to stay.

experience employees critical — *advantages*

A10

Clear, honest, ongoing communication is critical in dissipating the concerns of the CYOF staff. Perhaps there has been a lack of communication earlier that is responsible for the staff's sense of unease, especially since they are concerned that the former controller was privy to information they were not receiving. I would recommend that we first[R] meet with the entire group to give them a global message about our strategy going forward. Then we can[R] meet each employee individually to address specific concerns and to assure them that things are in control.[a]

meetings → group → individual — *why*

Performance Measurement for Evaluation of store managers[P]

- mix
- orders
- price

The Director of Operations and the store managers use the weekly analytical reports to make decisions on product mix, order quantities and pricing. In order to determine optimal product mix, it is important to identify the demand for each product and the price that can be charged.[b] The individual product gross margins are a key component used to establish the overall gross margin achievable through product mix. Order quantities are based on the level of inventory required to support the optimal number of weeks of sales in stock. The performance measure[R] should be based on results achieved after the Operations Department has made changes in pricing and order quantities with input from the store managers. Store managers input would ensure that product mix meets their clientele's needs. From that starting point, how they manage their staff and property will be reflected in the store's overall performance. These changes should result in increases in sales and gross profit, so the performance measure[R] should be based on results TY over LY same week, or perhaps based on increases to prior weeks.[c]

decisions ↓ performance ↓ measures

clientele's needs

demand + price ↓ optimal product mix ↓ gross margin

optimal stock turnover time ↓ quantities to order

financial impact: ↑ sales ↑ gross margin

comparative aspect to be considered

---

a In the case, the substitute controller, i.e. the candidate, mentioned that he was "surprised by the employees' concerns." (p. 4)

b In order to better understand this part of the proposed solution, simple diagrams were drawn in the margin. This allows, on the one hand, the bringing out of the link between the corporate objectives and the performance measures to be retained. On the other hand, it makes it easier to identify those variables to be considered when determining the optimal product mix and quantities to order.

c The annotations in this section of the proposed solution help with the drawing up of a list of elements that can be considered when determining what performance measures to use. Thus, one can:
- divide up: Sales figures - Gross margin - Inventory;
- evaluate the financial impact, such as an increase in sales or in gross profit;
- consider comparing income statements between periods. Since, in this case, Exhibit 1; provides a weekly analysis, a comparison by week is suggested.

non-financial

Non-financial factors to be considered in measuring firm-wide performance

To encourage behaviour and actions congruent with strategic objectives of the entity, I would recommend the Balanced Scorecard approach to measuring the non-financial performance of the company. Under this approach, performance is looked at from four perspectives:[a] *objectives*

- Learning and growth — Are our employees happy and productive? Are we retaining employees? Are employees getting the training they need? *Reminder: employees IMP*
- Internal business processes — What must we excel at to be effective and efficient in our business? *validation of suppliers*
- Customers — How do customers see us? How can we better target our market? *customers pay more*
- Financial — What do we look like to shareholders? Are we achieving our strategic financial goals? *GFI publicly accountable*

It should be pointed out that the discussion about performance measures is in two parts: financial and non-financial measures. This facilitates drafting and makes for a more complete analysis. A11

Payroll processing

practical aspect: This problem is urgent! A company absolutely must pay its employees on the date set down!

Use of spreadsheets for processing payroll could have several limitations, such as being end-user oriented, error-prone, inaccurate, and untimely. Given the circumstances, this may be a good time to invest in appropriate software for payroll or perhaps install the same software that GFI uses.[b] This would make the payroll processing automated, more accurate[c], less error-prone, and timely and facilitate accurate processing of statutory remittances. I would also recommend that CYOF consider direct deposit of payroll into employee bank accounts, wherever possible. *2 solutions* *advantages*

Disaster recovery and Business Continuity Planning

implicit problem

The fact that the former Controller has been using spreadsheets for various critical business functions and handing out only spreadsheets for the staff to process transactions has resulted in a panic among staff for lack of any input to perform their duties, upon the departure of the former Controller. This could have been avoided if there were sufficient backup and an IT recovery plan in place at CYOF. *impact*

1- spreadsheets (ST) *training*

There is an urgent need to address the issue of the information bottleneck created by the previous Controller. The staff responsible for the job must be in control of the information necessary to do the job. Step one will be to access the spreadsheets, whether on the former Controller's computer or by rebuilding them from the printouts that were being used.[b] All systems being put in place must have appropriate backup procedures including cross-trained personnel. These spreadsheets would be online, and there must be off-site back-up, which may be used to restore the original in the event of a data loss.[d] *2 solutions*

---

a The items listed from each of the four perspectives are described in fairly general terms. Note that in the margin the case facts identified are those that can be used to make a more tangible determination of these financial performance measures.

b RECOMMENDATIONS ARE CLEAR, SIMPLE AND PRACTICAL. Two solutions are offered.

c It is a good idea to list the advantages of using payroll software. However, one should note that these advantages are simply the reverse of the limitations of the current system, which were mentioned earlier.

d One must look for problems that are not made explicit in the case. Being unable to reconstitute the "spreadsheets" is not a problem in itself. It is rather an indication that the entity's activities have been disrupted by the controller's departure. One must make sure that the employees in place have access to data.

objective

2- recovery plan (MT)

concrete examples

CYOF must also work on having a business continuity plan to address contingencies in future. The plan should include a manual documenting policies and procedures of all the critical functions of the business. Such policies should include cross-training of employees so that a job will continue to be done even if staff leave. All data, including the policy manual, should be stored offsite. The manual should contain the key contact information for crisis management staff, general staff, customers, and vendors, and the location of the offsite data backup storage. It may also contain critical documents such as insurance policies. a

Manual:
- Policies
- Key contacts
- Documents

Suggested incentives and tax implications

employee + employer

The three options have different implications as noted below:

A12

point of view employees (✓)

- $100 cash bonus — a taxable benefit to the employee, 100% deductible by the company. With the cash bonus, employees can spend it the way they wish to, but the actual benefit would be net of the taxes payable on such bonus.
- $100 fruit basket — a non-taxable benefit to the employee (CRA allows a single $500 exemption that is applied against the total value of all the non-cash awards given to an employee, as long as all employees are eligible), 100% deductible by the company as the $100 is the cost of the basket.
- Dinner with the President — non-taxable to the employee (CRA does not consider this to be a taxable benefit to the employee because there is no element of choice), 50% deductible by the company. The perceived value of the dinner could be higher than actual cost due to the prestige factor of spending time with the President. b

Remember: net of tax

why

"dollar" value/"perceived" value

The choice of incentive to be awarded should be based on a trade-off between the incentive most highly valued by the employee and the lowest cost to CYOF. c

cost-benefit

key element: VALUE

practical aspect

Generally, employees prefer cash, which allows them to decide how they want to reward themselves. In this case, that option would be taxable in the hands of the employees. Most retailers provide employees with discounts on store merchandise so employees will likely be aware of the fruit basket's worth. In my opinion, the fruit basket would not satisfy the store managers' expectations of reward. I would suggest that although the meal with the President costs the most to the company, given the profile of the store managers, it may be the item of most perceived value to them. However, given the complexity of the issues, we could allow the employee to choose.

I look forward to discussing these issues in more detail at your earliest convenience. d

Personally, based on the previous analysis, I would recommend the cash bonus.

---

a This paragraph contains a series of recommendations that could be presented as a list of actions to be taken. One will notice that a number of practical examples are provided with respect to the contents of the procedures manual.

b In the United States, de minimus fringe benefits, such as the fruit basket, and occasional meals, such as the one with the President, are put down as non-taxable benefits to the employees, but deductible by the company.

c The analysis of the choice of incentive takes into account the cost-benefit constraint for the employee AND for the employer. The cost or the dollar value are after-tax amounts. The qualitative advantages, which have been ticked off, are considered from the point of view of the employees, i.e. the store managers.

d THE IDEAS PUT FORWARD IN THE ANALYSIS OF THIS ISSUE INDICATE A PRACTICAL ASPECT. It is "generally recognized" that employees prefer cash. It is also understandable that the manager of a fruit store might wish for something other than a basket of fruit. One needs to step back and ask oneself: "What would a store manager prefer?"

ASSESSMENT KEY *a*

a)

Core and core-related competencies: Assurance and other related services (PK:AS:09)
Did the candidate determine a program of controls to ensure supplier compliance with contractual requirements?

1- program of controls OR 2- appointment process

OR
Did the candidate describe appropriate controls in the vendor appointment process, in accordance with company policy?

major objective: compliance with agreement

There are two possible ways of achieving this competency.

It is important to determine the objectives prior to drawing up a "list" of controls.

A13

Performance level	Marking grid
0. *NR/Inc**	Did not attempt this competency or provided insufficient material to evaluate OR response was incorrect.
1. *Substantially below*	**Stated** that there is a 1- need for ensuring that vendors comply with the terms of the contract. *objective* **OR** **Stated** that the 2- vendor-appointment process needs to be reviewed, but did not elaborate. *check on "what doesn't work"*
2. *Below* *key aspect for CYOF*	**Identified** the 1- importance of the CYOF's marketing platform (proximity to market, organic produce) in extracting a premium price from customers **OR** **Stated** that the 2- vendor-appointment process should ensure that the criteria set by the company are met *objective*
3. *Meets* *passing standard: controls that need to be set up*	**Determined** 1- • the importance of the CYOF's marketing platform (proximity to market, organic produce) in extracting a premium price from customers 1- • that controls be put in place to ensure contract requirements are met on an ongoing basis *"list of" controls* **OR** 2- • **Described** controls in the vendor-appointment process, including validating that the vendors meet all the criteria and ensuring that they maintain the 250-kilometre standard
4. *Exceeds* *REC needed at this level*	**Outlined** important elements of a vendor compliance program specific to this case **AND** **Recommended** methods to ensure compliance with standards, including • Surprise visits to test facilities on the ability of vendors to meet the standards • "Dual sign-offs" on exceptions to standards *why*

* NR = No Response; Inc = Incorrect

objective → importance → controls

"described": identify and explain

2 criteria in the agreement:
- ORG
- < 250 km

impact on price

It is very IMPORTANT to integrate the ideas to the case.

practical control methods

Note the difference in the characteristics of the suppliers discussed in part a) of the suggested solution. The first supplier has used pesticides – if CYOF implements proper inspection controls and has confidence that this will not occur again there may be merit in keeping the supplier. This is a major supplier so there might be short-term supply shortages if the agreement is cancelled. The second supplier is shipping produce from more than 250 kilometres away and appears to be paying kickbacks – so regardless of the quality of the produce, the supplier's ethics are in question and the more than 250-kilometre distance is not in keeping with the company's stated marketing position.

} bio

} < 250

One needs to realize that failure to respect the agreement regarding the distance from the store does not mean that the other criterion regarding organic food is not respected, and vice versa.

a The order in which the competencies of the key are presented does not necessarily correspond to the order of importance of the problems or issues. One also needs to note that the indication "Other" is regularly present at levels 2, 3, or 4 of each marking grid. Although "Other" has been omitted here for purposes of presentation, one should not forget that any "other" idea can earn marks. In the current assessment key, the case facts are highlighted in yellow, whereas the theoretical concepts are highlighted in green. Comments that a candidate could write down when analyzing this key are written in the font used here.

One must always be honest and behave in an ethical manner.

ASSESSMENT KEY (continued)

a) **Core and core-related competencies: Management accounting** (PK:MA:03)

Did the candidate identify the implications of a lack of control over suppliers' adherence to requirements and terms of the contract and recognize the breach of trust with customers?

Structure P - I - R

One of the important specifics of the present case is the agreement with the producers.

It is important to differentiate the two criteria of the agreement that are under discussion.

A14

Performance level	Marking grid
0. *NR/Inc*	Did not attempt this competency or provided insufficient material to evaluate OR response was incorrect.
1. *Substantially below* identify the key facts in the case without commenting on them	**Stated**, without elaboration • That vendors are contractually bound to provide pesticide-free product. pesticide-free **OR** • That vendors are contractually bound to provide product grown within the established zone. established zone: 250 km
2. *Below*	**Identified** GFI's, and previously CYOF's, lack of control over suppliers. identification of the problem
3. *Meets* One needs to see the IMPACT on the customers.	**Identified** the implications of a lack of control over, or compliance testing of, suppliers' adherence to requirements and terms of the contract. The candidate **recognized** the breach of trust with customers due to the lack of due diligence with respect to ensuring standards were met.
4. *Exceeds* REC needed at this level	**Identified AND evaluated** the available data and information **AND made a recommendation** supported by the analysis, such as the following: • That a vendor compliance program be implemented

The brand image of CYOF is based primarily on compliance with the said agreement.

suppliers → customers

ethics

This is a major risk for CYOF; a risk that needs to be analyzed early in the response. The potential implication for customers absolutely needs to be considered at the "Meets expectations" level.

Make a tie-in with the "Business environment" competency (p. 22).

Professional qualities and skills: Stakeholder focus (PR:SF:01)

a) Did the candidate recommend internal controls that met the expectations of the customer but were consistent with the company's branding? Link up with the p. 13 "Audit" competency.

One needs to take a professional stance as regards the sales arguments. One must always ensure that one's behavior to, amongst others, customers and suppliers, is ethical in nature.

Performance level	Marking grid
0. *NR/Inc*	Did not attempt this competency or provided insufficient material to evaluate OR response was incorrect.
1. *Substantially below*	**Identified** customers as stakeholders. key aspect: customer trust
2. *Below* critical interest	**Identified** customers' demand for organic foods that reduce harm to the environment as stated in CYOF's marketing as a critical stakeholder interest.
3. *Meets* "list of"	**Recommended** internal controls that meet the expectations of the customer and that are consistent with the company's branding.
4. *Exceeds*	**Outlined** an action plan for implementing the recommendation.

REC needed at this level

We need to assess the ability of the candidate to identify what matters to CYOF. Here the message customers are receiving does not correspond to reality since the agreements with the producers are not being respected. The consequences may be very serious, in the short and medium term, for both CYOF and GFI.

When describing the controls that need to be set up, the candidate must show that he is aware of what is at stake by solving the problem rapidly and permanently. Personally, for the passing standard, I would expect at least three controls to be described. (see Part 8, p. 87)

PLAN:
WHO
WHAT
WHEN

ASSESSMENT KEY (continued)

a) **Core and core-related competencies: Assurance and other related services** (PK:AS:11)

Did the candidate identify possible "fraud" and analyze the facts of the case and suggest further investigation? *At the "Meets expectations" level, it is important to accumulate the facts in order to draw a conclusion regarding the controller's behavior.*

There's a difference between "dubious" behavior and "fraudulent" behavior.

Performance level	Marking grid
0. *NR/Inc*	Did not attempt this competency or provided insufficient material to evaluate OR response was incorrect.
1. *Substantially below*	**Restated** the facts of the case, but did not analyze further.
2. *Below*	**Identified** that the facts of the case indicate that the actions of the former Controller appear questionable, but did not state the possibility of fraud.
3. *Meets* *CONCLUSIONS*	**Identified** the facts of the case, including the following: • Given the circumstances, identified that sign-off of vendor appointment criteria exceptions by former Controller and higher rates charged by such vendors could mean possible fraud. • Suggested further investigation.
4. *Exceeds*	**Identified AND evaluated** the available information **AND made a recommendation** supported by the analysis.

It seems to me that the words "possible fraud" should certainly be used, so as to convey the idea clearly.

A15

REC needed at this level

There must be "further investigation" in order to confirm suspicions. It cannot be said here that all the suppliers chosen by the controller apply rates in excess of 20%. (p. 5)

a) **Core and core-related competencies: Ethics and trust** (PR:ET:01)

Did the candidate explain how to address the controller's potential breach of the Code of ethics?

Colleague? ⟶ Code of ethics

To achieve the passing standard, it is essential to present the steps to be taken, as laid out in the Code, since this ethical problem concerns a colleague.

Performance level	Marking grid
0. *NR/Inc*	Did not attempt this competency or provided insufficient material to evaluate OR response was incorrect.
1. *Substantially below*	**Restated** the facts of the case, or stated that there was an issue related to ethics without elaborating on the issue.
2. *Below*	**Identified** the potential ethical issues as arising from the following: • A cheque from a supplier made out to the former controller • The former controller's signature on a contract with a non-qualifying supplier
3. *Meets* *STEPS: 1) Attempt to make contact. 2) Inform the Association of the situation.*	**Explained** the ethical issue **and discussed** it, including the following: • The CGA candidate is bound by CEPROC. • The CGA candidate is bound to take actions in the sequence set out in CEPROC. • Because the former controller is also a professional accountant, the CGA candidate *1-* should first attempt to make contact with the former controller. • Failing to make contact with the former controller, or if the contact does not satisfy the CGA candidate, *2-* the CGA Association must be advised of the situation. • In addition, the vendors that aren't operating within CYOF guidelines *R* should be contacted because of the breach of policy, and CYOF *R* should stop doing business with them immediately.
4. *Exceeds*	**Explained** the ethical issue, **AND recommended** a realistic solution.

The case requires clearly that you indicate "what course of action should be taken." (p. 4)

REC needed at this level

HOW? concrete actions to be taken

N.B.: CEPROC: *Code of Ethical Principles and Rules of Conduct* of CGA-Canada

ASSESSMENT KEY (continued)

a) **Core and core-related competencies: Financial accounting and reporting** (PK:FA:03)
Did the candidate explain the appropriate IFRS accounting treatment for two buildings owned by CYOF, distinguishing between 1- PPE and 2- Investment Property and 1- Revaluation model versus 2- Fair Value model?

Performance level	Marking grid
0. *NR/Inc*	Did not attempt this competency or provided insufficient material to evaluate OR response was incorrect.
1. *Substantially below*	**Identified** that 1- Building 1 is Property, Plant, and Equipment (PPE) and 2- Building 2 Investment Property, but did not advise about the accounting treatment for valuing at fair value. minimum knowledge required
2. *Below* basic theoretical concepts	**Identified** that Building 1 is Property, Plant, and Equipment (PPE) and Building 2 Investment Property, **and stated** that 1- Revaluation model would be used for PPE (IAS 16) and 2- Fair value model would be used for Investment Property (IAS 40), but did not elaborate.
3. *Meets* The answer about accounting for the buildings at the time of acquiring CYOF is clear and explicit.	**Explained** that 1- • Building 1 is Property, Plant, and Equipment (PPE) and 2- Building 2 is Investment Property. 1- • Revaluation model would be used for PPE (IAS 16) and 2- Fair value model would be used for Investment Property (IAS 40). 1- • Building 1 has only been depreciated and not previously revalued; the revaluation increase is recorded in OCI – Revaluation Surplus. \$196,000 - \$48,200 = \$147,800 2- • For Building 2, \$32,000 (\$120,000 – \$88,000) may be credited back to the Income Statement.
4. *Exceeds* Go further than initial recognition and discuss subsequent revaluations.	**Explained** IFRS requirements, such as the following: 1- • Per IAS 16, revaluations shall be made with sufficient regularity to ensure that the carrying amount does not differ materially from that which would be determined using fair value at the end of the reporting period. 2- • Per IAS 40, the fair value must also reflect the rental income from current leases.

A16

Reminder: With the "revaluation model," a fixed asset is amortized. With the "fair value model," an investment property is not amortized.

A short calculation is presented between parentheses to better justify the ideas put forward.

N.B.: OCI: Other Comprehensive Income

Note that candidates will not be expected to quote standard numbers in an exam situation.

It is absolutely essential that the candidate be aware that the same accounting standards do not apply to both buildings. This is necessary at the "Substantially below expectations" level, which is very low in the marking grid. Which means that this is indispensable basic knowledge.

summary

Building #1: IAS 16
- property, plant and equipment
- revaluation model
- "revaluation surplus" in comprehensive income
- revaluations on a sufficiently regular basis

Building #2: IAS 40
- investment property
- fair value model
- revaluation surplus credited to the income statement
- fair value must (amongst other things) reflect rental income

ASSESSMENT KEY (continued)

a) **Core and core-related competencies: Financial accounting and reporting** (PK:FA:01)
Did the candidate identify that the cost of replacement of the roof would be treated as an asset and that it needs to be treated as a separate component for depreciation purposes, in accordance with IFRS?

A candidate who does not realize that we are dealing with an asset will simply achieve the "0" level.

Performance level	Marking grid
0. *NR/Inc*	Did not attempt this competency or provided insufficient material to evaluate OR response was incorrect.
1. *Substantially below*	**Identified** that the cost of replacement of the roof would be treated as an asset, but did not justify. The only acceptable solution: It's an asset!
2. *Below*	**Identified** that the cost of replacement of the roof would be treated as an asset and that the new roof would be treated as a separate component, but did not justify.
3. *Meets* This level requires a sufficient understanding and application of the following accounting concepts: 1- asset 2- separate component 3- amortization	**Identified and justified** that the cost of replacement of the roof would be treated as an asset because • The amount spent improves the lifetime of the asset. • The benefit from the new replaced roof would be derived by CYOF over several years. **AND** that per IAS 16, the new roof would be treated as a separate component because criterion: useful life • It has a different useful life than the building as a whole. • Its dollar value is significant when compared to the value of the building itself. criterion: dollar value **AND explained** that the cost of the new roof would be amortized over the useful life of the new roof.
4. *Exceeds*	**Identified and justified** the facts of the case **AND made a recommendation** supported by the analysis, in accordance with IFRS.

A17

The accounting treatment must be justified using the case facts.

practical aspect

32/196

It would be useless to argue or to discuss alternatives, since it is clear which accounting treatment should be adopted.

REC needed at this level

a) **Core and core-related competencies: Financial accounting and reporting** (PK:FA:06)
Did the candidate explain the accounting for the lawsuit?

Link up with the p. 22 "Business Environment" competency.

This is a major risk for CYOF; a risk that needs to be analyzed early in the response.

basic level of knowledge required for this level

Performance level	Marking grid
0. *NR/Inc*	Did not attempt this competency or provided insufficient material to evaluate OR response was incorrect.
1. *Substantially below*	**Stated** that because GFI purchased 100% of shares of CYOF, GFI assumes 100% of the liabilities of CYOF.
2. *Below*	**Identified** the following: • The outcome of the lawsuit is uncertain. • It should be disclosed in some manner.
3. *Meets* IMP to refer to the concept: "more likely than not"	**Explained** publicly accountable • IFRS requirements regarding accounting/reporting of the lawsuit • The need of a legal opinion to determine if the lawsuit should be accrued or disclosed in a note to the financial statements
4. *Exceeds*	**Explained** the available data and information **AND made a recommendation** supported by the analysis.

REC needed at this level

lawsuit → legal opinion → financial statements

The candidate should recognize the hint in the case about the purchase of shares – if Green Foods only purchased assets of CYOF then it would not be legally responsible for any prior claims against CYOF – although there would be some support for Green having an ethical responsibility. The comment made by the Director of Operations is incorrect. The candidate should not take comments at face value and should look carefully at the underlying facts.

1- legal
2- ethical

One should always pick up on mistakes, even when they are made by a Director!

ASSESSMENT KEY (continued)

b) **Core and core-related competencies: Financial accounting and reporting** (PK:FA:09) EMPLOYEES

financial measures

Did the candidate evaluate the performance measures that can be used in evaluating performance of the CYOF employees? The evaluation is divided into two parts: the financial and the non-financial performance measures.

Performance level	Marking grid
0. *NR/Inc*	Did not attempt this competency or provided insufficient material to evaluate OR response was incorrect.
1. *Substantially below*	**Referred** to the performances measures listed in Exhibit 1but did not elaborate on them, or relate them to the goals of the company.
2. *Below* Explicitly mentioned in b) to take corporate objectives into account	**Identified**, in general terms • Financial and non-financial measures commonly used in evaluating performance • The importance of using performance measures that align employee performance with organizational goals
3. *Meets*	**Evaluated** each of the performances measures given in Exhibit 1.
4. *Exceeds*	**Evaluated** the available data and information and **made a recommendation**, supported by the analysis, regarding specific performance measures that GFI could use.

A18

organizational goals → performance measures → employees' performance

REC needed at this level

Exhibit 1 attached to the case includes seven financial performance measures under consideration. At the "Meets expectations" level, the candidate needs to use his judgment to evaluate whether or not each one is valid in that specific CYOF context.

My personal belief is that a candidate who evaluates the most important measures, say four or five out of the seven, should be deemed to have achieved the passing standard.

b) **Core and core-related competencies: Management accounting** (PK:MA:04) ORGANIZATION

non-financial measures

Did the candidate identify the non-financial factors used to measure firm-wide performance?

When performance measures need to be discussed, one needs to adopt a balanced scorecard approach.

Performance level	Marking grid
0. *NR/Inc*	Did not attempt this competency or provided insufficient material to evaluate OR response was incorrect.
1. *Substantially below*	**Identified** two or less of the four factors as per the Balanced scorecard approach.
2. *Below*	**Identified** three of the four factors as per the Balanced scorecard approach.
3. *Meets* Identification of four factors	**Identified** all of the four factors as per the Balanced scorecard approach: • Learning and growth — Are employees getting the training they need? • Internal business processes — What must we excel at? • Customer — How do customers see us? • Financial — What do we look like to shareholders?
4. *Exceeds*	**Identified AND explained** the elements of the Balanced scorecard approach **AND made a recommendation** supported by the analysis.

1. one or two → 2. three → 3. four

REC needed at this level

The resolution of this issue could be presented as a table.

One needs to differentiate the "Below expectations" and the "Meets expectations" levels in order to assess the performance of the candidate who has identified four measures. As for the passing standard, I believe that at least one practical example should be provided for each factor of the scorecard. The examples selected need to reflect the specifics of the case in question.

ASSESSMENT KEY (continued)

b) **Professional qualities and skills: Organizational effectiveness** (LEAD:EE:04) *professionalism*

Did the candidate describe the need to ensure good communication between the employees and he management team?

Link up with the p. 22 "Business Environment" competency.

Since a general unease has been detected amongst the employees (p. 4), one should try to lessen this problem when resolving the "Transition" issue.

Performance level	Marking grid
0. *NR/Inc*	Did not attempt this competency or provided insufficient material to evaluate OR response was incorrect.
1. *Substantially below*	**Restated** the facts of the case regarding the employees' apprehension. *impact*
2. *Below*	**Identified** the risk of increased turnover if the employees' concerns are not addressed. p. 4: "good evaluations" ⟶ "skilled"
3. *Meets* In order to reach this level, the candidate needs to describe a number of the steps to be taken. I would suggest no less than three.	**Described** p. 4: "several years" ⟶ "knowledgeable" • The importance of retaining the skilled and knowledgeable CYOF employees • The need for ongoing communications with employees to alleviate their apprehension *individual/group* • Alternative approaches to communicating with employees — for example, singly, in a group, with the management team, with individual members of the management team, at different times, and so on *HOW - WHO - WHEN*
4. *Exceeds* REC needed at this level	**Discussed** the issue **AND recommended** a realistic solution for addressing employees' concerns.

A19

SIMPLE, PRACTICAL MEASURES

One may notice stressing the "importance" of a problem or issue is something to be found constantly in the marking grid. The analysis of the financial performance measures, on p. 18, is another example.

Personally, in order to achieve the passing standard I would provide concrete examples that take into account as much as possible the specifics of the case. For example, since the report is addressed to the President of GFI, I would suggest he issued an announcement to the employees.

a) **Core and core-related competencies: Information technology** (PK:IT:02)

Did the candidate explain the need for payroll software? *PAYROLL*

problem to be dealt with on a timely basis

ONE MUST RECOGNIZE THE NEED TO SETTLE THE PROBLEM.

Performance level	Marking grid
0. *NR/Inc*	Did not attempt this competency or provided insufficient material to evaluate OR response was incorrect.
1. *Substantially below*	**Identified** that spreadsheets being used for payroll processing are outdated, but did not elaborate.
2. *Below*	**Identified** that spreadsheets being used for payroll processing are outdated **and recommended** that CYOF looks for alternatives, but did not elaborate.
3. *Meets*	**Explained** that CYOF uses software to process payroll and justified the benefits: • automated • more accurate • less error-prone • timely • facilitates easier statutory remittances One needs to pick up on the need to use "payroll processing software" rather than "spreadsheets" that have to be redone each time.
4. *Exceeds* REC needed at this level *practical aspect*	**Explained** the circumstances **AND made a recommendation** supported by the analysis, including the following: • CYOF should consider direct deposit of payroll into employee bank accounts, wherever possible. *example*

The candidate who suggests alternative solutions for processing payroll is implicitly meeting the "Below expectations" requirements.

Although this is not specified in the case, one may imagine that the controller used calculation software such as Excel. When it comes to processing payroll this is an "outdated" system.

✓ see beyond the immediate problem

ASSESSMENT KEY (continued)

b) transition ST

Core and core-related competencies: Information technology (PK:IT:08)

Did the candidate explain the issue of IT recovery and recommend online systems and off-site back-up, cross-trained personnel?

other spreadsheets

One needs to understand that the pay spreadsheets are not the only problem.

One needs to act rapidly in order to ensure business continuity.

A20

Performance level	Marking grid
0. *NR/Inc*	Did not attempt this competency or provided insufficient material to evaluate OR response was incorrect.
1. *Substantially below*	**Identified** that the spreadsheets that were used by the former Controller need to be recreated for ongoing use, but did not elaborate.
2. *Below*	**Identified** that CYOF needs an IT recovery plan, but did not elaborate.
3. *Meets* At the passing standard, one must RECOMMEND solutions.	**Explained** the issue of IT recovery **AND recommended** • Accessing spreadsheets • Recreating based on print-outs and developing an online system • Offsite backup • Cross-trained personnel
4. *Exceeds*	**Explained** the risks being faced in the current situation **AND made a recommendation** supported by the analysis.

identification of the problem

WHAT HAS TO BE DONE + WHY

REC needed at this level

impact of taking no action

Personally, in order to achieve the passing standard I would provide concrete examples that take into account as much as possible the specifics of the case. For example, the off-site backup could be handled online at the parent company GFI.

b) transition MT

Core and core-related competencies: Business Environment (PK:BE:09)

Did the candidate identify the need for disaster recovery plan and Business Continuity Planning (BCP) and explain the basic steps that must be carried out for the same?

✓ see beyond the immediate problem

ST: disaster recovery
MT: business continuity

At the passing standard, I believe it is necessary to illustrate the "medium term" dimension, i.e. to plan out what needs to be done in order to minimize losses of information in the future.

Performance level	Marking grid
0. *NR/Inc*	Did not attempt this competency or provided insufficient material to evaluate OR response was incorrect.
1. *Substantially below*	**Identified** that the spreadsheets that were used by the former Controller need to be recreated for ongoing use, but did not elaborate.
2. *Below*	**Identified** that CYOF needs a disaster recovery plan and an ongoing BCP, but did not elaborate.
3. *Meets* One needs to indicate "why" a disaster recovery plan is necessary and "how" it should be implemented.	**Identified** the need for disaster recovery and Business Continuity Planning (BCP): • Recreating based on printouts • Accessing spreadsheets **AND explained** the basic steps in having a BCP: • Systems with appropriate back-up procedures • Computer/IT systems – separate recovery plan • Policies and Procedures Manual implementation
4. *Exceeds*	**Identified** the risks being faced in the current situation **AND made a recommendation** supported by the analysis.

need for a plan

impact of taking no action

REC needed at this level

Before identifying this issue, you really need to step back and reflect on what could be suggested to ensure that the departure of an employee does not impact negatively on the entity's operations.

The candidate who does not recall what tax concepts are involved should nevertheless attempt to come out with an analysis that leads to a justified recommendation.

ASSESSMENT KEY (continued)

b) **Core and core-related competencies: Taxation** (PK:TX:02)

implicit problem

Did the candidate explain the tax implications of the proposed incentives from the perspective of CYOF and the employees?

Performance level	Marking grid
0. *NR/Inc*	Did not attempt this competency or provided insufficient material to evaluate OR response was incorrect.
1. *Substantially below* maximum level if only one point of view is taken into consideration	**Identified** • Tax implications of the proposed incentives from either the employee's perspective OR the 1's perspective, but not both. **OR** • Tax implications of only one of the proposed incentives from both the employee's perspective and the employer's perspective.
2. *Below*	**Identified** the tax implications of two of the proposed incentives from both the employee's perspective and the employer's perspective.
3. *Meets*	**Explained** the tax implications of all three proposed incentive alternatives from both the employee's perspective AND the employer's perspective.
4. *Exceeds*	**Explained** AND **provided valid recommendations** related to proposed incentive alternatives.

two → three

One needs to choose from amongst the three!

A well-presented resolution of this issue could consist of a two-column table: employee AND employer.

A21

REC needed at this level

If this competency is to be mastered, it is essential to take into account both the point of view of the employee AND that of the employer. Nevertheless, my own experience has taught me that most candidates will analyze only one point of view, i.e. that of the employee. Since the role involves working within the firm, one needs to remember to take into account the employer's interests, i.e. to mention the tax implications for him.

b) **Professional qualities and skills: Integrative approach** (PR:IA:02)

Did the candidate recommend an incentive that integrated interests of employees and the company?

N.B.: "Money" value and "perceived" value are two concepts one needs to consider.

Performance level	Marking grid
0. *NR/Inc*	Did not attempt this competency or provided insufficient material to evaluate OR response was incorrect.
1. *Substantially below*	**Demonstrated** a limited understanding of the difference in perceived value to the employees of the alternative incentives.
2. *Below*	**Discussed** the after-tax cost and after-tax value of the alternative incentives to the company and to the employee, respectively.
3. *Meets* One needs to refer to relevant theoretical concepts when resolving the issue.	**Recommended** • An incentive that integrates interests of employees and the company • An incentive based on consideration of both cost to the company and perceived value to the employee • An incentive that optimizes after-tax cost and after-tax value to the company and to the employee, respectively.
4. *Exceeds*	**Outlined** the effect of the recommended incentive plan on other functions within the organization, such as HR and accounting.

always keep in mind the after-tax cost

REC needed at the passing standard

employee AND employer

cost/value

impact

This competency measures the "professionalism" of the candidate as concerns his analysis and his structuring of the recommendation. As in the workplace, the "best" recommendation may vary according to the point of view adopted. One needs, therefore, to identify the objectives--sometimes conflicting--of the stakeholders, and look for an optimal solution. And when doing so, one must not lose sight of the fact that one needs a priori to maximize the benefits for the employer for whom one works. By ensuring that the perceived value of the incentive offered to the employee is high, one is promoting better employee performance and, indirectly, the achievement of CYOF objectives.

ASSESSMENT KEY (continued)

b) **Professional qualities and skills: Problem solving** (PR:PS:02)

Did the candidate evaluate the alternative incentive proposals using both qualitative and quantitative factors? *Professionalism: This competency measures the candidate's analytical skills. He must come out with an enlightened judgment based on the case information and his general knowledge.*

A22

Performance level	Marking grid
0. *NR/Inc*	Did not attempt this competency or provided insufficient material to evaluate OR response was incorrect.
1. *Substantially below*	**Identified**, but did not evaluate, qualitative and/or quantitative factors.
2. *Below* three	**Evaluated** the three incentive proposals using either ONLY qualitative information, or ONLY quantitative information.
3. *Meets*	**Evaluated** the three incentive proposals using both qualitative and quantitative information.
4. *Exceeds*	**Evaluated** the three incentive proposals and made a recommendation supported by the analysis.

quant OR qual → quant AND qual

Structure – qualitative – quantitative – recommendation

REC needed at this level

At the "Below expectations" level, the candidate is required to analyze "the three" incentive proposals. To achieve this competency, the candidate must offer a full discussion of the issue. I do not believe this is easy to do within the time allotted.

ANALYZE AND RECOMMEND

a) + b) **Core and core-related competencies: Business Environment** (PK:BE:06)

Did the candidate evaluate risk factors associated with the acquisition of CYOF?

When there is an investment (purchase of CYOF), you should consider the risks involved.

Performance level	Marking grid
0. *NR/Inc*	Did not attempt this competency or provided insufficient material to evaluate OR response was incorrect.
1. *Substantially below*	**Stated** that there are risks associated with the acquisition of CYOF, but did not identify them.
2. *Below*	**Discussed** some of the risks, but did not elaborate: • Lawsuit • Sale of non-compliant products
3. *Meets* stated → discussed → evaluated	**Evaluated** • Risks associated with lawsuit because GFI purchased 100% of shares of CYOF. *why* • Risk of unfavourable publicity related to this lawsuit negatively impacting sales. *impact* • Risk of sale of non-compliant products due to reliance on suppliers' word in place of testing for compliance with agreements. *reliability* • Risk of loss of experienced CYOF employees due to the transition.
4. *Exceeds* *REC needed at this level*	**Evaluated** the risks associated with the acquisition **AND made a recommendation** supported by the analysis, such as the following: • Institution of a vendor compliance program • Management meetings with CYOF staff • A marketing strategy to counter negative publicity or a public statement acknowledging past breaches • Appropriate accounting options related to the lawsuit

The candidate who has correctly identified the issues that need to be dealt with on a timely basis in a) is certainly on the right path to determining the main risk factors associated with the acquisition of CYOF.

I do not believe it is necessary to provide a separate "Risk evaluation" section as a prerequisite to acquiring the competency in question. The elements required here can also be brought out during the problems or issues resolution process.

When playing the role of substitute controller, a good deal of information is obtained, information that was not available to the President of GFI at the time of the purchase of CYOF. When presenting the memo addressed to the President, one needs to inform him of the main risks noted, and follow up with solutions that will remove or lessen such risks. Personally, at the "Meets expectations" level, I would expect at least three procedures to be described.

ASSESSMENT KEY (continued)

a) + b) **Professional qualities and skills: Professional self-evaluation** (PR:SE:02)

Did the candidate explain the need to consult legal counsel and hire specialists to test vendor compliance of standards and product criteria? 1- legal counsel re lawsuit
2- specialists to check vendor compliance with standards

To achieve this level of competency one needs to take into account the impact of the lawsuit on the FS.

Performance level	Marking grid
0. *NR/Inc*	Did not attempt this competency or provided insufficient material to evaluate OR response was incorrect.
1. *Substantially below*	**Restated** the Director of Operations assessment of GFI's responsibility related to the lawsuit.
2. *Below* IAS 37	**Identified** the lawsuit as an issue that would affect GFI's financial statements. lawsuit ⟶ impact on FS
3. *Meets* One needs to recognize the need for outside assistance in both areas: lawsuit and agreements.	**Explained** the need to consult legal counsel regarding 1- • The lawsuit in order to inform GFI's decision regarding the accounting and/or disclosure related to the lawsuit 1- • Whether there is legal recourse to the vendor that supplied the pesticide-contaminated vegetables in violation of the agreement **Recognized** the 2- need to hire specialists to test vendor compliance with the standards and criteria.
4. *Exceeds* ✓ see beyond the immediate issue	**Explained** 1- • The relationship between seeking a legal opinion related to the lawsuit, and the audit professionals engaged by GFI. 2- • The role that experts in pesticide use and/or food production could play in a vendor-compliance program. 1- • That legal opinion be obtained about possible legal recourse to the vendor who violated the agreement to supply organic produce. 2- • That specialists would be able to test whether produce have in fact been organically grown.

immediate needs ST

needs and impacts MT

biological foods → pesticide-free → non-compliance with agreement

A23

see the "cause-to-effect" link

It is important that the candidate recognize that he is not an expert in all fields and that there are limits to his range of knowledge. Since he is not a legal consultant, he cannot evaluate the possibility of losing a lawsuit. His role will be rather to make appropriate use of the expert's assessment. Or again, as a professional accountant, he may certainly determine which of the agreement criteria need to be checked over; but when it comes to verifying whether or not biological foods are being grown, he will be unable to explain "how" this should be done.

Here are some other comments regarding the overall assessment key.

- The "professional qualities and skills" competencies should receive particular attention. THESE COMPETENCIES GO BEYOND THE CONTENTS OF THE RESPONSE PER SE, BECAUSE THEY DETERMINE HOW THE ANALYSIS WAS DRAWN UP, OR EVEN FURTHER, THEY EVALUATE THE SKILLS OF THE CANDIDATE WHEN IT COMES TO RESOLVING PROBLEMS OR ISSUES. Since these competencies allow one to measure the professional level of the candidate, one needs to pay particular attention to the differentiations between the "Below expectations" and "Meets expectations" levels. Personally, when in doubt, I do not award the candidate the passing standard.
- One needs constantly to remember that the quality of the analysis is an essential element if one is to achieve the "Exceeds expectations" level. Thus, the recommendations made MUST be integrated with the specifics of the case.

ASSESSMENT KEY (continued)

This competency is the only one in which the focus is more on the "appearance" or "form" than on the "substance" of the response.

a) + b)

Professional qualities and skills: Communication (PR:CM:02)
Did the candidate prepare a memo using appropriate characteristics?

Memo to the President

Performance level	Marking grid
0. *NR/Inc*	Failed to address this competency.
1. *Substantially below*	In the requested format (for example, memo) and had 0 characteristics.
2. *Below*	In the requested format and had one key characteristic.
3. *Meets*	In the requested format and had two key characteristics.
4. *Exceeds* One needs to inform the President of what is going on at CYOF.	In the requested format and had three key characteristics. Key characteristics • Appropriate ton • Appropriate language • Well-organized A "memorandum" is a document used inside the firm. It impacts the approach to resolving problems or issues.

one → two → three

A24

Personally, I give the passing standard to the candidate who communicates his response without making "major mistakes."

TONE: Since the memo is addressed to the President, there is no need to explain technical terms such as "disaster recovery plan."

LANGUAGE: Simple, precise and unambiguous wording, complete ideas, reasonable abbreviations, professional language, etc.

Unless they are really excessive, spelling or grammar mistakes are not really taken into account when assessing Communication competency.

ORGANIZATION: Appropriate presentation, titles and subtitles, structured discussion, conclusions or recommendations that stand out clearly, appropriate references, etc.

Professional qualities and skills: Communication (PR:CM:03)
Did the candidate communicate the issues identified in the case to the appropriate people in a timely, clear, and concise manner?

who when what

a) + b)

Performance level	Marking grid
0. *NR/Inc*	Failed to address this competency.
1. *Substantially below*	Answer was hard to follow.
2. *Below*	Answer was understandable (logical), although assessor needed to make *many* assumptions.
3. *Meets*	Answer was understandable (logical) AND written in a clear and concise manner, such that the assessor needed to make *few* assumptions.
4. *Exceeds*	Answer was understandable (logical) AND written in a clear and concise manner, such that the assessor needed to make *no* assumptions.

THE RESOLUTION OF PROBLEMS OR ISSUES NEEDS TO BE STRUCTURED LOGICALLY.

one idea → one sentence → one paragraph

"Clear" and "concise" are the key words!

The text of the response must flow well.

Coherent ideas.

The assessor needs to understand what he is reading without having to wonder "what did the candidate mean?" He cannot make presumptions about something that is not there in writing. The assessor who reads the candidate's response without having to wonder about the understandability of the ideas contained therein will probably award the "Meets expectations" level.

Assessment of a student response [a]

To: President of GFI
From: CGA
Date: February 20, 2009

OK

I suggest you list the most important problems under "Subject".

Subject: Problems related to the acquisition of CYOF, transition of the new employees, and performance measures.

Please find below the memo you asked me to write. I concentrated more specifically on the problems I believe have to be settled most urgently, along with a number of other issues you communicated to me. For more details or if there are other things you want to discuss, please contact me at your convenience.

This paragraph contains no relevant or new idea. So make it shorter.

Suppliers A25

intro not useful

Based on the information I have, I notice that five of your suppliers are located more than 250 km from the store. This does not respect your agreement. I think the problem should be settled without wasting time, since the difference between CYOF and its competitors is the fact that the former is committed to the environment and to selling local, organic produce. This, of course, means that CYOF can charge more, but still have a competitive advantage because more and more consumers are attracted to organic produce.

How can the problem be resolved?

"I rec that…" is preferable.

very good links to the case

The justification is too long; it sums up the case and becomes rather repetitive when you start talking about competitors.

ethics?

The problem appears to come from the fact that the previous CYOF controller had authorized these exemptions. Actually, a cheque was found to be made out to the controller. It might be worth finding out whether the supplier and the controller were acquainted.? Whatever the case, I don't think this type of exemption can be tolerated.

You just skim over the subject. What are the potential consequences? What actions need to be taken?

better to write a short title

Another problem has come up, this time due to a client-initiated lawsuit. It seems that one of the suppliers uses pesticides, which goes against the agreement. For the same reasons mentioned earlier, we cannot tolerate this because it could hurt both CYOF's brand image and the company. All this shows that these suppliers are not trustworthy and, in fact, are demonstrating bad faith. So, they should not be trusted in the future.

impacts well defined

A bit drastic. It might be difficult to replace so many suppliers.

clearly stated RECS

My recommendation is that you look for other suppliers to replace those who have not respected the agreement, to make sure that the 250 kilometers distance limit is respected and that no pesticides are used in the fruit and vegetable production. On top of that, in the future, you should set up controls to make sure that no supplier located over 250 kilometers away is approved. You could exercise these controls by getting another staff member to cross-check. I would also recommend product quality controls after the initial inspection, for example sampling products when they come in. There should be employees assigned to this task.

"km" is shorter

Since this is an important subject, you need to go further in developing steps that can be taken.
What is more, this is a "list" of recommendations that can be presented as a series, starting each item with a gerund or imperative.

relevant controls; well linked to context.

---

a This is a genuine student response, in fact he was a Certified General Accountant candidate, in the last term of his degree in Accounting. He simulated the case "Close to You Organic Foods" on a computer within the allotted time of 100 minutes. For presentation purposes, the assessor's comments are written in the font used here. Sometimes those comments could be presented more concisely.

Client-initiated lawsuit

There's no point in explaining to your employer things that don't apply to his own situation.

I wished to tell you that, since GFI has bought up the shares of CYOF, it is now responsible for any liabilities and lawsuits affecting the latter, even though the events that gave rise to these problems took place before the acquisition. If the company had purchased the assets, things would have been different. But, since GFI is now the owner, it has become liable for CYOF and must take responsibility for contingencies that were unknown at the time of the purchase. This means you need to keep a close eye on the lawsuit and that you should make sure nothing similar happens again. As I said above, at the very least, you need to replace the offending suppliers. This lawsuit bothers me because it means that the ecological image that CYOF has built up over the years could be more greatly damaged than we can anticipate.

Excellent!

O.K. but that's the same idea as the one in the 1st sentence.

Good link with earlier subject. Excellent that you picked up on "how do the customers see" CYOF.

already said

Here you are talking about "one" supplier and not about "all" of them. It's better that way!

A26 This is why it is even more important that something like this does not happen again. As accountants, we need to determine the probability of such lawsuit requiring a payment, in which case we will have to record a contingent liability. You should also ask your legal counsel whether there is any defense available as regards the accusation laid against CYOF, and whether the supplier can't be made liable for the contamination. Since there was a written agreement, it is possible that liability will lie with the supplier and not with CYOF.

With IFRS, the criterion is "more likely than not."

Excellent!

I would therefore recommend that you get in touch with your legal counsel so that this file may be followed closely. Additionally, if you have not done so already, you should get rid of the products responsible for the lawsuit. *VG*

New controller

case summary

Apparently, CYOF depended greatly on its controller. Indeed the accounting staff all appear a bit lost now the controller is no longer with them. For example, they are concerned about their possible lack of skill, and the payroll staffer wonders how she is going to manage to process the payroll. The very fact that the controller has resigned seems suspicious to me. *AND?* Perhaps there were things he did not want the new management to know about. You must hire a new controller as soon as possible, one who is very competent. It is also essential that, unlike his predecessor, he is absolutely trustworthy. This means he must have a high level of expertise as regards a company accounting cycle and that he can inspire confidence in his employees by working with them. Finally, it is important that the new controller can use his judgment, be creative when it comes to the problems that may arise at CYOF, and really understand the company's environmental policies.

impact?

Try rather to make use of the case data when drawing your conclusion on the former controller.

Pointless: the subject is not part of the requirements. Remember you are there to "replace" the controller.

It's not your job to deal with the hiring of a new controller. You should rather be talking about the impact the former controller's behavior has had on CYOF.

I would therefore recommend that you hire a new controller as soon as possible, but make a complete study of his biodata before hiring him, in order to check that he does have the skills I mentioned above. Amongst other things, this study should check out the applicant's past experience and make an assessment of his skills through a series of tests and structured interviews. References should also be obtained in order to verify the accuracy of the work experience described.

Your ideas are OK, but they are not necessary in the context of the requirements.

Your recommendation is not realistic. Do you sincerely believe that the former controller is going to cooperate under the circumstances? He made a quick departure!

Payroll system and missing documents

too long a summary of the case before getting round to a new idea

The payroll staffer at CYOF thinks she will no longer be able to process payments using the former system. Apparently, the former controller has possession of the spreadsheets required for making payments. This is a problem, because it means that payments may not be exact, or some might be forgotten about for the weeks or months before the acquisition. These spreadsheets need to be recovered, if possible, by getting in touch with the former controller.

Impacts OK

Too much about getting info from the former controller. You need to find faster, simpler solutions. He can't be relied on!

Additionally, it may be that the former controller holds other confidential information belonging to CYOF. It is very important to recover everything that relates directly or indirectly to CYOF financial information. This means that, as a first step, you should contact the former controller and ask him to return the CYOF pay spreadsheets and, at the same time, ask him whether he may not have "omitted" to hand over other documents. Should he not cooperate (which, I suspect, may happen), you should ask your legal counsel what you can do to ensure recovery of CYOF confidential, in-house information. Recovering such data is essential, since it directly affects financial information.

You are assuming that when he left he took confidential info with him. There is no indication of this in the case itself.

Furthermore, since GFI is publicly accountable, there will be an audit at the end of the period. Mistakes will then need to be justified, and this could be difficult. In such a case, the auditors might find themselves obliged to express a qualified opinion as regards the financial statements, more especially if there are documents missing and if the amounts involved are significant. The impact as concerns GFI could be worse that it may look at first.

You are "presuming" that mistakes were made. Not knowing how to produce spreadsheets doesn't mean that there are errors in the system.

Colleague? Take your code of ethics out!

A27

The payroll system also needs reviewing. Manual spreadsheets are too open to errors and difficult to monitor. The payroll system should be computerized *OK* just like the other items in the accounting cycle, if this has not already been done. Employees should fill in a time sheet that is then entered in the system, and all overtime hours have to be approved. Additionally, backup copies should be made on a regular basis so that no data is lost. *OK* Only authorized staff should be allowed to access accounting information, which should be password protected and impossible to copy, so that no information leaks outside the company. *OK*

impact OK

You have fully understood what is going on at CYOF. Good solution!

You are attempting to find solutions to CYOF's problems. Excellent! It would be easier to draft this in stages: 1- ST and 2- MT.

I would therefore recommend that everything be done to ensure recovery of the documents containing financial information. I would also recommend that the accounting system be computerized as soon as possible.

Your first REC is too general; suggest a practical "way" out.

Your 2nd REC lacks precision. It can only be done in MT. Try rather to focus on finding more solutions to the immediate problems.

<u>Accounting treatment of buildings</u>

First building

Good, because you don't cast doubts on the model

Since the *OK* company has adopted the revaluation model, such revaluation should be made on a regular basis. I have noticed that the fair value of the buildings is much higher than their net accounting value. This does not line up with the standard for the revaluation model of property, plant and equipment, because we are required to ensure that the fair value is not significantly different from the book value at the end of the financial period. This means that if we can trust the fair values indicated (i.e. they originate from the market and have been determined by an expert), then these values should be used when recording the buildings. *OK* If a revaluation is carried out, then the whole class will need to be revalued. *OK* This means that all the other buildings classified as tangible or fixed assets should also be subject to testing. You should note that these buildings must continue to be depreciated, even when recorded at their fair value, and that revaluation must be carried out over a period that takes into account the fluctuation in asset values. *OK* Since the real estate market is very unstable, you will probably have to revaluate the building every one or two years. *OK* After revaluation, the increase in value will be reflected in the comprehensive income and presented along with the shareholders' equity as a "revaluation surplus."

The $ amounts are provided, so use them. Bracket them (...) if you like.

??? 1st time for CYOF

GOOD!

Needs completing, since there are 2 ways of recording surpluses.

You have fully understood the accounting standard. To better integrate theory with case, try using the figures provided in the latter.

As regards the roof, its replacement cost can be capitalized because it will be used over several years, ensuring that the building continues to provide economic benefits to the entity, and because the cost of repairs can be assessed reliably. The entity <u>may decide</u>? to account for the roof as a component, since it makes up a significant part of the value of the building, i.e. 15%. *OK* However, GFI is not required to !!! do so. The advantage would be that you could then adopt a different depreciation period for the roof, i.e. a shorter one that would realistically reflect its wear and tear. But since the amount involved is low, adopting a different accounting approach might turn out to be more complicated and expensive than useful.

Revise! It is mandatory to separate according to components.

Unnecessary conclusion: there isn't any choice to be made.

Since the case explicitly requires you to indicate whether it's an asset or a repair and maintenance cost, I would like to see the term "asset" clearly included here. (p. 3)

Second building

Good integration of theoretical concepts with the case.

A28 Since this building is used to generate rentals, something that is not CYOF's main activity, it should be reclassified as investment property, according to IAS 40. Additionally, since the building in question generates rental income under the terms of a simple operating lease, the entity should use the fair value model to record it. Moreover, the fair value must be determined each year and the building must not be depreciated. Impairment losses or increases in value must be recognized during the period *OK* in which they occur. In the present case, CYOF should record the building at $120,000. This will represent an increase of $32,000 for purposes of reclassification.

Excellent

Be more precise! WHERE?

<u>Transition of new employees and performance measurement</u>

You are telling me what is missing. You should rather be trying to provide suggestions for improvements.

The intro is too long and doesn't offer any new idea.

Accounting staff seem to be ill-at-ease since the takeover. Some of them are afraid they may lose their jobs, and this may be, as I explained earlier, because they are a little bewildered. I also think that they are being abandoned and that no one is telling them what GFI intends to do to ensure that CYOF continues to operate prosperously and in a proper manner. One should remember that these employees have been with the company for a number of years and that you need them if you are to ensure the continuity of CYOF. *OK* Additionally, they are accustomed to working in a company whose purpose is transmitting social values and doing business with local merchants. Consequently, if they are to remain comfortable, it is necessary that you avoid depersonalizing their relationship with the company. This means listening to their concerns and paying attention to their needs. One of the worst things you can ask employees is to do their job without having the necessary tools. Measures must therefore be taken to facilitate their integration.

KSF seen

good

general

Financial measures can most certainly be used to motivate employees and improve their performance on an ongoing basis. It is very important that the incentive offered depend on the performance of individual stores and not of the company as a whole. If the assessment is based on the overall performance of the business, it could lead to dysfunctional situations where some take advantage of the good performance of others, and <u>vice versa</u>. ???

1st sentence general

A good justification of the need to retain the employees. But your only recommendation is too general. You need to suggest more STEPS that can be taken to assist in making the transition easier.

useless intro

<u>Following this same line of argument</u>, the financial measures would use are the following:

- Increase in the number of units sold
- Increase in sales figures
- Increase in the gross margin (decrease in costs)
- Faster inventory turnover

Excellent choices. But you still need to justify them!

You need to make more use of the information in Exhibit 1 in order to determine the key elements that will allow you to evaluate the store managers. For example, you could suggest a product-by-product analysis.

Why? If you don't justify your idea, you are simply repeating the requirement.

However, it is also very important to use non-financial measures. Here are some that I consider to be relevant:

- Client satisfaction
- Diversification and quality of products
- Respect for the environment (product production)
- Suppliers who respect the conditions in their agreements.

Well linked to the context specifics, but the practical side is missing. How will performance be measured?
E.g.: Website survey to measure customer satisfaction.

useless intro

I would also say that I do not believe that $100 per quarter is a very significant incentive. If you cannot increase this amount, I would recommend choosing between the three currently under consideration for each Director, each quarter: OK

- $100 cash bonus: This amount would be exchangeable for any product or service. TAX?
- A fruit basket (cost to the store of $100): This requires that the employee accept predetermined products that may be of no interest to him. A29
- I'm out of time! Try to plan out your response better so that you can handle everything requested. This is an easy subject and you only glanced at it!

Don't write this sort of comment in your response.

Here are some other suggestions that could make the transition easier:

- Hold a meeting with the accounting staff to introduce the new owners and tell them as much as possible about the direction in which the latter wish CYOF to move. OK
- Tell them that a new controller will be hired and will meet with the staff before taking up his duties.
- Tell them that no staff members will lose their jobs and that they are all important employees as far as CYOF is concerned. OK
- Collect information about staff operational concerns, in order to fix all problems as soon as possible. Explain that this information will be examined and steps taken to ensure they can continue doing their tasks as before. OK

good links with subjects previously discussed

Text too general here. You could have used certain case facts to illustrate your idea, for example the fact that spreadsheet procedures will be simplified.

ASSESSOR'S COMMENTS

TO REMEMBER:

- All your analyses end with recommendations.
- The problems that should be dealt with on a timely basis were correctly identified.
- Several good links with the specific CYOF context.

TO IMPROVE:

- Take the time to properly identify the problem or issue to be discussed. To this end, review the section about "spreadsheets." The case facts sometimes indicate the "consequences" of a problem. At that point you need to step back and identify what the problem really is.
- Do not presuppose the existence of problems devoid of facts. We do not know whether there are system errors or even whether the controller took confidential information with him when he left. You need to stick with the case facts!
- Review your recommendations, because some of them are not very solid or realistic. Also, you need to structure your text so that the ST solutions precede the MT ones. Try and provide a reasonable response to all the case requirements.

Good work!

REPORT ON ASSESSMENT [a]

Competency	Marking grid
Assurance 3 only just nature of the controls properly understood	1. **Stated** that there is a need for ensuring that vendors comply with the terms of the contract OK **OR stated** that the vendor-appointment process needs to be reviewed, but did not elaborate. OK 2. **Identified** the importance of the CYOF's marketing platform in extracting a premium price from customers (org, 250 km) VG **OR stated** that the vendor-appointment process should ensure that the criteria set are met. +/- 3. **Determined** the importance of the CYOF's marketing platform OK and that controls be put in place to ensure contract requirements are met on an ongoing basis OK **OR described** controls in the vendor-appointment process. +/- 4. **Outlined** important elements of a vendor compliance program **AND Recommended** methods to ensure compliance with standards. insufficient controls
Management accounting 3	1. **Stated** that vendors are contractually bound to provide pesticide-free product **OR** to provide product grown within the established zone. 2. **Identified** GFI's, and previously CYOF's, lack of control over suppliers. OK 3. **Identified** the implications of a lack of control. **Recognized** the breach of trust with customers due to the lack of due diligence with respect to ensuring standards were met. YES ~~4.~~ **Identified AND evaluated** the available information **AND made a recommendation** supported by the analysis. incomplete
Skateholder focus 3	1. **Identified** customers as stakeholders. 2. **Identified** customers' demand for organic foods that reduce harm to the environment as a critical stakeholder interest. YES 3. **Recommended** internal controls that meet the expectations of the customer and that are consistent with the company's branding. YES 4. **Outlined** an action plan for implementing the recommendation. NO context properly understood
Assurance 2	1. **Restated** the facts of the case, but did not analyze further. p. 25 2. **Identified** that the facts of the case indicate that the actions of the former controller appear questionable, YES but did not state the possibility of fraud. ~~3.~~ **Identified** the (relevant) facts of the case. (> 250 km, 20% higher rates, cheque) 4. **Identified AND evaluated** the available information **AND made a recommendation** supported by the analysis. no perception of possibility of "fraud"
Ethics and trust 1	1. **Restated** the facts of the case, or stated that there was an issue related to ethics. p. 25 2. **Identified** the potential ethical issues (cheque, non-qualifying supplier). 3. **Explained** the ethical issue and discussed it (Code, contact colleague/Association). 4. **Explained** the ethical issue, **AND recommended** a realistic solution. Ethical aspect unnoticed
Financial accounting 3	1. **Identified** that Building 1 is Property, Plant, and Equipment (PPE) and Building 2 is Investment Property, but did not advise about valuing at fair value. 2. **Stated** that Revaluation model would be used for PPE (IAS 16) and Fair value model would be used for Investment Property (IAS 40), but did not elaborate. 3. **Explained** the accounting treatment for Building 1 and Building 2. VG ~~4.~~ **Explained** IFRS requirements concerning revaluations and fair value. lack of clarity in discussion regarding fair value
Financial accounting 2 towards 3	1. **Identified** that the cost of replacement of the roof would be treated as an asset. 2. **Identified** that the cost of replacement of the roof would be treated as a separate component. +/- 3. **Identified and justified** that the cost of replacement of the roof would be treated as an asset **AND** that per IAS 16, the new roof would be treated as a separate component YES **AND explained** that the cost of the new roof would be amortized over the useful life of the new roof. YES 4. **Identified and justified** the facts of the case **AND made a recommendation** supported by the analysis, in accordance with IFRS.

[a] This "shortened" assessment key, used to inform the student of how he is assessed, is based on the marking grids on pages 13 to 24. It could, of course, be more concise and limited to one page, as necessary.

REPORT ON ASSESSMENT (continued)

Competency	Marking grid	
Financial accounting 3	1. **Stated** that because GFI purchased 100% of shares of CYOF, GFI assumes 100% of the liabilities of CYOF. YES 2. **Identified** that the outcome of the lawsuit is uncertain and should be disclosed in some manner. YES 3. **Explained** IFRS requirements and the need of a legal opinion (accrued/disclosed). YES 4. **Explained** the available information **AND made a recommendation** supported by the analysis.	
Financial accounting 2	1. **Referred** to the performance measures, but did not elaborate on them, or relate them to the goals. 2. **Identified** measures commonly used in evaluating performance and the importance of using measures that align employee performance with organizational goals. YES 3. **Evaluated** each of the performances measures given in Exhibit 1. 4. **Evaluated** the available information **AND made a recommendation** supported by the analysis regarding specific performance measures that GFI could use.	A31 lack of explanations
Management accounting 1	1. **Identified** two or less of the four factors as per the Balanced scorecard approach. 2. **Identified** three of the four factors as per the Balanced scorecard approach. 3. **Identified** all of the four factors as per the Balanced scorecard approach, (Learning and growth, Internal business processes, Customer, Financial) indirectly p. 29 4. **Identified AND explained** the elements of the Balanced scorecard approach **AND made a recommendation** supported by the analysis.	
Organizational effectiveness 2	1. **Restated** the facts of the case regarding the employees' apprehension. 2. **Identified** the risk of increased turnover if the employees' concerns are not addressed. Importance of the employees is understood 3. **Described** the importance of retaining the employees and the need for ongoing communications, and described alternatives approaches to communicate. NO 4. **Discussed** the issue **AND recommended** a realistic solution for addressing employees' concerns.	general and incomplete
Information technology 2 generous	1. **Identified** that spreadsheets being used for payroll processing are out-dated. OK 2. **Recommended** that CYOF looks for alternatives, but did not elaborate. OK 3. **Explained** that CYOF uses software to process payroll and justified the benefits. (automated, more accurate, less error-prone, timely, easier statutory remittances) +/- 4. **Explained** the circumstances **AND made a recommendation** supported by the analysis.	lack of explanations
Business environment 2	1. **Identified** that the spreadsheets that were used by the former controller need to be recreated for ongoing use. YES 2. **Identified** that CYOF needs an IT recovery plan. 3. **Explained** the issue of IT recovery **AND made a recommendation.** incomplete (accessing spreadsheets, recreating data, offsite backup, cross-trained personnel) 4. **Explained** the risks being faced in the current situation **AND made a recommendation** supported by the analysis.	
Business environment 2	1. **Identified** that the spreadsheets that were used by the former controller need to be recreated for ongoing use. OK 2. **Identified** that CYOF needs a disaster recovery plan and an ongoing Business Continuity Planning (BCP). 3. **Identified** the need for disaster recovery plan and BCP (recreating data, accessing spreadsheets) **AND explained** the basic steps in having a BCP (back-up, computer/ IT systems, Manual). 4. **Identified** the risks being faced in the current situation **AND made a recommendation** supported by the analysis.	indirectly p. 27

REPORT ON ASSESSMENT (continued)

Competency	Marking grid
Taxation 0	1. **Identified** tax implications of the incentives from either the employee's perspective **OR** the employer's perspective, but not both **OR identified** tax implications of only one of the incentives from both the employee's perspective **AND** the employer's perspective. 2. **Identified** the tax implications of two of the proposed incentives from both the employee's perspective and the employer's perspective. 3. **Explained** the tax implications of all three proposed incentive alternatives from both the employee's perspective AND the employer's perspective. 4. **Explained AND provided** valid recommendations related to proposed incentive alternatives. *Easy issue!*
Integrative approach 1	1. **Demonstrated** a limited understanding of the difference in perceived value to the employees of the alternative incentives. *OK* 2. **Discussed** the after-tax cost and after-tax value of the alternative incentives to the company and to the employee, respectively. *NO* 3. **Recommended** an incentive that integrates interests of employees (perceived value, after-tax value) and of the company (cost, after-tax cost). 4. **Outlined** the effect of the recommended incentive plan on other functions within the organization (human resources, accounting). *Lack of justification for REC*
Problem solving 1	1. **Identified**, but did not evaluate, qualitative and/or quantitative factors. 2. **Evaluated** the three incentive proposals using either ONLY qualitative information, **OR** ONLY quantitative information. 3. **Evaluated** the three incentive proposals using both qualitative **AND** quantitative information. 4. **Evaluated** the three incentive proposals **AND made a recommendation** supported by the analysis.
Business environment *excellent* 4	1. **Stated** that there are risks associated with the acquisition of CYOF, but did not identify them. 2. **Discussed** some of the risks, but did not elaborate. *OK* 3. **Evaluated** the risks associated with the acquisition. (lawsuit, unfavourable publicity, non-compliant products, loss of employees) *major risks identified and evaluated* 4. **Evaluated** the risks associated with the acquisition **AND made a recommendation** supported by the analysis. *YES* *REC supported for each risk*
Professional auto-evaluation 2	1. **Restated** the Director assessment of GFI's responsibility related to the lawsuit. 2. **Identified** the lawsuit as an issue that would affect GFI's financial statements. 3. **Explained** the need to consult legal counsel regarding the lawsuit (accounting treatment, legal recourse to the vendor) **AND Recognized** the need to hire specialists to test vendor compliance with the standards and criteria. *YES* 4. **Explained** the need to consult other professionals and experts (lawsuit and audit professionals, vendor-compliance program, legal recourse to the vendor, whether produce have been organically grown).
Communication 3	1. In the requested format (for example, memo) and had **0** characteristics. 2. In the requested format and had **one** key characteristic. 3. In the requested format and had **two** key characteristics. 4. In the requested format and had **three** key characteristics. Key characteristics: Appropriate tone, Appropriate language, Well-organized *Some terms need review; Text sometimes too general.*
Communication 3	1. Answer was hard to follow. 2. Answer was understandable (logical), although assessor needed to make **many** assumptions. 3. Answer was understandable (logical) *OK* **AND** written in a clear and concise manner, *OK* such that the assessor needed to make **few** assumptions. 4. Answer was understandable (logical) **AND** written in a clear and concise manner, such that the assessor needed to make **no** assumptions. *some ideas are too general*

EXHIBIT

CASE B

StarNova

B1

CASE B

StarNova

(5 hours)

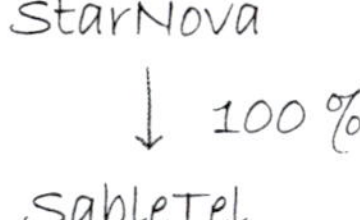

StarNova (5 hours) a

StarNova is a publicly traded company that operates exclusively in Canada. Its revenue exceeded $800 million for the year ended August 31, 2010. The company has a diversified portfolio of businesses ranging from consumer goods to high technology. All of StarNova's businesses operate independently and must be self-sufficient. Typically StarNova expects all of its businesses to generate a 15% return on investment.

IMP objective 15%

SableTel Limited (SableTel) is a 100%-owned subsidiary of StarNova and operates in the telecommunications industry. SableTel sells long-distance, local telephone access, mobile, and Internet and data services to end users. SableTel's reporting document (Exhibit II), as well as its 2010 financial statements (Exhibit III) provide more information about its operations. Each subsidiary's reporting document is expected to meet StarNova's Management Discussion and Analysis (MD&A) requirements so that StarNova's senior management can easily incorporate it in StarNova's annual report to shareholders. b

IMP

The telecommunications industry in Canada is strictly regulated, and each year SableTel must have its operating licence renewed by the Canadian Radio-television and Telecommunications Commission (CRTC) c. Further information about the telecommunications industry is provided in Exhibit IV.

yearly licence

On September 13, 2010, Dan Wilson, Chief Executive Officer (CEO) of SableTel, presented an overview of SableTel's 2010 financial results and 2011 strategic plan (Exhibit VII) to the executive committee (EC) of StarNova. The EC was confused by the results for 2010 and concerned about the 2011 strategic plan, particularly because SableTel is requesting funding from StarNova of $21 million. d e

IMP dates

21 M !!!

ROLE

Today is September 14, 2010. You, CA, work in StarNova's finance department. You were copied on an email (Exhibit I) from John McReynolds, the Chair of the EC, to Dan Wilson, outlining concerns raised by the EC. John has asked you to drop everything to respond to the issues raised in the email.

email EXH I

B3

John M., Chair EC
↓
Dan Wilson, CEO

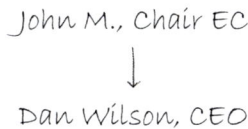

a When reading, the relevant case facts were highlighted in yellow, whereas everything that concerned the requirements was highlighted in green. Comments that a candidate could write down on the case itself were written in the font used here.
N.B.: Since annotations are used by the candidate only, words are abbreviated. Thus, one will find "IFRS", "M" (millions), "IMP" (important), "EXH" (Exhibit), "proc" (procedure), "FS" (financial statement), "rev" (revenue), "NRV" (net realizable value), "IC" (internal control), "MARK" (marketing), "strat" (strategic), "info" (information), "obj" (objective)", "tax" (taxation), etc.

b The words "expected to meet" must be noticed, since the "reporting document" is probably not meeting StarNova's MD&A requirements.

c The US counterpart of the CRCT is the "Federal Communications Commission."

d The fact that the Committee is "confused" by the results of 2010 must be picked up. In Exhibit III, we note that SableTel goes from a loss of ($1,287,860) in 2009 to a profit of $1,178,000 in 2010. Since the Committee is "confused" by these results, one must pay attention to the facts that explain, confirm or refute them.

e The fact that the Committee is "concerned" about the strategic plan must be noted. A priori, this means that it contains elements that are lacking in precision or are erroneous. One should not forget this when reading the text.

INDEX TO EXHIBITS

B4

[a] The word "draft" must be noticed, since this means that the financial information is likely to be incomplete or contain errors.

EXHIBIT I a

EMAIL FROM JOHN MCREYNOLDS TO DAN WILSON

To: Dan.Wilson@SableTel.com **09/14/2010 08:14am**
Cc: CA@StarNova.com
Bcc:
Subject: Follow-up to yesterday's presentation

Hi Dan:

key element

As you are aware, SableTel is the key to strategic growth within the technology segment of StarNova's business. Based on your presentation yesterday, the EC would like further information and analysis. We have asked CA to prepare the following on our behalf and report back to us at our next meeting: b

techno: rapid obsolescence

- An evaluation of SableTel's operating performance relative to its competitors; EXH III + IV
- Comments on the reporting document, including suggested improvements; EXH II + III
- A more thorough analysis of the variance in results between 2010 and 2009; 15/16/17
- Comments on the points raised in the 2011 strategic plan, including suggested improvements to the plan; and
- An evaluation of the 2011 budgeted financial information and of the likelihood of the result being achieved. c

EXH VII

In addition to these issues, we reviewed the letter from the CRTC regarding its fee calculations. We are not sure if the initial calculations prepared are accurate. d We have asked our internal audit group to perform procedures to ensure that the CRTC submission is correctly calculated. e CA will participate in this work by preparing an audit plan for SableTel's 2009 CRTC resubmission and 2010 CRTC submission, including a preliminary estimate of the error, a risk analysis, and a description of procedures that will need to be performed.

EXH V + VI

CALC

B5

Please assist CA by providing whatever information may be helpful.

Audit plan:
→ estimate error
→ risk analysis
→ description proc

ACCURACY

John McReynolds, FCA
Chairman, StarNova Executive Committee
Chairman, StarNova Audit Committee

---

a A quick look at this page allows us to see that the year is often mentioned (2009, 2010, 2011). One must pay attention to the year of reference when drafting the response for each problem or issue.

b These are the main case requirements. Since the candidate will read this page more than once, it is normal that it should contain a greater number of annotations.

c There is a mention of the case exhibits or pages that can help resolve the various requirements. Thus, as one reads on, it would be a good idea to come back to the present page in order to write in the appropriate references.

d The fact of not being "sure if the initial calculations prepared are accurate" means the probable presence of errors to be corrected.

e It must be noted that "Accuracy" will be the key assertion of the audit plan.

comments + suggestions

EXHIBIT II

SABLETEL REPORTING DOCUMENT FOR THE YEAR ENDED AUGUST 31, 2010

Report to StarNova's executive committee

The following is dated September 13, 2010, and should be read in conjunction with the financial statements of SableTel for the year ended August 31, 2010.

check on "what doesn't work"

SableTel had an outstanding year in 2010. We turned the corner from a loss in 2009 to profitable operations in 2010 despite difficult economic conditions. We continue to benefit from decisions our excellent management team has implemented over the past several years.

!!! EC confused

Highlights from fiscal 2010 include:

check on FS

- Net income of $1,178,000 based on robust revenue of $65,072,224
- Reduction in operating costs of $2,783,365 due to cost restraint
- Cost of sales were contained
- Strong liquidity at year-end based on liquid assets totalling $16,215,519 WRONG
- Solid balance sheet at year-end, with shareholder's equity totalling $26,338,280

B6 impact project

We plan to do even better in the future by increasing revenue and decreasing expenses. We also expect the impact of our new Wireless Technology Project to be substantial in the short term. HOW?

? 2012

impact hurricane

Unfortunately, Hurricane Baylee hit Nova Scotia in August 2010. Although no injuries were reported by SableTel employees, a number of communication towers were damaged and the mobile telephone network was disabled.

We have also taken steps to decrease our risk profile. We established an occupational health and safety committee in 2010, which decided to remove all fried foods from the cafeteria menu and installed hand sanitizers at all doorways as a result of the H1N1 pandemic. Reducing our risk was mandated by our parent company, StarNova, and we believe we have met this objective. not a business risk!

lawsuit

past?

We are not aware of any new significant lawsuits to which SableTel has been named defendant.

We continue to focus on evolving our core business. We have no significant new projects planned for the foreseeable future.

??? contradictory

Finally, we would like to request that StarNova's MD&A thank a long-time employee of our company who will be retiring next month. Mr. Dudley Oldmun has been working with our sales department for 25 years.

not relevant

Dan Wilson

EXHIBIT III

submission
ratios
reporting doc
variances

EXCERPTS FROM 2010 SABLETEL LIMITED DRAFT FINANCIAL STATEMENTS [a]

DRAFT STATEMENT OF FINANCIAL POSITION
As at August 31
(unaudited)

	2010		2009	
Assets	errors?			
Current assets	16.2 M (EXH II)			
Cash (low - project?)	$ 351,018		$ 8,320,677	stable revenue receivables increased twofold
Accounts receivable	15,864,501	↑	6,788,745	
Inventory (Note 3) (high inventory techno?)	3,219,431	↑	883,318	
	19,434,950		15,992,740	
Non-current assets				
Property, plant and equipment (Note 6)	62,532,502		65,643,101	
Deferred taxes	35,629		35,629	
Intangible assets (Note 4)	10,753,709	↑ IMP	1,654,530	
	$ 92,756,790		$83,326,000	
Liabilities				
Current liabilities				current ratio < 1.0 worsening
Trade and other payables (↑ IMP)	$ 13,065,938		$ 8,718,978	
Current portion of long-term debt	9,200,000		7,800,000	
	22,265,938		16,518,978	
Non-current liabilities				
Long-term debt (high leverage required 21M!)	44,152,572		41,646,742	
	66,418,510		58,165,720	
Capital				
Common shares	3,000		3,000	
Retained earnings (no dividend)	26,335,280		25,157,280	
	26,338,280		25,160,280	
	$ 92,756,790		$ 83,326,000	

B7

a When analyzing financial statements provided in a case, one must consider the most significant items (in terms of changes and percentage), items that are at the greatest risk (those whose future benefits are least certain or that require an estimate of the situation), unusual items, inconsistencies and contradictions, non-compliance with accounting standards, laws and business practices, key ratios (more especially those of interest to a creditor or to management), questionable operations, etc.

submission
ratios
reporting doc
variances

EXHIBIT III (continued)

EXCERPTS FROM 2010 SABLETEL LIMITED DRAFT FINANCIAL STATEMENTS

DRAFT STATEMENT OF COMPREHENSIVE INCOME
For the years ended August 31
(unaudited)

		2010		2009
Revenue (Note 1)		$ 65,072,224	stable	$ 65,176,742
Cost of sales (Note 2)		30,714,869		30,591,682
Gross profit		34,357,355		34,585,060
Expenses				
Selling and marketing	↑ 291,588	16,875,413		16,583,825
Administration (Note 5)	↓ 3,074,953	13,336,292		16,411,245
		30,211,705		32,995,070
		↓ 2,783,365		
Operating profit		↑ 4,145,650		1,589,990
Financing				
Interest expense		2,967,650		2,877,850
Profit (loss) before income taxes		1,178,000		(1,287,860)
Income taxes		– ?		–
Profit (loss) and comprehensive income (loss)		$ 1,178,000	↑	$ (1,287,860)

1,178/26,338
4.5% < 15%

difficult economic
conditions
and
stable revenue

B8

check for errors!

EXHIBIT III (continued)

EXCERPTS FROM 2010 SABLETEL LIMITED DRAFT FINANCIAL STATEMENTS

Additional Information [a]

IFRS

Since 2008, the financial statements for SableTel have been prepared using International Financial Reporting Standards (IFRS) in order to consolidate with its parent company, StarNova. StarNova has been preparing IFRS financial statements since 2008 in order to access global capital markets.

Note 1 - Revenue [b]

	2010	2009
Long-distance ↓ IMP	$ 28,050,628	$ 33,069,103
Local access	24,567,800 ↑	23,679,870
Mobile	4,238,967	3,963,200
Internet and data services	3,789,070	2,896,739
Internet and data services – routers and modems	1,675,759	1,567,830
IMP Government grant (see below)	2,750,000	-
	$ 65,072,224	$ 65,176,742

grant in revenue?

TOTAL steady IMP changes by product line

criteria

During the year, SableTel received $2,750,000 from Industry Canada (IC) to assist with the development of its Wireless Technology Project. Once the project is complete, SableTel must share its technology with IC. IC will then formally approve the technology and will use the technology to support its own wireless initiatives.

B9

Note 2 - Cost of sales [b]

rev ↓ 5M
cost ↓ 0.6 M
???

	2010	2009
Long-distance	$ 11,943,020	$ 12,561,728
Local access	11,067,818	10,684,562
Mobile	2,204,529 ↑	2,087,618
Internet and data services	1,002,159	795,119
Internet and data services – routers and modems	679,859	619,870
CRTC Fee	3,817,484	3,842,785
	$ 30,714,869	$ 30,591,682

Included in long-distance expenses is $897,500 (2009 – $788,000) that was paid to a US supplier for infrastructure charges and $1,357,850 (2009 – $1,458,760) paid to a related party for telecommunication distribution services. [c]

---

a By highlighting the important items in yellow, the candidate can immediately identify the main elements to be analyzed in his response.

b It is important to notice that the information is broken down by product line. One must consider solving the problems or issues according to such classification.

c The information contained in this paragraph must be read carefully. Expenses are paid to non-Canadian entities and to a related party, and those costs must be excluded from the calculation of the CRTC Fee. One should not, however, conclude that there are revenues from non-Canadian entities or from related parties simply because it is not mentioned. It should also be noted that these costs are excluded only when calculating the Fee. For example, it would be inappropriate to exclude these same costs for the purpose of calculating ratios or variances. Each situation is different.

EXHIBIT III (continued)

EXCERPTS FROM 2010 SABLETEL LIMITED DRAFT FINANCIAL STATEMENTS [a]

Note 3 - Inventory

Inventory consists of routers and modems that SableTel typically sells to end users to support its Internet and data services. Inventory is carried at cost. SableTel realizes a gross margin of approximately 60% on these items. Inventory tends to have a short life (typically 12 months) because of rapid technological change. In September 2009, SableTel paid $2.5 million for inventory, which it purchased at a substantial discount. SableTel has not provided for obsolescence in the inventory balance at August 31, 2009 or 2010 because on an overall basis the inventory is still generating a profit.

Note 4 - Intangible assets

	2010	2009
Software	$ 1,593,459	$ 1,654,530
Deferred research and development costs (Note 5)	9,160,250	–
	$ 10,753,709	$ 1,654,530

Note 5 - Research and Development

B10

Research and development (R&D) expenditures include projects in process that may or may not become commercially viable. All research and development costs are expensed as incurred in Administration on the Statement of Comprehensive Income unless they have been capitalized as noted below.

The largest project is the Wireless Technology Project, which is expected to improve margins by 5% for all products and services due to more efficient distribution methods. In 2010, management declared its intention to carry this project to market. All costs associated with this project are now being capitalized. In 2010, $5,702,390 was spent on this project, and the entire amount was capitalized. As well, costs of $3,457,860 that were originally expensed in 2009 were reversed and capitalized in 2010.

Note 6 - Hurricane Baylee

On August 24, 2010, a Class 4 hurricane (Hurricane Baylee) devastated the south shore of Nova Scotia. Sixty of SableTel's 340 communication towers were damaged, disabling the entire mobile network. Each tower had a carrying value of $35,000. SableTel is currently assessing whether the mobile network can be fixed. It is also contemplating replacing the entire tower system with a faster system. While these assessments are ongoing, no accounting adjustments have been made. Revenues from the mobile network will be negligible until it is restored.

---

a As one read the four pages of Exhibit III, the subjects to be discussed and their importance were noted.

EXHIBIT IV

FURTHER INFORMATION ABOUT THE TELECOMMUNICATIONS INDUSTRY

The telecommunications industry in Canada is dominated by three major public companies, each with large investments in infrastructure across the country. There are also many regional operators, like SableTel, that provide services to residents regionally. Regional operators pay a fee to one of the "big three" operators for the right to access their infrastructure.

Telecommunications Industry Ratios (Regional Operators Only)

	2010	2009
Profitability ratios		
Return on equity	9.6%	10.5%
Margin analysis		
Gross profit	52.2%	53.0%
Selling, marketing and administration	40.5%	40.3%
Operating profit	11.7%	12.7%
Turnover		
Accounts receivable turnover	6.7×	6.9×
Short-term liquidity		
Current ratio	0.8×	0.8×
Long-term solvency		
Operating profit/interest expense	8.1×	8.3×
Growth over prior year		
Revenue growth *	(2.6%)	(3.2%)

* Industry analysts expect revenue to grow by 1.5% in 2011.

B11

recalc Fee audit plan

EXHIBIT IV (continued)

FURTHER INFORMATION ABOUT THE TELECOMMUNICATIONS INDUSTRY

Canadian Radio-television and Telecommunications Commission (CRTC)

see errors 2009 + 2010

As defined in the table below, SableTel, like all other telecommunication companies, is required to contribute a percentage of its adjusted margin (the Fee) to a fund administered by the CRTC. The Fee subsidizes services to rural and remote regions of Canada. On September 1, 2008, the calculation of the Fee changed in an effort to better balance the cost of the Fee with the services subsidized. [a]

Description	Until August 31, 2008	After August 31, 2008
Revenue	100% of revenue.	100% of net Canadian telecommunications revenue (after any discounts) from long-distance, local access and mobile services. Related-party revenue is excluded.
Less: Qualifying costs	Qualifying costs are amounts paid that are directly attributable to providing telecommunications services to customers.	Qualifying costs are defined as cost of sales associated with long-distance, local access, and mobile services. Costs paid to non-Canadian entities and related parties are excluded from this calculation.
Add: 200% of the negative margin for any customers with a negative margin	Negative margin customers are defined as customers where any product is priced below cost.	No change.
Fee rate	10 %	12 %

see note 2

B12

Fees, along with supporting calculations, are due three months following the year-end.

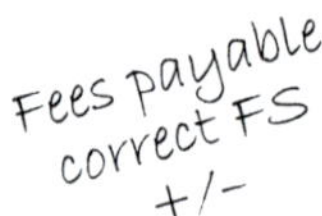

a It is relevant to notice the fact that the calculation of the Fee changed in 2008, since there are likely to be some errors in 2009 and 2010. Particular attention should be paid to the changes made by the CRTC.

EXHIBIT V

LETTER RECEIVED FROM CRTC

September 5, 2010

Third Notice

Mr. Dan Wilson, CEO
SableTel Limited
2435 Highwayman Road
Westbrook, NS B4D 1H4

Regarding: Violations of CRTC Regulations

Mr. Wilson:

This letter is to inform you of our intention to revoke your operating licence based on your continuing failure to comply with CRTC regulations regarding your 2009 CRTC Fee. Your licence will be revoked on November 30, 2010, if you do not provide us with the following:

1. Submission of your revised 2009 CRTC Fee calculation.
2. Submission of your 2010 CRTC Fee calculation.
3. Payment of all amounts owing for 2009 and 2010.

Should you have any questions, you may reach us at the number provided below.

Sincerely,

Ima Bulldog
Assessment manager
1 888 555-1234
CRTC

recalc Fee
audit plan

EXHIBIT VI

INFORMATION REGARDING SABLETEL'S 2010 DRAFT CRTC SUBMISSION

check for errors!

SableTel's 2009 Fee calculation (submitted to the CRTC on June 6, 2010) and the draft 2010 Fee calculation are as follows: [a] p. 12

includes
- internet
- grant!

note 2 p. 9
- US supplier
- related party

		2010	2009
Revenue	=$ p. 8/9	$ 65,072,224	$ 65,176,742
Less: Qualifying costs	=$ note 2 - CRTC	26,897,386	26,748,892
Add: 200% of negative margin customers		0	0
Base as calculated		38,174,838	38,427,850
CRTC Fee rate	rather 12%	10%	10%
CRTC Fee		$ 3,817,484	$ 3,842,785

IC

The information technology (IT) department produced a margin report on a per-customer and a per-product basis for the Finance department from the Finance database. The report showed that there were several customers with negative margins, that totalled $1,130,000 for the 2010 fiscal year. This report was reviewed by the Marketing department, which used its own database to produce a similar report. The Marketing report showed no negative-margin customers, and this report was used in the CRTC Fee calculation. In explaining the discrepancy, IT said that the difference is in the databases, but they were not sure why the databases differed. !!!

B14

2010 IT: $1,130,000
MARK: $0

2009 ?

[a] This page must be read taking into account the fee calculation formula presented on p. 12 and the information provided in the financial statements. Establishing a relationship between the various pieces of information allows one to pick out most of the mistakes while reading the case.

ratios
reporting doc
variances
strat plan
budget

EXHIBIT VII

PRESENTATION FROM DAN WILSON a

The following presentation of the 2010 financial results and the 2011 strategic plan for SableTel was given to StarNova's EC on September 13, 2010, by Dan Wilson, CEO of SableTel. After each slide there are notes regarding discussions that ensued between Dan and the EC.

SABLETEL LIMITED
EXECUTIVE SUMMARY
HAVING OUR DUCKS IN A ROW

2010 Financial Results

2011 Strategic Plan

- Return to profitable operations in 2010
- In 2011 a further $20 million will be spent on the Wireless Technology Project — budget p. 21
- 2011 budgeted revenues – $75.4 million
- 2011 budgeted profit – $4.22 million — 2010: 1.2 M
- 2011 required funding from StarNova – $21 million

5 IMP points

REVENUES: 101.5% x 65 M = 66.05 M < 75.4 M

21M VS 20M ?

1

Discussion:

EC – "Why did you choose the slogan *Having our Ducks in a Row*"? — really? p. 11 analysts 1.5%

Dan – "Having our ducks in a row contributes to our preparation for growth and prosperity following difficult times." — revenues; difficult economic conditions p. 6

EC – "How confident are you that $20 million will be enough to complete the Wireless Technology Project? — note 4: 9M in 2010

Dan – "That's a great question. I am not sure how accounting came up with that number. I will have to get back to you with an answer." !!!

a This eight-page Exhibit contains information useful for the analysis of a number of problems or issues. It is therefore efficient to pick up those subjects concerned while reading the case; subjects written at the top of each page, on the left-hand side.

EXHIBIT VII (continued)

PRESENTATION FROM DAN WILSON [a]

2010 FINANCIAL RESULTS

	2010 Actual	2009 Actual
Revenue ($000's)	65,072	65,177
Gross profit ($000's)	34,357	34,585
Gross margin (%)	53%	53%
SM&A [(1)] and interest ($000's)	33,179	35,873
Profit (loss) ($000's)	1,178	(1,288)
Key financial ratios:		
Profit as a % of revenue	1.8	(2.0)
Profit as a % of Gross profit	3.4	(3.7)
Profit as a % of SM&A and interest	3.6	(3.6)

(1) SM&A — Selling, Marketing and Administration

2

Discussion:

Dan – "I am proud to announce that SableTel generated a profit for 2010 and improved all its key financial ratios despite the difficult economy."

EC – "Why is 2010 revenue slightly lower than 2009 revenue?"

Dan – "Revenue has decreased for two reasons. First, the sales team didn't meet its quota because of high staff turnover. Second, and more importantly, two large customers, each with monthly recurring revenue exceeding $25,000, were lost in June 2010. These customers have not yet been replaced, but we plan to hire additional sales staff to increase sales. On a good note, our margins are holding up pretty well."

EC – "Why did we lose those customers?"

Dan – "I'm not sure. I believe pricing was the main issue. I haven't spoken directly to the customers to find out what happened."

---

a When reading the case, it is useful to notice the possible impact on the budget. Thus, the mention of "↓ revenue" or "↑ costs" will facilitate the evaluation of the financial information presented in the budget, as well as the calculation of the adjusted profit (loss).

VARIANCES

EXHIBIT VII (continued)

PRESENTATION FROM DAN WILSON

adjust FS before analysis!

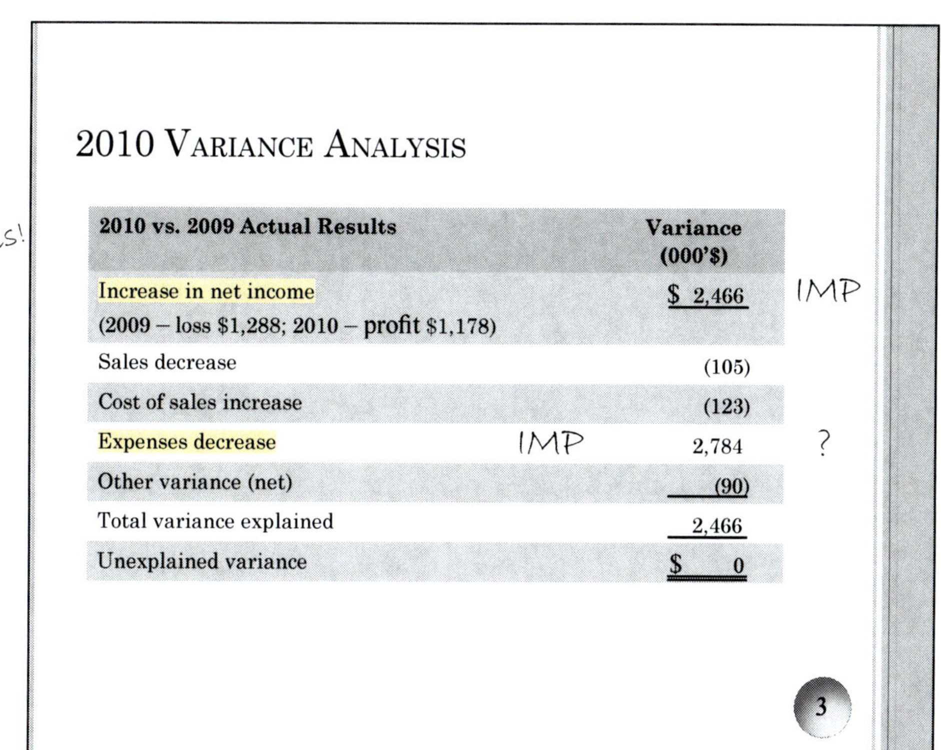

2010 Variance Analysis

2010 vs. 2009 Actual Results		Variance (000'$)	
Increase in net income (2009 – loss $1,288; 2010 – profit $1,178)		$ 2,466	IMP
Sales decrease		(105)	
Cost of sales increase		(123)	
Expenses decrease	IMP	2,784	?
Other variance (net)		(90)	
Total variance explained		2,466	
Unexplained variance		$ 0	

Discussion:

EC – "I see that overall expenses have declined, which on the surface is a good thing. Can you provide me with further details regarding what specific expenses were reduced?" a

The CEO is not sure!

Dan – "I understand from our Marketing department that the reduction is the result of their cost containment."

? ↑ costs p. 8

EC – "Do you know what accounts for the Other variance of $90,000?"

Dan – "I think it may be made up of many smaller expense items such as lower depreciation charges, but I will check and get back to you." b

again ?!? p. 15

---

a This is an indication that one should look in detail at the mix of expenses and not simply focus on the overall amount.

b At this point, there are sufficient indications that the CEO does not know how to answer the questions that are put to him. More precisely, he attempts to give answers, but his explanations are not convincing.

EXHIBIT VII (continued)

PRESENTATION FROM DAN WILSON

SableTel 2011 Strategic Plan

Information Technology (IT)

- Goal – To introduce new technology to reduce cost of sales
  - Completion of the Wireless Technology Project to improve margins by 5%
  - Implantation date – January 1, 2012
  - IT will focus all of its resources on this project in 2011

Human Resources

- Goal – Increase retention of existing employees
  - Introduce new executive bonus plan in 2011 to ensure we retain our top talent

4

Discussion:[a]

EC – "Does the IT department have the resources it needs to complete the Wireless Technology Project on a timely basis?"

Dan – "Yes I think they have all the brain power they need. They just need the money to complete the project. Without the financial support of StarNova we would not be able to proceed."

EC – "How sound is the technology supporting this project?"

Dan – "We are currently waiting for a third-party feasibility assessment of the project which we expect within the next 60 days."

EC – "How many employees will be covered by the new executive bonus plan, and how much are you expecting it to cost?"

Dan – "The plan will cover seven employees. The total bonus could range anywhere from $500,000 to $1,000,000 based on our future profitability."

---

a The following information must be integrated into the discussion about capitalizing (or not) development expenditures. Two uncertainties are raised: funding and feasibility. These both suggest that costs will be expensed. It will however be necessary to come out with an in-depth discussion of this major accounting issue.

EXHIBIT VII (continued)

PRESENTATION FROM DAN WILSON

strat plan budget

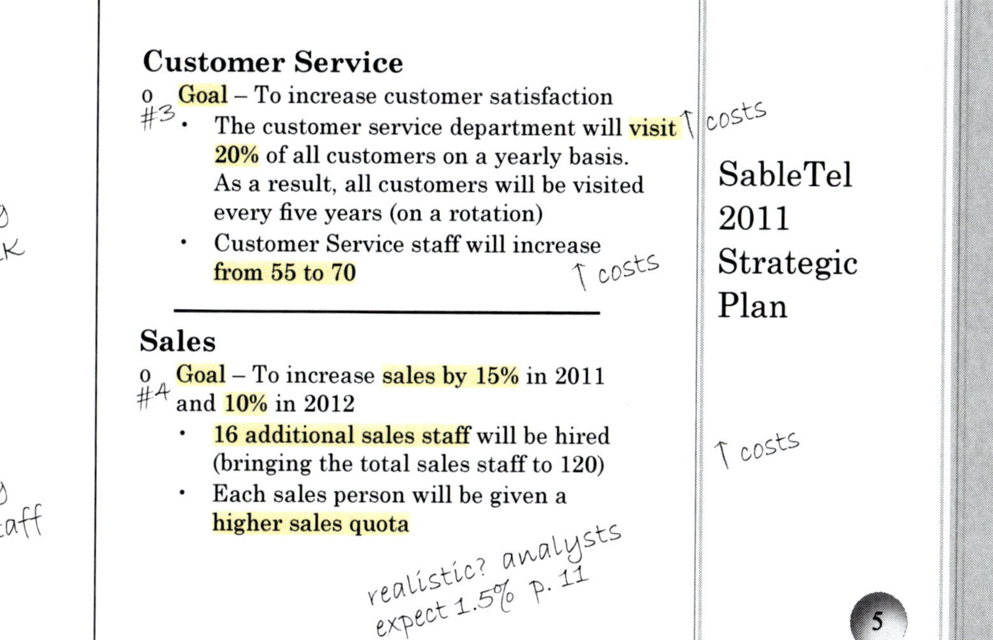
Customer Service
o Goal – To increase customer satisfaction
#3
• The customer service department will visit 20% of all customers on a yearly basis. As a result, all customers will be visited every five years (on a rotation)
↑ costs
• Customer Service staff will increase from 55 to 70
↑ costs
Sales
o Goal – To increase sales by 15% in 2011 and 10% in 2012
#4
• 16 additional sales staff will be hired (bringing the total sales staff to 120)
• Each sales person will be given a higher sales quota
realistic? analysts expect 1.5% p. 11
↑ costs
SableTel 2011 Strategic Plan
5

hiring MARK

hiring sales staff

B19

Discussion:

EC – "How many customers does SableTel have? How will you decide which customers to visit first?"

Dan – "Currently SableTel serves approximately 25,000 customers. Revenue from each of the largest customers is approximately \$300,000 annually. Smaller customers provide annual revenue of \$1,000 each. Customer service staff will first visit any customers that are close to our main office to keep travel costs down."

p. 16 $ customer visits other? \$1,000 is low

EC – "How do you plan to increase sales as budgeted?"

sales quotas

Dan – "To meet targets, sales staff will be given higher quotas. Senior sales staff will be asked to lead by example, and hopefully when they are successful, there will be a trickledown effect."

realistic? ↑ rev?

turnover p. 16 – retiring p. 6

EC – "How do the wages paid to the sales force compare with industry norms?"

Dan – "Our salespeople are paid a base salary of \$45,000 per year. If they meet their quota, they can earn up to \$85,000 per year including commissions. Comparable positions in the industry are paid a base salary of \$65,000 plus commissions. I believe that keeping our sales force motivated to earn commissions through a lower base salary encourages them to make more sales."

base salary sales staff $ CHECK

EXHIBIT VII (continued)

strat plan
budget

PRESENTATION FROM DAN WILSON [a]

Marketing — realistic?

p. 11 industry 52%
p. 16 2010 53%

margin - standard

- o Goal #1 – 60% gross margin
  #5A
  - 60 % will be used for all standard pricing — same margin for all?
  - Implementation of a "non-standard pricing policy" that will be used under specific circumstances
- o Goal #2 – Increase cross-selling
  #5B
  - Insert a targeted advertising flyer with monthly invoices to cross-sell products and services – $450,000 required to modify billing software — ↑ costs

cross-selling

$

Finances

- o Goal – Increase profitability
  #6
  - See budget (attached)

SableTel 2011 Strategic Plan

6

B20

Discussion:

EC – "Can you explain the non-standard pricing policy?"

Dan – "This policy will allow discounts to be offered to larger, higher-volume customers. Non-standard pricing requests will be approved by the Vice-President Marketing. Discounts could range from 1% to 15%. We expect to make up these discounts through increased sales volume."

IMP discounts — $

EC – "How will the cross-selling program increase sales?"

Dan – "Our IT department will develop software that will allow us to identify trends in phone, data, and Internet usage so we can make sales based on each customer's habits."

p. 6 no new project?

advantages not clear

---

a There is uncertainty as to most elements in the strategic plan, something that is inherent to the planning of any future activity. However, in this case, one must pick up on a number of facts that cast serious doubt as to the likelihood of SableTel achieving the desired results. On this page, for example, the development of software that will allow to identify customer trends does not appear to be based on any cost-benefit analysis.
The Chief Executive Officer's presentation includes the goals of six Departments. Their numbers (#1 to #6) help the candidate to understand what is going on and, eventually, to better structure and diversify his response.

EXHIBIT VII (continued)

PRESENTATION FROM DAN WILSON

BUDGETED FINANCIAL INFORMATION

	2010 Actual (000'$)	2011 Budget (000'$)
Revenue	$ 65,072	$ 75,400
Gross profit	34,357	41,470
Gross margin %	53%	55%
SM&A and interest	33,179	37,250
Profit	1,178	4,220
Add back: Depreciation and amortization (included above)	10,790	7,500
Less: Capital expenditures	(19,858)	(32,000)
Cash flow	(7,890)	(20,280)
Financing requested	N/A	21,000

Discussion:

EC – "Why is there a significant increase in Selling, marketing, administration and interest expenses for 2011?"

Dan – "We have budgeted an inflationary increase of 2% for 2011. Plus we anticipate hiring 31 additional employees."

EC – "Where are the costs associated with the Wireless Technology Project?"

Dan – "In 2011, the $20 million of expenditures will all be capitalized."

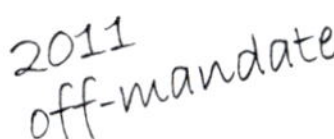

EXHIBIT VII (continued)

strat plan budget

PRESENTATION FROM DAN WILSON

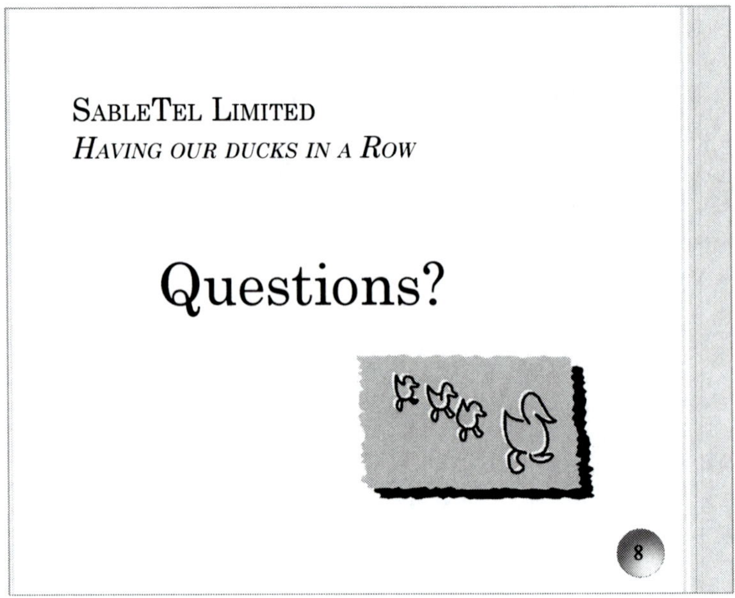

SABLETEL LIMITED
HAVING OUR DUCKS IN A ROW
Questions?
8

Discussion:

B22

EC – "What information is provided to the Vice-Presidents for them to execute the strategic plan?"

Dan – "They receive all the information required to complete their functions. Marketing receives product margin information. Finance monitors budget and actual financial results. Sales gets monthly sales. Human Resources receives staff-count information. As a result each department will focus on accomplishing its individual goals. Information resides in various departmental folders on the file server. IT has estimated that it would cost $50,000 to provide cross-functional access to the files. However, the cost of this project is not justified given my belief that access to information should be restricted."

access information

whole organ vs indiv depts

$

$50,000 minor – cost-benefit?

EC – "Are there any regulatory or legal issues that we should be aware of?"

Dan – "We received a letter from the CRTC asking us to resubmit our Fee calculation for last year. I will send the EC a copy of the letter following this meeting."

CRTC – URGENT!

"As well, we received a reassessment from the Canada Revenue Agency (CRA) on July 15, 2010. The reassessment relates to losses that we utilized in 2008 to offset taxes payable. On January 1, 2008, SableTel acquired all the shares of an inactive shell company, Spacolli Enterprises Inc. (Spacolli), a former cell phone manufacturer and distributor. The two corporations were amalgamated that day. Spacolli had $500,000 in unutilized non-capital tax losses. SableTel used these losses to save $160,000 of taxes in 2008. The CRA has denied these losses but I am not sure why or if there is anything we can do about it."

TAX reassessment losses (+/–)

delay: 90 days

similar business?

Example of work sheets or checklist (CASE B)

CONTEXT	Evaluation budgeted info Likelihood result achieved	Comments + Improvements Strategic plan 2011
Sept. 14, 2010	budget (p. 15 + p. 21)	FUTURE ***
		p. 16
ROLE: Finance Dept	hurricane ++	high sales staff turnover
	revenues? costs? (p. 6-4) (note 6)	2 big clients lost ++
public co (p. 3-1)	lawsuits? (p. 6-7)	hire sales staff ++
IFRS!		
revenues 800 M	long-time salesman retiring (p. 6-8)	p. 18
YE Aug 31		IT focus: wireless project ±
	Wireless Tech. (note 5) 20 M (p. 15) ++	executive bonus plan +
OBJ: (p. 3-1)		
15% return invest.	industry: (p. 11) revenue grows: 1.5%	p. 19
		hire new mark staff
Industry strictly regulated	CRTC fee calc. error (Exh. V and VI)	hire more sales staff ++
(p. 3-3)		customer visits +
	EXHIBIT VII	higher sales quotas } ++
(p. 3-4)	budg. revenues > analysts' expectations (p. 15)	sales staff compensation }
EC confused by 2010 results	2 big customers lost (p. 16) ++	
concerned about 2011	hire sales staff (p. 16) + (p. 19)	p. 20
strategic plan	NEW executive bonus plan 500 to 1M (p. 18)	standard gross margin 60% +
funding 21 M!	hire MARK 55 to 70 employees (p. 19)	discounts non-standard (> 60 %?)
	sales staff quotas (p. 19)	cross-selling –
	? sales staff salaries? (p. 19)	
	margin 60%? (p. 20) industry 52% (p. 11)	p. 21
	discounts major clients?	31 more employees ++
	cross selling (p. 20)	
	31 more employees (p. 21) ++	p. 22
	$50,000 cross-functional access (p. 22) ±	access to information +
		individual dept. goals ±

EXAMPLE OF A RESPONSE PLAN (CASE B) [a]

			min.
Reading and plan			90
→ Accounting errors	QUANT	10-15	
Obsolescence provision			
Deferred R&D costs			
Grant			
Impairment of Mobile network	QUAL	30	40-45
→ Audit plan			
Preliminary estimate of error	QUANT	10	
materiality approach — Risk analysis			
Description of procedures to be performed	QUAL	25	35
→ Analysis of variance in results between 2010 and 2009	calc comm conc		20
→ Evaluation of operating performance — calc ratio 2 yrs/ind analysis			20-25
→ Comments on the reporting document AND suggestions	comm explan REC		20-25
→ Comments on the 2011 strategic plan AND suggestions	P-I-R		20
→ Evaluation of 2011 budgeted information AND LIKELIHOOD of the result being achieved — YES or NO!			20
Secondary:			
→ Reassessment — if time!			5
Overall conclusion			10
extra time			5-10
TOTAL			300

[a] I think that it is important to stay as close as possible to the case "words" when planning out the response. While drafting the response, it helps a great deal to regularly go back to the case and reread the requirements so as NOT TO LOSE SIGHT OF WHAT IS ESSENTIAL.
The response plan can be integrated into the Subject on the Presentation page of the response.

The CRTC Fee is the most important issue of this case. However, the candidate may well have decided to adjust the financial statements before dealing with any other issue.

EVALUATION GUIDE [a]
PRIMARY INDICATORS OF COMPETENCE

Memo to: StarNova Executive Committee
From: CA
Subject: SableTel's 2010 Year-End and 2011 Strategic Plan

As requested, I have assessed the strategic plan as formulated by the CEO of SableTel, Dan Wilson. I have also identified issues associated with the 2010 financial results and I have assessed the financial condition and future prospects of SableTel.

Primary Indicator #1 *(VI-1, VI-2.2, VI-2.4, VI-2.5, VI-2.10)*
The candidate provides an audit plan, recalculates the CRTC Fee, and provides auditing procedures to test the accuracy of the Fee calculation.
The candidate demonstrates competence in Assurance.

same words EXH 1

SableTel has received a letter from the CRTC, which has threatened to revoke its operating licence based on the 2009 CRTC Fee as calculated by SableTel. The letter, dated September 5, 2010, requires SableTel to recalculate and submit its 2009 Fee, as well as calculate and submit its 2010 Fee by November 30, 2010. Since SableTel cannot operate without a licence, this matter requires my immediate attention. John McReynolds has specifically asked me to carry out this work, further emphasizing its importance.

The importance of the subject must be justified.

B25

I have been asked to plan an audit of SableTel's 2009 CRTC resubmission and 2010 CRTC submission, including a preliminary estimate of the error, a risk analysis, and a description of procedures that will need to be performed. I have not been asked to perform the procedures because they will be carried out by the internal audit group of StarNova. [b]

role and responsibilities

The CRTC requires telecommunications companies to contribute a portion of their adjusted margin to a fund administered by the CRTC. The CRTC changed the calculations associated with this Fee on September 1, 2008. [c] It would appear that SableTel did not change the way that it calculated this Fee and therefore is in violation of the CRTC agreement based on its 2009 submission. Its calculations and submission have been based on the rules in effect before September 1, 2008.

impact

"attempted to address" → The candidates probably had difficulty reaching the "Competent" level.

(Candidates clearly recognized that SableTel's calculation of the CRTC fee contained errors and attempted to address John McReynolds' requests.)

---

a In this evaluation guide, the case facts are highlighted in yellow, whereas the theoretical concepts are highlighted in green. Comments that a candidate could write down during the analysis of this proposed solution are written in the font used here. The following abbreviations: "P" (identification of problem), "I" (impact, consequences), and "R" or "REC" (recommendation) are used frequently. Marker's observations are in bold-type and in italics.

b This last sentence is true, but not necessary, since the focus should be rather on resolving the problems or issues. However, I am aware that by including elements that are not part of the requirement, some candidates find it easier to understand what has to be done. From this point of view, it may be useful.

c So far, the text of the proposed solution is basically a summary of the case facts. Of course, it is important to understand what is going on before starting an analysis. Nevertheless, references to the case could be more succinct.

Overall Risk

CONC

The risk associated with this engagement is high because the CRTC licence is required in order for SableTel to continue operations. Should SableTel submit an inaccurate or incomplete Fee, there is a significant risk that the CRTC will revoke its operating licence, forcing SableTel to shut down its business (at least temporarily).

importance of risk clearly brought out

Preliminary Materiality

key users → materiality

Given the sensitive nature of this engagement, the overall high risk associated with the engagement, and the scrutiny that this engagement will receive from its key users (the CRTC and the EC), preliminary materiality should be set at a low level. I will determine preliminary materiality based on 1% of the 2009 Fee as originally calculated by SableTel. One percent of $3,842,785 is $38,428.[a] Materiality will be initially set at $38,000 and should be reviewed during the engagement to ensure it is still appropriate.[b]

calculate materiality

basis of the calculation: CRTC Fee

conclusion

Approach/Understanding the Environment

Structure:
- Risk
- Materiality
- Approach
- Calculation
- Procedures

The approach to the assurance regarding the components of the CRTC Fee can be a combination of substantive and compliance procedures. The use of compliance testing will be tempered with the knowledge that there are discrepancies between the Finance and Marketing customer databases. Tests will need to be designed to determine if these systems feed into the general ledger, and if they do, whether the systems are accurate.

link with case facts about control p. 14

ACCURACY: key assertion

objective

First, an accurate and full understanding of the rules for the calculation will need to be determined. The information that is available must be verified with documentation from the CRTC that defines the calculation. It is likely that there is signed communication from the CRTC that will explain the impact of the changes to the calculation to SableTel. If not, we can contact the CRTC to ensure we use the most up-to-date information. It may also be advisable to confirm with the CRTC whether the calculation should be based on financial information using International Financial Reporting Standards or another appropriate basis of accounting, such as Accounting Standards for Private Enterprises.

✓ procedure

how

B26

Check whether these standards are the same as those for FS.

It is also possible that the internal audit group has performed an analysis on the systems at SableTel that may be useful for this engagement so as to avoid unnecessary duplication of testing.

understanding of the role needs to be demonstrated

practical aspect

Internal audit should perform a detailed review of the systems and controls over the data used in the calculation and perform walkthroughs of the key controls. Since the 2009 financial statements were audited (at the group level), there is already some assurance that the financial accounting systems are producing accurate results. However, the systems may have been audited only at the group level (with a much higher materiality), so this may not provide a great deal of comfort regarding SableTel's systems.

professional judgment

StarNova group versus SableTel subsidiary

(Virtually all candidates addressed the risk of the engagement and recognized the gravity of SableTel losing its operating licence. Most of the risk factors discussed were valid and supported with case facts. However, the only audit planning issue most candidates discussed was engagement risk. Some candidates went on to calculate a preliminary materiality level for the engagement and discussed some of the factors that would affect the audit approach, such as the discrepancies noted in the different databases, but only a minority did so.)

materiality and approach are part of an audit plan

will probably not be required at the "Competent" level

---

a We notice that a short calculation is integrated into the text of the solution.

b The internal auditor could determine a different performance materiality level.

insider point of view

(Some candidates seemed to misinterpret the case facts or misunderstand their role since they raised a non-existent independence issue with respect to the engagement. The Board cautions candidates to take the necessary time to fully understand the context of the simulation before beginning to respond.)

Beware of automatisms! Different role here!

Preliminary Estimate of Error a

calculation objective determined from the start

We have been asked by John to determine a preliminary estimate of the error. This calculation is based on preliminary information and the main purpose of this calculation is to determine if a material misstatement is likely. This may influence the remaining planning activities for the engagement and may also influence the audit procedures suggested.

info p. 9 — This calculation could be placed in an Exhibit.

Description of Input	2010 Calculation	2009 Calculation
Revenue from long-distance, local, and mobile services (see Note 1 to the financial statements)	$ 56,857,395	$ 60,712,173
Less: Related-party revenue (assume = $0)	0	0
Less: Qualifying costs (see Note 2 to the financial statements)	(25,215,367)	(25,333,908)
Add: Fees paid to non-Canadian entities (see Note 2 to the financial statements)	897,500	788,000
Add: 200% of negative margin customers (assume that the finance database is correct and assume 2009 = $0)	2,260,000	0
Add: Related-party costs (see Note 2 to the financial statements)	1,357,850	1,458,760
Fee base	36,157,378	37,625,025
Contribution rate	12%	12%
Preliminary fee calculation	4,338,885	4,515,003
Fee as calculated	3,817,484	3,842,785
Adjustment required	$ 521,401	$ 672,218

no hint? suppose $0

choice to be made between the two databases p. 14

1,130 x 2

p. 14

estimate of the "error" → calculation of the difference

extra amount to pay → FS

IMP: profit 1,178M (p. 8)

conclusion

From the above calculations it is apparent that the Fee as calculated is materially misstated. Adjustments will be required to the submission based on our preliminary estimate of the error. In addition, SableTel's 2009 financial statements are likely materially misstated. These will need to be corrected, and we should determine whether SableTel's statements are provided to any external users. Thankfully, this error should not have a material impact on StarNova: the company's annual revenue exceeds $800 million, so StarNova's 2009 financial statements are not materially misstated. b

go back to the initial objective

2009 + 2010

impact

(Most candidates were able to apply the new formula correctly, calculate a revised fee, and estimate the amount of the error. However, the Board was disappointed to see some candidates making careless errors, such as including all types of revenue or making unsupported assumptions, such as assuming that the related party costs have related party revenues associated with them.) c

Read the case facts carefully!

I find it hard to see how one can reach the "Competent" level without recalculating the Fees payable.

a Since all the components of the calculation contain errors, it would be preferable to completely redo the calculation rather than to directly adjust the CRTC Fee amount presented in Exhibit VI (p. 14).

b This is the second time that the solution includes a comparison between how important it is for StarNova at the Group level and how important it is for the subsidiary SableTel. A notion to remember for the next case!

c This comment reminds one to read case information carefully. Each word that describes the calculation presented on p. 12 is important. There has to be a reason for breaking down Revenue and Cost of sales by category in Exhibit III (p. 9).
DO NOT FORGET: THERE IS NO POINT IN MAKING PRESUMPTIONS ABOUT WHAT IS GOING ON. ONE SHOULD NEVER EXTRAPOLATE WITHOUT THE FACTS.

The "how" and the "why" of each procedure is made clear.

Specific Risks and Procedures

link to role

requirement p. 5

overall objective

The internal audit group would need to perform many audit procedures to ensure that the CRTC Fee calculations are not materially misstated. Many of these procedures would be similar to any audit engagement, and the internal audit group would likely have standard audit programs for these procedures.[a] In addition to these standard procedures, the internal audit group should perform the following procedures, which have been tailored to this unique engagement:

standard/ specific

To remember: list the procedures related to assertions or specific risks.

risk → procedure

✓ procedure

Risk Areas	Assertion	Specific Risks	Procedures/Extent
Qualifying Revenue	Classification IMP	Revenue includes services not included in the CRTC calculation.	The formula specifies that only revenue associated with long-distance, local access, and mobile services needs to be included in the calculation. It would appear as though SableTel's general ledger (based on Note 1 to the financial statements) can track revenue in this fashion. The internal audit team will need to ✓test a sample of the revenue to source documentation to ensure the system is accurately tracking revenues by product line
	Classification IMP	Related party revenue is incorrectly included in the calculation.	The amount of revenue received from related parties will need to be determined to ensure that it is properly excluded. The starting point will be any working papers prepared for the external auditors and the preparation of the financial statements at year-end. The internal audit team will need to ✓determine the definition of related parties for regulatory purposes to verify if the same companies that were considered related parties for financial statement purposes are considered related parties for regulatory purposes. Note that this is a new exclusion as of September 1, 2008, and therefore is a high risk area of the audit.

CLASSIFICATION IMP assertion, since the CRTC Fee calculation does not use FS figures per se. One needs to differentiate the different product lines.

objective (obj)

ACCURACY IMP assertion, as referenced in the requirements (p. 5).

focus: changes 2009 + 2010

Risk Areas	Assertion	Specific Risks	Procedures/Extent
Qualifying Costs	Accuracy +/- imp	Foreign exchange amounts have not been properly calculated.	There is evidence that some of the purchases have been made in US dollars. The internal audit team needs to ✓test these purchases, and any balances outstanding at year-end, to ensure the amounts have been translated into Canadian dollars using the appropriate exchange rates and to ensure the resulting foreign exchange gain or loss has been properly recorded. obj

Structure: - Revenue - Costs - Negative Margin Customers - Rate

N.B.: Each component of the Fee calculation is examined and the assertion of its ACCURACY is discussed each time.

---

a This is not the first time that the solution refers to the fact that the accountant who normally works at the Finance Department participates in the work of the internal audit group. It is important to determine one's role at the very start so as to carry it out adequately throughout the resolution of the problems or issues.

✓ procedure

The procedures mentioned are straightforward and practical.

It will be noticed that the "source document" is mentioned regularly.

Also see working papers prepared for external auditors.

Qualifying Costs	Classification IMP	All non-Canadian costs are not captured.	The internal audit team will need to determine if there are any transactions with non-Canadian entities. First, they will need to determine the definition of non-resident entities for regulatory purposes. Then they can scan the purchase documents or disbursement journals for any amounts paid to non-residents. They could then ask for a report based on the addresses of payees from the payables system, because the address would be a good indication of where the payee is resident. The report would show all payments to all payees with non-Canadian addresses. They could test the accuracy of the report through a sample. They could also ask management in charge of the purchasing function if there are other suppliers that are non-resident that are not on the report, or if there are payees on the report that are resident in Canada but that have a non-Canadian mailing address for some reason.
	Classification IMP	All related party costs are not captured.	Finally, the internal audit team should determine what costs included in the qualifying costs above were paid to related parties. They can use the list of related parties that was generated for the sales testing to identify the appropriate related parties. Then they can exclude these costs from the calculation. During the revenue testing (above), there should be a comprehensive list of related parties documented. This list should be used to test for additional related party costs. The source documents, such as a purchase journal or similar document, could be scanned for related party purchases.

practical aspect

link with Rev proc

The solution procedures are directly in line with this unique engagement.

Negative Margin Customers	Accuracy IMP	Negative margin customers — the general ledger is not reflecting the underlying entries of the proper database.	Test the accuracy of the upload from the billing system into the general ledger. It is possible that there are some inaccuracies, given the discrepancies in the databases for the negative margin customers, so additional work may need to be performed to ensure that the uploads are accurate. Select a sample of invoices from the billing system and trace them through to the general ledger to ensure they are recorded properly.

Negative Margin Customers *more difficult subject*	Accuracy *IMP*	Negative margin customers are not identified or are recorded inappropriately.	Testing negative margin customers will be difficult. There are already indications that discrepancies exist between the database used by Marketing and the database used by Finance. Therefore, it is unlikely that the internal audit team will be able to rely on the systems and must use a substantive approach. The first step may be to review the agreement with the CRTC to clarify what amounts are considered negative margin amounts for purposes of the CRTC calculation. Select a sample of inputs into each database and trace the amounts back to source documentation. This procedure will attempt to verify if one of the databases is accurate by performing manual recalculations on a sample basis. If one of the databases proves to be reliable using the sample, then this is the system that should be used for further testing.
Fee rate	Accuracy *+/- imp*	Arithmetical errors are included in the Fee calculation.	Test the overall mechanical accuracy of the Fee calculation and ensure that the proper calculations have been made by tracing the amounts back to the definitions in the agreement. Ensure the new rate of 12% is included in the calculations and not the old rate of 10%.

One can see that the drafting of the audit procedures is in line with the following phrase: "Test this... by..."

✓ procedure — *link with Approach* — *obj* — *obj* — *choice based on reliability* — *obj*

B30

(Most candidates attempted to provide valid procedures but many fell short in this regard. Where most candidates faltered was in providing procedures that were specific to this engagement. Candidates should have focused on the areas of risk based on the errors committed by SableTel in their initial submission. For example, revenue is a significant component of the formula, so it will need to be audited. But more specifically, there is a significant risk with regards to the classification of revenue. Based on the new formula, only certain types of revenue are to be included, whereas SableTel has continued to incorrectly include all revenue. As a result, it would be important to perform procedures to test that types of revenue are properly classified. Instead of zeroing in on the elements of the CRTC formula and the significant risks involved, some candidates only provided generic procedures that would apply to virtually any engagement. For example, instead of trying to test the classification of revenue, they focused on testing revenue cutoff when there were no facts presented in the case to indicate that cutoff was an issue for SableTel.) a

Providing valid procedures is not something easy.

Every component of the fee calculation must be ANALYZED.

ALWAYS integrate the response with the case!

classification → key assertion

USELESS discussion if not based on facts!

a Analysis of comments regarding the Assurance indicator reveals that:

- The audit objective is mentioned for each assertion: "What do we wish to audit?" Mentioning the assertion or the risk area makes it easier to describe valid procedures.
- The procedures listed are simple, practical and ALWAYS linked to the specifics of the case. They answer the question: "How should it be done?" The procedures are also justified ("Why?"). Where necessary, the source document containing the target information is clearly mentioned.
- It is essential to take note of those case specifics that affect the audit plan. For example, the 2009 financial statements were audited by an external auditor, there is an internal audit group in place, and the SableTel information system already provides information by product line.

For Primary Indicator #1 (Assurance) the candidate must be ranked in one of the following five categories:	Percent Awarded
Not addressed — The candidate does not address this primary indicator.	0.0%
Nominal competence — The candidate does not attain the standard of reaching competence.	6.7%
Reaching competence — The candidate discusses some of the audit issues surrounding the CRTC Fee calculation.	41.5%
Competent — The candidate discusses audit planning issues or makes a reasonable recalculation of the Fee AND provides some relevant audit procedures.	51.5%
Highly competent — The candidate discusses audit planning issues, makes a reasonable recalculation of the Fee, and provides several relevant audit procedures.	0.3%

A candidate who has not recalculated the Fee may nevertheless reach the "Competent" level.

Procedures make the difference. ←

SEVERAL procedures, not just SOME.

(Candidates were asked to prepare an audit plan for SableTel's CRTC submission. They were asked to include a preliminary estimate of the error, a risk analysis, and a description of procedures that would need to be performed. To demonstrate competence, candidates were expected to provide some relevant procedures that would help the internal audit group audit the CRTC submission, and to either recalculate the CRTC Fee or discuss some of the planning issues with regards to the engagement.)

explicit requirement

two ways of achieving the passing standard

(Most candidates recognized the errors that had been made in SableTel's calculation of the CRTC Fee, and recalculated the Fee using the new formula and the appropriate amounts to determine a preliminary estimate of the error. Candidates who addressed the planning issues related to this engagement were also able to identify what factors affect risk, what materiality should be, and what approach should be used. Candidates sometimes struggled to provide specific and relevant audit procedures. Some candidates failed to focus on the specific risks involved in the audit of the submission, and instead provided generic procedures that would apply to any audit engagement. Candidates who used case facts to tailor their procedures to this particular situation had stronger responses.) [a]

B31

describe specific and relevant procedures

focus: RISKS

INTEGRATION!

---

[a] Comments:

- To reach the "Competent" level it is essential to describe relevant audit procedures. Such procedures are part of the context of this unique engagement, whose objective is to ensure that the CRTC Fee is correctly calculated. One must not lose sight of this objective and describe, for example, period-end generic audit procedures. It seems evident to me that the quality of the procedures described takes precedence over their quantity, when it comes to meeting the passing standard. It is important to give some thought to the specifics of the calculation, in order to better determine the revenues, the costs, and what adjustment to make for negative margin customers. Dealing with these three components seems essential to me.
- Fee recalculation needs to be "reasonable", though not necessarily perfect. To this end, I believe it is necessary that the amount of the revenues and costs include only the long-distance, local access and mobile services. Additionally, costs paid to non-Canadian entities or to related parties should be excluded from Qualifying Costs.
- There are three parts to the preparation of the audit plan: RISK, MATERIALITY, APPROACH. This is a familiar response structure. I believe it is important to provide a reasonable discussion for each part.

One should avoid general sentences that can be applied to just any entity!

Primary Indicator #2 *(V-2.2, V-2.5)*

The candidate discusses the significant accounting issues related to the 2010 financial statements.

The candidate demonstrates competence in Performance Measurement and Reporting.

identify IMP issues

I have identified the following accounting issues with respect to SableTel's 2010 financial statements and, where possible, I have estimated the misstatement. I have adjusted the financial statements as presented to better reflect the actual financial condition and financial results of SableTel for its 2010 fiscal year.

There is clear support for recording an obsolescence provision. Simply stating that one is needed because the balance is high is not enough!

clear, accurate title

Inventory — Obsolescence Provision IMP

Guidance for accounting for inventory can be found in IAS 2 — *Inventories*. Inventory shall be measured at the lower of cost and net realizable value.

Inventory at SableTel consists of routers and modems that SableTel sells to its customers. Total inventory at August 31, 2010, had a book value of $3,219,431. The continuity of the inventory for the 2010 fiscal year can be presented as follows: [a]

1- Determining whether or not to record a provision
2- Estimating the writedown amount

B32

Inventory — Opening	$	883,318	p. 7
Purchases — Discounted Product		2,500,000	note 2
Purchases — Other (Regular)		515,972	note 3
Cost of Sales — Routers and Modems		(679,859)	
Inventory — Closing	$	3,219,431	

The inventory level at year-end would appear to be extremely high and [P] may require a writedown. According to IAS 2, paragraph 28, *"the cost of inventories may not be recoverable if those inventories are damaged, if they have become wholly or partially obsolete, or if their selling prices have declined."* The main reason for the substantial increase in inventory relates to the $2,500,000 of inventory that was purchased in September 2009. Given that the inventory tends to have a short life (typically 12 months), it is not clear why SableTel would purchase such a large quantity of inventory since its annual sales do not justify such a large purchase. It is now 12 months after this discounted product was purchased, so it is likely that much of this inventory can no longer be sold.

link inventory and cost of sales

realistic and reasonable assumptions

case data used to establish provision

impact on FS

Sales of routers and modems for the 2010 fiscal year totalled $1,675,759. The costs associated with these sales totalled $679,859. Assuming similar sales in future years, SableTel has inventory on hand at August 31, 2010, that represents 4.74 years of sales ($3,219,431 ÷ $679,859). Given that these items have a short life (typically 12 months), a portion of the inventory is likely obsolete and [R] requires a writedown. Further details would need to be gathered regarding the specific inventory items to determine an accurate obsolescence provision, but as an initial estimate, we could assume that items representing sales greater than one year will likely [R] require a writedown. Therefore, the estimated obsolescence provision is $2,539,572 ($3,219,431 − $679,859). SableTel should reduce its inventory balance on the financial statements by $2,539,572 and increase its cost of sales by a similar amount (see the adjusted financial statements below).

It would certainly be preferable to obtain more details, but this does not prevent the candidate from making a precise recommendation.

---

a The calculation provided summarizes what has taken place during the year. There doesn't seem to be any need for it when analyzing the obsolescence provision issue. As shown in the subsequent paragraphs, this issue can very well be resolved without having to reconcile the amounts. However, I understand that this could help some candidates to visualize what is going on, and therefore to develop a better analysis.

conclusion: writedown is needed

(This issue was generally well done by candidates. The majority of candidates concluded that an obsolescence provision was needed and adjusted the financial statements accordingly. Where the quality of discussions varied was in the explanation of why a provision was needed. Some candidates reasoned that a writedown was needed simply because there was a large amount of inventory at year-end. However, there were much stronger arguments to support a writedown, such as the amount of inventory on hand compared to average sales or the short life of the goods.)

adjusted FS

VERY IMP +++

Deferred Research and Development Costs

IMPORTANT to use case facts to justify conclusions and recommendations.

Guidance for research and development costs can be found in IAS 38 — *Intangible Assets*

It is necessary to refer to the theoretical concepts, but standard numbers are not indispensable.

Deferred research and development costs represent costs associated with the Wireless Technology Project from 2009 and 2010 that have been capitalized. The amounts have been capitalized as management has "declared its intention to carry this project to market." However, this is only one of the criteria that must be met in order for research and development costs to be capitalized. notes 4 + 5

P

IAS 38, paragraph 57 states: [a]

1- Determining whether the 2010 costs can be capitalized
2- Knowing what to do with the 2009 costs
3- Discussing the presentation in the financial statements

"An intangible asset arising from development (or from the development phase of an internal project) shall be recognised if, and only if, an entity can demonstrate all of the following:

(a) the technical feasibility of completing the intangible asset so that it will be available for use or sale.

(b) its intention to complete the intangible asset and use or sell it.

(c) its ability to use or sell the intangible asset.

(d) how the intangible asset will generate probable future economic benefits. Among other things, the entity can demonstrate the existence of a market for the output of the intangible asset or the intangible asset itself or, if it is to be used internally, the usefulness of the intangible asset.

(e) the availability of adequate technical, financial and other resources to complete the development and to use or sell the intangible asset.

(f) its ability to measure reliably the expenditure attributable to the intangible asset during its development."

Every criterion for which the case provides facts must be analyzed.

B33

The analysis of this issue should be carried further, even though its first criterion is not met.

p. 9 The first criterion requires that the technical feasibility be assured. Dan has indicated that SableTel is currently awaiting a third party feasibility study for this project. Therefore it is unlikely that this criterion has been met at year-end.

Recommending as of now that development costs be expensed would be premature.

p. 10 The second criterion requires an intention to complete the intangible asset. Management has indicated that they intend to complete the Wireless Technology Project, so this criterion is likely met.

p. 9 The next criterion requires SableTel to prove that it will use or sell the intangible asset. We can assume that this criterion is met, and the Industry Canada grant may provide further evidence supporting this criterion since Industry Canada wants to use the technology (indicating that SableTel may be able to sell the technology as well).

conclusions

---

a I don't think it is necessary to quote the whole paragraph 57 of IAS 38. It does contain all the relevant theoretical concepts, but it would be preferable to make use of them rather than simply to reproduce them. In fact, each of the six criteria is subsequently mentioned again in relation to the case facts. This simultaneous integration of theory and case is an example that should be followed. Finally, we notice that a firm stand was taken as to whether or not each criteria was met.

note 5

cost-benefit

The fourth criterion requires management to demonstrate how the asset will generate probable future economic benefits. SableTel will use the wireless technology internally, presumably to decrease costs and increase margins. Therefore, SableTel likely meets this criterion because the technology is supposed to increase margins by 5% across all of its product lines. This would provide substantial benefits (5% of $65 million is $3.25 million on an annual basis). SableTel would [R] need to provide some evidence to support this assertion. This may be available once the third party feasibility assessment has been completed.

link with the analysis of a previous criterion

p. 18, 21

The fifth criterion requires adequate technical, financial, and other resources to complete the project. Dan has indicated that SableTel does not currently have the financial resources to finish this project and requires funding from StarNova to complete the project. Therefore, this criterion is likely not met currently since StarNova has not committed itself to the funding. However, should SableTel be able to provide support that StarNova or some other source will fund the remainder of the project, then this criterion may be supportable.

Other sources of funding? human resources OK p. 18

conclusions

p. 15

Finally, SableTel must be able to demonstrate that it can reliably measure the expenditures attributable to the project. It is not clear if SableTel can do this. Dan has indicated that accounting came up with the $20 million necessary to complete the project, but he is not sure how they came up with this number. As well, SableTel would also [R] need to demonstrate that it had the necessary systems in place to track the costs associated with this project reliably. Therefore, this criterion may be met, but more information is required.

clear and precise REC

impact on FS

Since all six criteria must be met in order to capitalize the costs, and at least two of the criteria were likely not met at year-end, the costs cannot be capitalized and [R] must be expensed. As a result, SableTel [R] should reduce the deferred research and development costs from $9,160,250 to nil and increase administration expenses by the same amount (see the adjusted financial statements below).

adjustment amount justified

B34

2009 +/- imp

Even if SableTel met all of the criteria for capitalization of the development costs, it would not be able to go back to 2009 and capitalize those research and development costs in 2010. IAS 38, paragraph 71 states *"Expenditure on an intangible item that was initially recognised as an expense shall not be* [R] *recognised as part of the cost of an intangible asset at a later date."*

From a presentation standpoint, we would also have to separate the research and development costs from the administration expenses on the statement of comprehensive income since it is a significant amount and is likely of interest to users of the financial statements.

theoretical concepts ⇆ case facts

(Candidates performed best on this accounting issue. Most candidates seemed familiar with the recognition criteria for deferred research and development costs and were able to apply them to the case facts. Where a few candidates got confused was in their conclusion, as they seemed to forget that all of the criteria needed to be met in order for the costs to be capitalized.) [a]

Reminder: FS USERS

It is important to discuss the accounting treatment for R&D expenses prior to that of the grant. This is because the presentation of the grant depends directly on the recommendation regarding the R&D expenses. This means IT IS IMPORTANT TO PAY ATTENTION TO THE SEQUENCING OF THE SUBJECTS AND TO PICK UP THEIR INTERRELATIONSHIPS, amongst other things when it comes to conclusions or recommendations.

---

a Given the large amounts involved and the uncertainty of the project, this is the most important accounting issue. However, the discussion with regard to the costs expensed in 2009, along with the presentation of the R&D costs in the financial statements, are less important aspects. In other words, not all the aspects of a given subject have the same importance and, consequently, do not all require the same depth of analysis.

Industry Canada Grant

Guidance for government assistance can be found in IAS 20 — *Accounting for government assistance and disclosure of government assistance.*

There are two issues associated with the government grant. The first issue is whether SableTel has met the criteria for recognition of the government grant. IAS 20, paragraph 7 states:
"Government grants, including non-monetary grants at fair value, shall not be recognised until there is reasonable assurance that:

(a) the entity will comply with the conditions attaching to them; and

(b) the grants will be received."

SableTel has received the $2.7 million, so we can safely state that the second criterion has been met. However, it is not clear if the first criterion, related to satisfying all of the conditions attached to the grant, has been met. There is some evidence that the conditions have not been met since SableTel must share its technology with Industry Canada (IC) and IC must formally approve the technology. However, we would need to gather further details relating to the grant in order to determine whether the first criterion has been met and, as a result, whether the amount can be recognized.

Assuming that the above two criteria have been met, the second issue regarding the government grant relates to its presentation. IAS 20, paragraph 24 states:
"Government grants related to assets, including non-monetary grants at fair value, shall be presented in the statement of financial position either by setting up the grant as deferred income or by deducting the grant in arriving at the carrying amount of the asset."

This government grant relates to the Wireless Technology Project. This project was initially recorded as an intangible asset. If the Wireless Technology Project was still recorded as an asset then SableTel would need to reverse the amount as revenue and record the amount as either deferred income or by deducting the amount from the carrying value of the Wireless Technology Project.

B35

However, due to the adjustment proposed above (see Deferred Research and Development Costs), the Wireless Technology Project is now expensed as administration on the statement of comprehensive income. The presentation of grants related to income is discussed in IAS 20, paragraph 29, which states:
"Grants related to income are sometimes presented as a credit in the statement of comprehensive income, either separately or under a general heading such as 'Other income'; alternatively, they are deducted in reporting the related expense."

I would recommend that the amount be recorded as a reduction of the related expense because it is clearly attributable to these expenditures. Therefore, the amount should be removed from revenue and recorded as a reduction of the research and development expenses (administration expenses) on the statement of comprehensive income (see the adjusted financial statements below). Note that the adjustment will have no net effect on the profit (loss) of SableTel. IAS 20, paragraph 12 states, *"Government grants shall be recognised in profit or loss on a systematic basis over the periods in which the entity recognises as expenses the related costs for which the grants are intended to compensate."* Therefore, the reduction of the expense should be recognized in proportion to the costs incurred in 2009, 2010, and the future.

(Most candidates did a good job of analyzing this accounting issue by either discussing whether the grant could be recognized by SableTel or by explaining how the grant should be recognized in the financial statements. The Board was pleased to see that many candidates linked their discussions of the proposed accounting treatment of the grant with the conclusion they had reached with regards to the recognition of the deferred research and development costs. This is the type of integration that the Board likes to see.)

Impairment of Mobile Network

Guidance for the impairment of assets can be found in IAS 36 — *Impairment of assets.*

subject IMP but difficult to analyze

note 6 In August 2010, Hurricane Baylee damaged several of the communication towers associated with SableTel's mobile network, disabling the entire network. In total, 60 of the 340 towers were damaged. Each tower has a carrying value of $35,000.

P SableTel must determine whether the communication towers require a writedown at year-end.

1- Determining whether or not to record an impairment

IAS 36, paragraph 9 states:
"An entity shall assess at the end of each reporting period whether there is any indication that an asset may be impaired. If any such indication exists, the entity shall estimate the recoverable amount of the asset."

conclusion

Clearly there is an indication that the assets may be impaired since the towers have been damaged. Therefore, SableTel R should estimate the recoverable amount.

2- Determining whether this is an individual asset or a cash-generating unit

For a full discussion, it is important to identify the various steps.

IAS 36, paragraph 18 states:
"This Standard defines recoverable amount as the higher of an asset's or cash-generating unit's fair value less costs to sell and its value in use."

IAS 36, paragraph 22 states:
"Recoverable amount is determined for an individual asset, unless the asset does not generate cash inflows that are largely independent of those from other assets or groups of assets. If this is the case, recoverable amount is determined for the cash-generating unit to which the asset belongs (see paragraphs 65–103), unless either:

(a) the asset's fair value less costs to sell is higher than its carrying amount; or

(b) the asset's value in use can be estimated to be close to its fair value less costs to sell and fair value less costs to sell can be determined."

B36

IMP uncertainties

It would appear from the facts of the case that the towers, as a whole, make up a cash-generating unit because the entire mobile network has been disabled by the damage to 60 of the towers. Therefore, it may be necessary to R estimate the recoverable amount for the entire mobile network (the 340 communication towers) and not just the 60 towers that have been damaged. 60 or 340?

3- Determining the recoverable amount AND estimating the impairment loss

IAS 36, paragraphs 66 and 67 state:
Paragraph 66 — "If there is any indication that an asset may be impaired, a recoverable amount shall be estimated for the individual asset. If it is not possible to estimate the recoverable amount of the individual asset, an entity shall determine the recoverable amount of the cash-generating unit to which the asset belongs (the asset's cash-generating unit)."

Paragraph 67 — "The recoverable amount of an individual asset cannot be determined if:

(a) the asset's value in use cannot be estimated to be close to its fair value less costs to sell (for example, when the future cash flows from continuing use of the asset cannot be estimated to be negligible); and

(b) the asset does not generate cash inflows that are largely independent of those from other assets.

In such cases, value in use and, therefore, recoverable amount, can be determined only for the asset's cash-generating unit."

recoverable amount
- individual asset
- cash-generating unit

1- FV - selling costs
2- Value in use

As stated above, there are two possible ways to determine an asset's (or group of assets') recoverable amount.[a] The first is to determine the asset's fair value less costs to sell. We do not have a lot of information to determine this amount, but it is unlikely that SableTel could sell the damaged towers for any significant amount. As well, there is no indication that SableTel could sell its entire mobile network, but it is possible that another telecom company would want this network. The mobile network in its current state has no value because the entire mobile network has been disabled. It is important to note that the value in use is generally determined by its estimated future cash flows in its *current condition*. Therefore, SableTel's decision to fix or replace the network is irrelevant. IAS 36, paragraph 44 states:

logical — link case fact note 6

"Future cash flows shall be estimated for the asset in its current condition. Estimates of future cash flows shall not include estimated future cash inflows or outflows that are expected to arise from:

(a) a future restructuring to which an entity is not yet committed; or

(b) improving or enhancing the asset's performance."

60 towers — decision — simple assumption: pro rata — impact on FS

Note that it is possible that all 340 towers and the entire mobile system (the cash-generating unit) would need to be written down to nil or the estimated recoverable amount (fair value less costs to sell) since the mobile network has no value in use based on its current condition. Further information would need to be gathered to determine the exact amount of the impairment, but as an estimate we could approximate that the recoverable amount of the 60 damaged towers is likely nil. SableTel should therefore recognize an impairment loss for this amount. The total for these sixty towers would be \$2.1 million (60 × \$35,000) (see the adjusted financial statements below).

N.B.: Impairment loss estimated despite lack of information.

340 towers possibility — high amount

If the mobile network cannot be sold (in other words, the fair value less costs to sell is minimal) and SableTel does not plan to fix the network, then the entire network should be written down to nil. At a minimum, this amounts to \$11.9 million (340 towers × \$35,000 per tower) for the towers, and may need to be higher if there are additional capital assets associated with the mobile network.[b]

B37

The impairment loss should be recorded as an impairment loss as stated in IAS 36, paragraph 59: *"If, and only if, the recoverable amount of an asset is less than its carrying amount, the carrying amount of the asset shall be reduced to its recoverable amount. That reduction is an impairment loss."*[c]

Reminder: insurance!

We should also determine if SableTel is likely to receive any insurance proceeds as a result of the damage to the towers. Any proceeds would reduce the loss.

after 2010 — of little IMP

Finally, once the towers are repaired or replaced, the impairment recognized can be reversed up to the extent that the value in use or the fair value of the towers after repair and replacement equals the original carrying cost (plus any betterments).

---

a The analysis of the recoverable amount used to determine the loss of value is tinged with uncertainty. This is because the case offers few facts regarding the value of the Mobile network (60 or 340 towers). Therefore, several points of view need to be taken into consideration, using simple assumptions based as far as possible on case facts

b The solution takes into consideration two possibilities: recognizing an impairment loss of 2.1M for the 60 damaged towers, or 11.9M for the entire network. Given the lack of information, it would be better, at least for now, to suggest the lesser of the two, as it appears in the adjusted financial statements (p.39).

c The analysis of the impairment of the Mobile network includes several references to accounting standards. I don't think it is necessary to reproduce these standards. It is more important to focus on the appropriate theoretical concepts and analyze how they can be applied to the specifics of the case.

data backing!

Alternatives should be analyzed prior to concluding. ***

(The impairment of the mobile network was one of the complex issues in the case. The Board was not looking for perfection in this area. Rather, the Board was hoping candidates would question the value of the mobile network and use case facts to consider multiple viewpoints. Unfortunately, most candidates prematurely concluded that the 60 towers needed to be written off. Strong candidates took a step back and, in light of the circumstances, considered whether the entire network might be impaired. The Board reminds candidates that not all accounting issues are black or white. In some cases, the real value of a candidate's response is in a discussion that considers all of the possible accounting treatments and the reasons they may or may not be valid, not in a recommendation of a single treatment.)

justified analysis + REC

of little IMP

Accounting Errors — CRTC Fee and 2009 R&D [a]

IAS 8, paragraph 42 states, *"an entity shall correct material prior period errors retrospectively in the first set of financial statements authorised for issue after their discovery by:*

(a) restating the comparative amounts for the prior period(s) presented in which the error occurred; or

(b) if the error occurred before the earliest prior period presented, restating the opening balances of assets, liabilities and equity for the earliest prior period presented."

+/- IMP

CRTC Fee

link previous issue

We have already recalculated the estimated misstatement in the 2009 and 2010 CRTC Fees. The total estimated misstatement is $1,193,619. Of this amount, $672,218 relates to 2009 and $521,401 relates to 2010. The amount relating to 2009 ($672,218) is an accounting error and, as such, should be added to accrued liabilities and should reduce the 2010 opening retained earnings. The amount for 2010 ($521,401) should be added to cost of sales (CRTC Fee) and be added to accrued liabilities at August 31, 2010, since this amount relates to the 2010 fiscal year.

IMPACT

2009 + 2010

B38

N.B.: Keeping debit-credit in mind makes one less likely to forget one part of the required adjustment.

of little IMP

2009 R&D

The R&D expenses that were capitalized in 2009 are also considered to be an accounting error and therefore need to be treated similarly (in other words, retrospectively).

few case facts → of little IMP

A justified recommendation is sufficient if the subject is of little importance.

Deferred Revenue

link with specific case context

practical aspect

There is no deferred revenue listed on the statement of financial position. Given the nature of the company — a telecommunications company — we would expect that some of its revenues would be billed in advance (it is typical for companies in this industry to bill a month of service in advance and, some also require substantial deposits). This should be investigated further. It is possible that this amount is buried in the "trade and other payables" line item on the statement of financial position. It is also possible that these amounts have been incorrectly recorded as revenue. Further information would need to be gathered to determine if an error exists.

(The treatment of the accounting errors and the lack of deferred revenue on the statement of financial position were minor issues, and most candidates appropriately did not address these.)

The less important elements, presented on page 38, are not necessary to master this competency.

---

a I am not suggesting presentation of the text of an accounting standard with the assumption that it is self-evident. ONE SHOULD RATHER DISCUSS THE APPLICATION OF THE THEORETICAL NOTIONS TO THE CASE.

calculation objective determined from the start

Adjusted Financial Statements

Mentioning the impact of accounting adjustments, more especially on the income, is necessary in order to master this competency. However, preparing "adjusted" financial statements in due form is not.

The financial statements for 2010 R will require adjustment due to the cumulative material effect of the misstatements noted above. The following schedule adjusts the financial statements: a

to be presented as exhibit

Item Description	2010 Actual F/S's (unadjusted)	Required IFRS adjustments	JEs	2010 Actual F/S's (adjusted)
Current assets				
Cash	$ 351,018			$ 351,018
Accounts receivable	15,864,501			15,864,501
Inventory	3,219,431	(2,539,572) IMP	1	679,859
Total current assets	19,434,950	(2,539,572)		16,895,378
Property, plant and equipment	62,532,502	(2,100,000)	4	60,432,502
Deferred taxes	35,629			35,629
Intangible assets	10,753,709	(9,160,250)	2	1,593,459
Total assets	$ 92,756,790	(13,799,822)		$ 78,956,968
Current liabilities	$ 22,265,938	1,193,619	5	$ 23,459,557
Long-term debt	44,152,572			44,152,572
Total liabilities	66,418,510	1,193,619		67,612,129
Total shareholders' equity	26,338,280	(14,993,441) IMP	(A),5	11,344,839
Total liabilities and shareholders' equity	$ 92,756,790	(13,799,822)		$ 78,956,968
Revenue	$ 65,072,224	(2,750,000) IMP	3	$ 62,322,224
Cost of sales	30,714,869	3,060,973 IMP	1,5	33,775,842
Gross profit	34,357,355	(5,810,973)		28,546,382
Expenses:				
Selling and marketing	16,875,413 IMP			16,875,413
Administration	13,336,292	8,510,250 IMP	2,3,4	21,846,542
Interest expense	2,967,650			2,967,650
Total expenses	33,179,355	8,510,250		41,689,605
Profit (loss)	$ 1,178,000	(14,321,223)	(A)	$ (13,143,223)

To speed things up, some terms can be abbreviated. E.g. "S&M" instead of "Selling and Marketing."

WOW!

conclusion

The adjusted financial statements present a much different financial picture for SableTel for its 2010 fiscal year. These adjusted financial statements should be used when analyzing SableTel further.

important adjustments → much different financial picture

a Comments:

- When adjusting financial statements, subsequent use of the results obtained must be taken into account. As concerns the case, obtaining reliable and exact information is a prerequisite to the estimate of the error in the CTRC Fee, to the evaluation of the operating performance (ratios), to the analysis of the variance in results, and to the evaluation of the likelihood of the result being achieved.
- The statement of comprehensive income is the most important because, amongst other things, the criterion for evaluating SableTel's operating performance is its return on investment, and because the 2010 results "confused" the Committee. The column showing the "unadjusted" amounts can be left out, in order to speed up drafting. Only the adjustments and the adjusted amounts are necessary.
- In order to validate understanding of the adjusted financial statements, one can redo the calculation, beginning with the net unadjusted profit of $1,178,000, which will be adjusted subsequently. (see Part 6, p. 65)
- The statement of financial position (balance sheet) has a limited usefulness and, in my opinion, may be left out of the response. ONLY ITEMS THAT MAY LATER PROVE USEFUL FOR OTHER ANALYSES SHOULD BE ADJUSTED, such as Inventory (current ratio) and Retained earnings (profitability ratio). The statement doesn't have to balance out to the nearest dollar.

Journal Entries (JEs) [a]

	JE #	Account Description	Debit [b]	Credit [b]	
IMP	1	Cost of sales (routers and modems)	$ 2,539,572		
	1	Inventory		$ 2,539,572	
		To set up a provision for inventory obsolescence			
IMP	2	Administration (R&D expenses)	$ 9,160,250		2009 and 2010 costs expensed
	2	Intangible assets		$ 9,160,250	
		To reverse expenditures associated with the Wireless Technology Project that were capitalized			
This accounting adjustment does not change the net result but does change the ratios and variances.	3	Revenue (government grant)	$ 2,750,000		
	3	Administration (R&D expenses)		$ 2,750,000	
		To reclassify the Industry Canada grant received during the year			
	4	Administration (impairment charge)	$ 2,100,000		the lesser of two possibilities p. 37
	4	Property, plant and equipment (mobile network towers)		$ 2,100,000	
		To record an impairment charge on the mobile network towers [c]			
correct errors retrospectively	5	Cost of sales (2010 CRTC Fee adjustment)	$ 521,401		
	5	Retained earnings (opening – 2009 CRTC Fee adjustment)	672,218		link previous issue
	5	Current liabilities (accrued liabilities)		$ 1,193,619	
		To record the estimated misstatement in the CRTC Fee for 2009 and 2010			

full impact of adjustments

(Most candidates were able to quantify the necessary accounting adjustments or explain the financial statement impact in the case where an exact number could not be determined. However, some candidates provided "one-sided" entries; in other words, they explained the impact on the statement of financial position or on the statement of comprehensive income, not both. Candidates were not expected to fully restate the financial statements and show the adjusting journal entries, as shown here. However, they were expected to fully understand the impact of the adjustments they were recommending.)

It is important to mention the impact on the financial statements. This may be done in the qualitative analysis OR in the quantitative one, via the adjusted financial statements. However, useless repetition of ideas should be avoided as much as possible.

---

[a] Journal entries are presented for information purposes. They do not need to be included in the case response. If the operation happens to be particularly complex, the candidate can always make one or two entries on a worksheet. It is very rare, however, that journal entries are taken into consideration when assessing a case.

[b] THINKING IN TERMS OF DEBIT-CREDIT WHEN ADJUSTING FINANCIAL STATEMENTS IS A GOOD WAY OF AVOIDING ERRORS OR OMISSIONS. IT IS EFFICIENT, EVEN WHEN ONLY A FEW ITEMS NEED ADJUSTMENT.

[c] The suggested solution assumes that the impairment loss of the Mobile network is 2.1M. Should it become necessary to carry out a sensitivity analysis, it would be a good idea to indicate what the profit (loss) would be if the loss were 11.9M instead.

For Primary Indicator #2 (Performance Measurement and Reporting) the candidate must be ranked in one of the following five categories:	Percent Awarded
Not addressed — The candidate does not address this primary indicator.	0.1%
Nominal competence — The candidate does not attain the standard of reaching competence.	4.0%
Reaching competence — The candidate identifies some of the relevant accounting issues.	26.5%
Competent — The candidate discusses some of the relevant accounting issues and their impact on the financial statements.	68.9%
Highly competent — The candidate discusses most of the relevant accounting issues and adjusts the financial statements for most of the accounting adjustments.	0.5%

Nominal competence: ↓ lack of integration OR no mention of impact on FS

in accordance with IFRS

IMPACT

← requires in-depth analysis

implicit problem

(Candidates were required to recognize that the manner in which SableTel had recorded some of its transactions was not in accordance with IFRS. While candidates were not directed explicitly to this indicator, they were presented with SableTel's financial statements as well as relevant excerpts from the notes, which provided a description of these transactions. There were a number of accounting issues associated with SableTel that candidates could have discussed, ranging from the need for an obsolescence provision for inventory to how costs incurred for the Wireless Technology Project (WTP) and the related grant received from Industry Canada should be recorded.)

facts available in the case

3 IMP subjects:
- Inventory
- R&D
- Grant

R&D analysis is indispensable

B41

(Most candidates performed well on this indicator and seemed to be comfortable applying the relevant IFRSs. In general, candidates recognized most of the accounting issues relating to SableTel and discussed them in sufficient depth. More specifically, most candidates included good discussions of deferred research and development costs related to the WTP, applying case facts to the criteria that need to be met before such costs can be capitalized. Most candidates also discussed how to recognize the related grant and realized that this discussion should be linked to their proposed treatment of the WTP costs. Finally, most candidates concluded that an obsolescence provision was needed for the large year-end inventory balance and were able to explain why.)

link R&D and Grant

(The accounting issue candidates had the most difficulty with was the impairment of the mobile network. While there were several case facts provided to allow candidates to provide a generous discussion of this issue, most candidates jumped to the conclusion that the 60 damaged towers needed to be written off without considering whether the entire mobile network might be impaired as a result of the hurricane.) a

When the subject is important, one should take the time to look at the alternatives.

An analysis should not be cut short on the grounds that the conclusion is already known!

60/340 towers

---

a Comments:

- It is not necessary to adjust the financial statements in order to achieve the "Competent" level. In fact, as will be seen later, obtaining adjusted figures, although preferable, is not required to meet the passing standard for competencies concerning the evaluation of the operating performance (ratios) and the analysis of the variance in results.
- Personally, to meet the passing standard I believe that an analysis with a sufficient recommendation regarding development costs is essential. I would also expect that two of the three following subjects be reasonably well discussed: inventory obsolescence, grant (one of the two aspects) and Network impairment. A sufficient discussion is one that identifies and integrates the relevant theoretical concepts with the case facts. IT IS CLEAR THAT THE EFFECT (OR IMPACT) ON THE FINANCIAL STATEMENTS MUST BE MENTIONED, ALL THE MORE SO SINCE THIS HAS AN INFLUENCE ON THE ANALYSIS OF SEVERAL OF THE PROBLEMS OR ISSUES THAT FOLLOW.

Conclusions must be justified. ALWAYS

For a complete analysis, it is important to regularly ask oneself whether the adjustments to the financial statements (p. 40) should be taken into consideration.

Explicit requirement EXH 1: "thorough" analysis of the variance in results.

Primary Indicator #3	*(VIII-1.1, VIII-4.1, VIII-4.3)*
The candidate performs a variance analysis on the 2010 financial statements.	
The candidate demonstrates competence in Management Decision-Making.	

variance between 2010 and 2009

We have reviewed the variance analysis for the 2010 financial results of SableTel provided by Dan Wilson in the presentation (slide 3) that he made to StarNova's executive committee. We have noted a number of deficiencies in the variance analysis.

overall comment on the Chief Executive Officer's variance analysis (p. 17)

While the approach that was taken seems logical (explaining the difference in the bottom line between 2009 and 2010), there is no detail provided in the variance analysis and the explanations for the items contained in the analysis are inadequate.

Sales The variance analysis is divided into parts. Revenue and Cost of sales are separated by category, as in Notes 1 and 2 in the financial statements.

There is no point in calculating the variance in grant, since it is not recurrent.

Dan has identified a small negative variance as a result of decreased sales but has not provided any further explanation. Note 1 to the financial statements provides further relevant details on this variance. From this note we can determine the following more detailed variances: a

B42

note 1

Revenue Category	2010 Amount	2009 Amount	Variance	% Change	
Long-distance	$ 28,050,628	$ 33,069,103	$ (5,018,475)	(15.2%)	IMP
Local access	24,567,800	23,679,870	887,930	3.7%	
Mobile	4,238,967	3,963,200	275,767	7.0%	
Internet and data services	3,789,070	2,896,739	892,331	30.8%	IMP
Routers and modems	1,675,759	1,567,830	107,929	6.9%	
Industry Canada grant	2,750,000	–	2,750,000	100.0%	
Total	$ 65,072,224	$ 65,176,742	$ (104,518)	(0.2%)	

Bring out relationship with %s.

conclusion

From the above analysis it is apparent that all of the revenue categories are growing except for the long-distance services. This is the largest revenue category for SableTel, and it has shrunk by more than 15% in 2010 versus 2009, which is a significant concern. As well, if the Industry Canada grant is excluded from revenue (as proposed in the adjusting journal entries above), then the overall negative variance increases to $2,854,518, which equates to 4.4% year over year. On a positive note, the Internet and data services category grew by more than 30% in 2010.

- Compare between years
- Check whether rise or fall

link previous issue

Further relevant details would include whether these variances relate to lower sales volumes (volume variances) or a change in selling prices (pricing variances). Given the lack of a similar percentage decrease in cost of sales (noted below), b we expect that most of this decrease would be related to a pricing decrease. Some of this decrease may be related to decreased volumes. R Further details would need to be obtained to determine the exact breakdown of these variances.

link cost of sales

Some possible explanations for the decreased sales volume may be the loss of key sales personnel and the high turnover in the sales department. The decreased sales may also be attributable to the loss of key customers throughout the year. R Further investigation into the specific decrease in the long-distance segment should be undertaken to pinpoint the decrease.

p. 6, 16

CONCLUSION based on case facts

a There is no point in copying out--neatly or not--the 2010 or 2009 amounts in the response. What really matters is the variance (in terms of changes or percentage). Repetitions of the case should be minimized and more time given over to new ideas.

b SINCE THE CANDIDATE WILL PROBABLY START HIS ANALYSIS WITH THE SALES, THIS MEANS HE WILL NEED TO GO BACK AND COMPLETE IT A LITTLE LATER WHEN HE ANALYZES THE COST OF SALES.

The cost of sales variance for the long-distance service is not very high but nevertheless requires some discussion, since the variance in the revenue from this category is significant.

Cost of Sales

comparable

An analysis of cost of sales, similar to the one for sales, should be provided. Note 2 to the financial statements provides relevant information on cost of sales. From this note we can determine the following more detailed variances: a

Take into account the cost of sales/sales

Cost of Sales Category	2010 Amount	2009 Amount	Variance	% Change
Long-distance	$ 11,943,020	$ 12,561,728	$ (618,708)	(4.9%) to discuss
Local access	11,067,818	10,684,562	383,256	3.6%
Mobile (note 2)	2,204,529	2,087,618	116,911	5.6%
Internet and data services	1,002,159	795,119	207,040	26.0%
Routers and modems	679,859	619,870	59,989	9.7% IMP
CRTC Fee	3,817,484	3,842,785	(25,301)	(0.7%) ***
Total	$ 30,714,869	$ 30,591,682	$ 123,187	(0.4%)

conclusions

From the above analysis we can see that costs in the long-distance segment of the business are decreasing somewhat. This is not surprising given the large decrease in revenue associated with the long-distance services. Given that both revenue and costs are decreasing in this category, we would expect that part of this variance would be the result of lost customer volumes (volume variances). However, the sales within this category decreased by 15.2% while costs decreased by only 4.9%, lending support to the assertion that the margin is shrinking as well (pricing variance).

link to sales

One needs to explain the possible CAUSES of the variances, using case facts.

Non-recurrent or unusual events should be excluded.

Note that the cost of sales for the routers and modems category in the above analysis has not been increased by the $2,539,572 representing the suggested adjustment for obsolete inventory at August 31, 2010. We have not made this adjustment because it is considered an isolated adjustment and would not provide any further meaningful information for this analysis. Similarly, the CRTC Fee has not been adjusted. If the CRTC Fee had been adjusted based on the adjustment proposed above, then the 2009 CRTC Fee would be $4,515,003 ($3,842,785 + $672,218) and the 2010 Fee would be $4,338,885 ($3,817,484 + $521,401), which equates to a decreased Fee of $176,118 or 3.9%. This is reasonable given the decreased sales of 4.4% noted above. b

link with previous issues

One needs to make choices and to focus on what matters.

While the individual variances for revenue and cost of sales provides some additional detailed variance information, an analysis of the gross margins for each category by product line may provide even more information. This information is readily available by combining the information in Notes 1 and Note 2 as follows:

For greater efficiency, it is certainly possible to include variances that need to be analyzed in one and the same table.

It would be acceptable to present the gross margin directly as a percentage, without giving the amount per se (1st and 3rd columns).

Product Category	2010 Gross Profit	2010 Gross Margin %	2009 Gross Profit	2009 Gross Margin %	Change in Margin
Long-distance	$ 16,107,608	57.4%	$ 20,507,375	62.0%	IMP (4.6) p.p.
Local access	13,499,982	54.9%	12,995,308	54.9%	0.0 p.p.
Mobile	2,034,438	48.0%	1,875,582	47.3%	0.7 p.p.
Internet and data services	2,786,911	73.6%	2,101,620	72.6%	1.0 p.p.
Routers and modems	995,900	59.4%	947,960	60.5%	(1.1) p.p.
Total	$ 35,424,839	56.8%	$ 38,427,845	59.0%	(2.2) p.p.

p.p. = points de pourcentage

---

a IT IS IMPORTANT TO COMPARE VARIANCES IN SALES WITH VARIANCES IN THE COST OF SALES. A PRIORI, VARIANCES IN % SHOULD BE ROUGHLY THE SAME. SINCE THIS IS NOT SO, A WAY OF EXPLAINING THE SITUATION, USING CASE FACTS, MUST BE FOUND.

b Since the CRTC Fee is not controlled by SableTel, discussing this variance does not seem to me very useful.

Note that the Industry Canada grant and the CRTC Fees are not included in the above analysis as they do not directly relate to one another and a comparison would not provide any useful information.

long-distance service → most important service

From the gross margin analysis we can see that the long-distance services, in addition to losing substantial revenue, have a significantly lower gross margin percentage in 2010 than in 2009. This is very troubling. For this product category, the analysis indicates that sales volumes are decreasing and costs (as a percentage of sales) are increasing.
The other product lines seem to have held their gross margins or are very close. Therefore, the significant negative variances identified can be primarily attributed to the long-distance services.

other: of little importance

Sales, cost of sales and gross margins need to be related to one another.

Expenses

IMP because of CEO's comments

Dan has noted that there is a positive variance of $2,784,000 related to decreased expenses. However, no further details have been provided. Dan has indicated that this is likely due to cost containment in the marketing area.

p. 17

case facts need to be related to one another.

p. 6, 16

conclusion

From the draft financial statements and the related notes provided in Exhibit III we can further determine the source of this variance. From the draft income statement we can see that the variance is actually the result of positive variances in the administration expenses totalling $3,074,953 ($16,411,245 − $13,336,292) offset partially by a negative variance in the selling and marketing expenses of $291,588 ($16,875,413 − $16,583,825). Therefore, Dan's explanation that this variance is a result of cost containment in the marketing area is likely not accurate. *a*

The conclusion concerning the Chief Executive Officer's comments is tempered.

B44

Note 5 provides further information on the administration expenses. This note indicates that $9,160,250 of R&D expenditures have been capitalized in 2010. In prior years, R&D expenditures were expensed in the administration line item. If the R&D costs were expensed in 2010 like they had been in prior years (and as we have proposed in our adjusting journal entries), then the administration expenses in 2010 would actually have increased by $6,085,297 ($3,074,953 less $9,160,250). This represents a significant increase in administration expenses over the prior year and needs to be investigated further. Certainly one explanation for this large negative variance is the increased expenditures on the Wireless Technology Project, which increased by $2,244,530 in 2010 ($5,702,390 in 2010 versus $3,457,860 in 2009). *b* This may not necessarily be a bad thing as R&D expenditures are typically made to increase sales or income many years into the future. However, this is only one part of the negative variance and the remaining negative variance should be researched further. We would need more details on the expenses for 2010 and 2009 to pinpoint additional sources of this variance. *c*

9 M − 6 M VERY IMP

link with earlier conclusion

It is not enough simply to say that R&D costs push up the expenses. The situation needs to be analyzed.

Other Variance

Dan has explained that he believes that the other negative variance of $90,000 is made up of "smaller expense items such as lower depreciation." However, this is not the source of the variance. The variance is made up completely of the negative variance of $89,800 ($2,967,650 − $2,877,850) in interest.

of little importance

Note that we used the unadjusted financial statements to perform our variance analysis in order to ensure we were comparing apples with apples. We wanted to analyze SableTel's performance year over year, not the impact of accounting treatment decisions. *d*

---

a The comments of a case stakeholder need to be confirmed or, more often, refuted.

b A telecommunications business usually needs to invest in its projects in process. Thus, it would be preferable, for the purpose of the variance analysis, to present these costs and administration expenses separately.

c One will notice that recommendations to carry out further investigation or to obtain more information (details) come up regularly. (p. 42) This is also noticeable in the analysis of accounting issues such as the impairment of the Mobile network. (p. 37)

d In fact, when one looks at the LIST OF ADJUSTMENTS AT P. 40, ONLY THE ONE CONCERNING R&D COSTS HAS AN EFFECT ON THE VARIANCE ANALYSIS. The other adjustments are linked to events that are easy to isolate, once the analysis by product line is made.

There would be no point in analyzing variances in the statement of the financial position (balance sheet), quite simply because this was not required! (p. 5)

unnecessary at the "Competent" level

We should also note that the variance analysis provided by Dan compares the 2010 results with the actual results for 2009. While this provides some meaningful information, it would also be appropriate to compare the actual results for 2010 with the budgeted results for 2010. Variances could then be calculated and explained against the approved budget for the year, which would provide StarNova with additional information on the results compared with what was expected.

budget variances

justification

All important requirements need to be dealt with in a reasonable manner.

(This proved to be the most challenging indicator for candidates. a ***It should be noted that the Board was not expecting anything as comprehensive as the analysis performed above. What the Board was looking for when they developed this indicator was for candidates to use the product line detail as well as other information provided in the case to make some insightful comments about SableTel's results year over year. While some candidates rose to the occasion and provided StarNova with a very meaningful analysis, the majority of candidates struggled.)***

compare between years

N.B.: In my opinion, the variance analysis is a fairly simple issue, more especially when the discussion is divided into parts.

The context is important here: relevant information should be provided.

THE SOLUTION OFFERS SOME THOUGHTS ABOUT THE CALCULATED VARIANCES; IN OTHER WORDS, IT PROVIDES EXPLANATIONS BASED ON THE CASE FACTS. THIS IS A REQUISITE AT THE "COMPETENT" LEVEL.

For Primary Indicator #3 (Management Decision-Making) the candidate must be ranked in one of the following five categories:	Percent Awarded
Not addressed — The candidate does not address this primary indicator.	4.6%
Nominal competence — The candidate does not attain the standard of reaching competence.	56.4% ←
Reaching competence — The candidate attempts to analyze areas of variance that provide relevant information to the executive committee.	25.1%
Competent — The candidate analyzes areas of variance that provide relevant information to the executive committee.	13.9%
Highly competent — The candidate analyzes the areas of variance that provide relevant information to the executive committee and recognizes that a comparison with the approved budget would provide additional meaningful information.	0.0%

An idea to retain in order to improve the reporting document.

Calculating or identifying is not enough! ↓ Explain! Analyze! Interpret!

(Candidates were asked to perform a more thorough analysis of the variance in results between 2010 and 2009. Candidates were expected to expand on Dan's high-level variance analysis, which did not provide any useful information to StarNova's executive committee. To demonstrate competence, candidates were required to identify some of the significant variances between the two years and provide some insight into the variance, such as why the variance occurred, why the variance was important, and how the variance could be addressed.)

One needs to take into account what makes up the essential part of SableTel's telecommunication activities.

(Candidates did not perform well on this indicator. Despite the directedness of the requirement, many candidates did not address this indicator. Most candidates either missed this indicator altogether, made passing comments on a variance or two as part of their work on other indicators, or deferred this work back to Dan or management for further explanation. Information provided in the simulation allowed the competent candidates to perform some meaningful variance analysis. For example, the simulation contained a breakdown of the revenue and cost of sales by product line. A comparison of revenues by product line to the prior year should have directed candidates to make more insightful comments, such as a comment on the large decrease in SableTel's most significant product line, long-distance service revenue.) b

The breakdown by product line is an indication in itself.

One should go beyond what is evident and suggest improvements to the employer.

---

a Even if more than 60% of the candidates have not attempted to make the analysis, one still needs to take the time to study this part of the evaluation guide. The requirement to analyze variances is made explicit in Exhibit I. The candidates did not plan out the response well or simply did not wish to discuss this subject, often perceived as difficult.

b AT THE "COMPETENT" LEVEL, IT SEEMS TO ME THAT ONE SHOULD HAVE PICKED OUT THE MAJOR VARIANCES, CARRIED OUT THE ANALYSIS BY PRODUCT LINE, AND PROVIDED A REASONABLE INTERPRETATION OF THE CALCULATIONS, TAKING THE CASE FACTS INTO ACCOUNT. (see Part 7, p. 77)

In a case, the candidate plays the lead role.

The list of financial ratios includes ratios linked to the financial condition AND ratios linked to the operating performance. It would be preferable to PRESENT A SOLUTION THAT TAKES INTO ACCOUNT BOTH ASPECTS.

explicit requirement EXH I

Primary Indicator #4 *(VII-4.1, VII-2.2)*

The candidate calculates financial ratios to determine the financial condition and operating performance of SableTel relative to its competitors.

The candidate demonstrates competence in Finance.

To determine the financial results and the financial condition of SableTel at August 31, 2010, we can compare certain key ratios with the industry ratios provided. Below is a comparison of the key ratios for 2010 followed by an explanation of the information that these financial ratios contain: [a]

These are the same ratios as those provided in the case. (p. 11) No new ratio has been calculated.

	Financial Ratio	SableTel 2010 Actual (unadjusted)	SableTel 2010 Actual (adjusted)	SableTel 2009 Actual (unadjusted)	Industry Ratios (2010) [b]
IMP	**Profitability ratios**				
	Return on equity (1)	4.5%	(115.9%)	(5.1%)	9.6%
IMP	**Margin analysis**				
	Gross margin % (2)	52.8%	45.8%	53.1%	52.2%
	Selling, marketing, and administration % (3)	46.4%	62.1%	50.6%	40.5%
	Operating profit % (4)	6.4%	(16.3%)	2.4%	11.7%
	Turnover				
	Accounts receivable turnover (5)	4.1×	3.9×	9.6×	6.7×
	Short-term liquidity				
	Current ratio (6)	0.9×	0.7×	1.0×	0.8×
	Long-term solvency				
	Operating profit/interest expense (7)	1.4×	(3.4×)	0.6×	8.1×
	Growth over prior year				
	Revenue growth (8)	(0.2%)	(4.4%)	Note 1	(2.6%)

p. 11

obj.: 15%

The most significant categories of ratio have been identified.

B46

The definitions may be abbreviated and entered directly on the table of ratios. Thus, "SM&A/rev" can replace line 3.

Details of calculations (see numbers from financial statements in Primary Indicator #2): p. 39

(1) Return on equity = profit ÷ total shareholders' equity
(2) Gross margin % = gross profit ÷ revenue
(3) Selling, marketing, and administration % = (Selling and marketing + administration) ÷ revenue
(4) Operating profit % = operating profit (before interest) ÷ revenue
(5) Accounts receivable turnover = revenue ÷ accounts receivable
(6) Current ratio = current assets ÷ current liabilities
(7) Operating profit/interest expense = operating profit (before interest) ÷ interest expense
(8) Revenue growth = (2010 revenue ÷ 2009 revenue) − 1

Note 1: No information on 2008 revenue or net income was provided, so this ratio cannot be calculated.

---

a IT IS PREFERABLE TO CALCULATE RATIOS FROM ADJUSTED FINANCIAL STATEMENTS (p. 39) IN ORDER TO PRESENT THE MOST ACCURATE POSSIBLE EVALUATION OF THE OPERATING PERFORMANCE. PROCEEDING IN THIS WAY, THERE IS NO LONGER ANY POINT IN CALCULATING AND THEN INTERPRETING THE "UNADJUSTED" RATIOS IN THE FIRST COLUMN.

b When writing his response, the candidate does not need to repeat this column, provided as is in the case. He can simply refer to the industry ratios as he proceeds.

comparison: - inter-year
- with industry

✓ comment

OVERALL COMMENT

The above ratio analysis indicates that SableTel is not performing as well as its peers, both from an operational (income statement) point of view and from a financial condition (balance sheet) point of view. The analysis also indicates that SableTel's financial condition has deteriorated over the past year.[a] This assessment is based on the following:

The positive or negative "sense" should be stressed.

IMP

- Profitability Ratios — SableTel's return on equity ratio is below the industry average, and after adjustments it is negative. This indicates that SableTel is not earning an adequate return for its shareholder (StarNova). StarNova has indicated that it typically expects all of its investments to earn a return of at least 15%. SableTel is not earning a return that is anywhere close to this percentage. As well, after the 2010 adjustments, SableTel's ratios have deteriorated significantly from 2009 due to the large loss in 2010.

link earlier issue

One needs to go back to the 15% return target because this is one of the important specifics of the case.

IMP

- Margin Analysis — SableTel's margin analysis indicates that it is earning a gross margin that is slightly higher than its peers (before adjustments). This margin (before adjustments) is also similar to the prior year.[b] However, its big problem appears to be its high SM&A percentage. This is causing SableTel to have a lower operating profit relative to the industry. SM&A expenses are 6% higher at SableTel then its peers (before adjustments) and after adjustments are almost 22% higher. This is one of the largest reasons for the poor financial results and we should investigate further why this is the case. Some of this will be due to the R&D at SableTel. Relative to the prior year, SableTel appears to have a better SM&A percentage before adjustments. However, this amount relates to the reversal of the R&D expenditures related to the Wireless Technology Project. Once these capitalized expenditures are reversed, the SM&A percentage is significantly higher in 2010 than in 2009.

1- Gross margin
2- SM&A

note 2 p. 44

Not to be forgotten: R&D costs are included in the SM&A.

link ACCT issue

The solution attempts constantly to explain SableTel's 2010 operating loss.

There are few indications about rec. in the case.

- Turnover[c] — SableTel is not "turning over" its accounts receivable fast enough. This is particularly true with respect to its accounts receivable in 2010, which appear to be abnormally high at August 31, 2010. This has also resulted in a turnover that is considerably worse than the prior year. SableTel appears to be tying up a significant amount of cash in its accounts receivable. If SableTel were able to increase its accounts receivable turnover to the average turnover in the industry, it would generate significant additional cash and would need to borrow less money from StarNova in order to meet the needs identified in its strategic plan. This low accounts receivable turnover may be an indication that SableTel has uncollectible accounts receivable. We would need to obtain further information to assess the amount for reasonableness and to determine if additional write-offs are required.

impact

required funding p. 15

suggested solution

Customers ⟶ CASH ⟶ Funding

- Short-Term Liquidity — SableTel appears to meet the industry norms with respect to its current ratio. This is in part due to the high accounts receivable balance at year-end. The ratios are slightly worse than the prior year but all above the industry norms and are acceptable (before adjustments). After the adjustment to write off a portion of the inventory at year-end, the current ratio is worse than the industry average.

link with high client balance

explanations

positive current ratio

N.B.: Making a link with recommendations from a previous issue is relevant. However, one should remember THAT AN OBSOLESCENCE PROVISION IS NOT A RECURRENT ITEM.

---

a This is an overall comment on the analysis of the ratios. Myself, I would present this comment at the very end, after having analyzed the important subjects of the issue.

b Personally, my analysis would be based solely on the adjusted financial information. However, as we will see later, the "Competent" level in the evaluation guide may be achieved with an analysis of the "adjusted" OR "unadjusted" ratios. Naturally, one does not need to provide both.

c The discussion of this ratio offers fewer concrete links than that of the two previous ratios. This is because there are less case facts concerning accounts receivable. I believe the analysis of this ratio to be less important, though it is easy to carry out.

few case facts ↓ of little importance

✓ comment

Interest coverage ratio? ↓ loss in 2010 ↓ limited usefulness

I believe it is important to point out that SableTel's operating activities resulted in a loss in 2010.

- Long-Term Solvency — Its interest coverage ratio is worse than the industry average and has deteriorated further in 2010, meaning that it may have trouble meeting its interest payments in the future. This is very troubling and indicates that, without some form of financial assistance, SableTel may not be able to meet its financing obligations in the near future.

- Growth Ratios — The industry has contracted over the past year and SableTel has contracted with the industry. Sales at SableTel have decreased by more than the industry (after adjustments), indicating a loss of market share as well. Note that the 2008 sales and profit figures were not available. These growth ratios should be computed over several years and trends identified and compared with the industry. Economic conditions are difficult (p. 6). Nevertheless, a priori, the impact is the same for all the entities within the industry.

impact

overall comment

Dan's comments and the ratios presented to the StarNova executive committee are, at the very least, not informative and may even be misleading. The three ratios provided to the executive committee in Dan's presentation all essentially report the same information. All compare the net income of SableTel relative to some other balance so, since SableTel initially reported an increase in net income, appear to be better in 2010 than in 2009. However, none of the ratios presented explains anything related to the financial condition of SableTel or how SableTel compares with its peers in the industry. a

The Chief Executive Officer's ratios are incorrect, since there was a profit and not a loss. (p. 6, 46)

An idea to retain in order to improve the reporting document.

To provide significantly enhanced information to the executive committee, SableTel should monitor and track some additional ratios and indicators, such as the following. These are all common indicators within the telecommunications industry: b

- Churn rate — new customers ÷ customers lost
- Customer mix — % of small customers versus % of large customers
- Capex intensity — total capital expenditures ÷ total revenue

practical aspect

ratios specific to the industry

B48

(Candidates also struggled with this indicator, but unlike the previous indicator, virtually all candidates attempted to address it. Candidates seemed to clearly understand that they were to use the ratios provided to compare SableTel with its competitors. Most candidates were able to calculate the ratios for SableTel and compare them to the industry figures provided. However, candidates seemed to be less familiar with the return on equity (ROE) and accounts receivable (A/R) turnover ratios as evidenced by errors in calculating these ratios. The next step in the analysis should have been to interpret the ratios. Unfortunately, most candidates did not push their analyses this far. The Board was disappointed because the interpretation of results could have taken many forms: an explanation of what the ratio means, the possible causes for the difference with the industry, or a suggestion as to how the ratio could be improved.) c

BEWARE OF CALCULATION ERRORS THAT MAKE THE ANALYSIS MORE DIFFICULT! ONE NEEDS TO CHECK OUT THE PLAUSIBILITY OF A CALCULATION BEFORE USING IT.

There are several ways of demonstrating analytical ability.

In the course of analyzing the suggested solution, one will notice that some points come back again and again: profitability (revenues, margin), the fact that SableTel incurred a loss, and the required funding as regards the Wireless Technology Project.

---

a As mentioned in Exhibit I, the case clearly required an evaluation of SableTel's operating performance relative to its "competitors."

b The following suggestions are valid but, in my opinion, not indispensable to the achievement of the "Competent" level.

c When one looks at the solution offered with respect to the evaluation of operating performance (ratios), one may notice that the following structure was adopted to resolve the issue:

1- Calculation of the ratio
2- Inter-year comparison/Comparison with industry
3- Analysis and interpretation (explanations, suggestions)

N.B.: The evaluation of operating performance is based on the case facts and regularly refers to the conclusions and recommendations for the preceding problems or issues.

It is not difficult to calculate and subsequently to comment on the ratios.
↓
Reaching competence

For Primary Indicator #4 (Finance), the candidate must be ranked in one of the following five categories:	Percent Awarded
Not addressed — The candidate does not address this primary indicator.	0.6%
Nominal competence — The candidate does not attain the standard of reaching competence.	5.8%
Reaching competence — The candidate calculates relevant financial ratios for SableTel.	57.2% ←
Competent — The candidate calculates relevant financial ratios for SableTel and performs a meaningful analysis, comparing SableTel to the industry.	36.0%
Highly competent — The candidate calculates relevant financial ratios, including a full range of ratios related to the financial position (i.e. balance sheet) and the operations (i.e. income statement) of SableTel, and performs a meaningful analysis comparing SableTel to industry.	0.4%

meaningful analysis

financial position AND operations

complete analysis of all the ratios (p. 11, 46)

(Candidates were asked for an evaluation of SableTel's operating performance relative to its competitors. To enable candidates to perform this analysis, they were provided with industry ratios for the past two years. To demonstrate competence, candidates were required to calculate some of the ratios for SableTel, compare those to the industry, and provide some value-added analysis.)

VALUE-ADDED

A more accurate description goes beyond:
- "Higher"
- "Lower"
- "Better"
- "Not as good"
- etc.

(Most candidates understood how the ratios were calculated and were able to use SableTel's financial statements to calculate some of the ratios for the company. After calculating SableTel's ratios, candidates then compared them to the industry and commented on whether SableTel's performance was better or worse than its competitors. This was a good first step; however, what was generally lacking was any type of value-added analysis. Candidates needed to step back and think about what the ratios were telling them about SableTel's operating performance.) [a]

One needs to use the information available in the case.

B49

It is surprising to observe the low percentage (36%) of candidates who have achieved the "Competent" level. Clearly it would be PREFERABLE TO CALCULATE FEWER RATIOS AND ANALYZE THEM CORRECTLY RATHER THAN TO CALCULATE THEM ALL AND LACK THE NECESSARY TIME FOR SUCH ANALYSIS. There should be some balance between breath and depth. Finally, when one takes a step back, one is not surprised to discover that the passing standard requires reflection and judgment. IT IS NOT SO MUCH THE CALCULATION OF THE RATIOS THAT MAKES THE DIFFERENCE, BUT THE USE TO WHICH ONE PUTS THEM.

---

a Comments:
- The most important ratios, as identified on the table on p. 46, will be found under the categories "Profitability ratios" and "Margin analysis." To reach the "Competent" level, I think it is essential to have calculated a number of ratios, say four or five, that would come from these two categories and elsewhere. Apart from calculating the ratio itself, one needs to compare it from year to year, and then compare it with the industry itself.
- At the "Competent" level, one needs to carry out a meaningful analysis of the ratios calculated, i.e. one needs to do more than just make a statement concerning the positioning of SableTel in relation to its peers. ONE NEEDS TO EXPLAIN WHAT IS HAPPENING, USING CASE FACTS, TO INTERPRET, AND THEN TO RECOMMEND SOLUTIONS, where appropriate. I believe it would be necessary to base such an analysis on at least three ratios.

  Finally, one must not forget the "diversity" aspect when drafting a response, which means that only analyzing the three ratios in the "Margin analysis" category would not be sufficient. (see Part 8, p. 87)

FOCUS: - how to improve the CONTENT of the reporting document.
- how to correct the statements in the report.

It is essential to take the time to define what must be contained in the reporting document, and to whom it is directed, in order to better specify the deficiencies.

Primary Indicator #5	*(V-1.3, V-2.7, V-2.8)*
The candidate identifies weaknesses within the executive reporting document as presented and recommends improvements.	
The candidate demonstrates competence in Performance Measurement and Reporting.	

explicit requirement EXH 1

use: Annual report to shareholders

The executive reporting document prepared by Dan is not informative and may in fact be misleading. a The purpose of the executive reporting document is to provide meaningful, high level analyses for StarNova so that StarNova can prepare its external MD&A included in its annual report to shareholders. Therefore the information presented should be relevant for this group.

OVERALL COMMENT

The essential elements of what is stated in Exhibit II must be reexamined and analyzed.

I have identified the following weaknesses in the executive reporting document: b

- IMP "[B]ased on robust revenue of $65,072,224" — This would imply that revenue was very good in 2010. However, revenue has actually decreased from the prior year and is not "robust." As well, $2,750,000 of the revenue relates to a government grant. Without this revenue (which I have recommended allocating to offset expenses instead of increasing revenue in my accounting adjustments above), the revenue has actually decreased significantly.

  link ACCT issue

- IMP "Reduction in operating costs of $2,783,365 due to cost restraint" — This statement implies (impact) that management has done a good job of controlling costs through management decisions. This is not true. The actual source of the decreased costs is a reduction in R&D expenses since these expenditures were capitalized in the current period (in prior periods these costs were expensed). In fact, we know that in general the administrative costs of SableTel are higher in 2010 than in 2009 and are significantly higher than the industry averages. As well, the administration expenses have increased by a very significant amount in 2010 after we consider the adjustments recommended above.

  ONE SHOULD NOT BE AFRAID TO ADOPT A POSITION ONCE THE CONCLUSION IS CLEAR.

  B50

  links with previous issues: Variance analysis + Adjusted FS

- IMP "Cost of sales were contained" — While based on the cost of sales balance on the income statement this is true, it is clear that margins in the long-distance segment of the business (its most significant segment) are decreasing at a significant rate. As well, after we remove the government grant from revenue we know that overall the gross margin decreased by 2.2%. A better analysis in the executive reporting document would highlight the gross margin and compare the margin with prior years and with industry averages in order to provide meaningful explanations. p. 43

  comparison: - inter-year - with industry

- IMP "Strong liquidity at year-end based on liquid assets totalling $16,215,519" — While it is true that SableTel has considerable liquid assets (cash and accounts receivable), this is primarily the result of an increase in accounts receivable that is tying up cash. It is not clear if these assets are "liquid." The statement implies that SableTel could turn its assets into cash quickly if necessary to meet financial obligations or to take advantage of other investment opportunities. This may not be the case. For example, we know that SableTel only turns its accounts receivable into cash about four times each year. This does not imply liquidity.

  What are the liquid assets? To be compared with balance sheet "Cash" item.

  This REC stems from the preceding analyses of the solution, analyses that have provided information much more useful to the Committee.

  link previous issue p. 46

---

a This is an overall comment on the analysis of the reporting document. Myself, I would present this comment at the very end, after having analyzed the important subjects of the issue.

b This is a "list of problems" and the discussion of each one requires a separate paragraph. In the course of the analysis of the suggested solution, the "important" problems are identified. It may be noted that the five highlights from fiscal 2010, presented in Exhibit II (p. 6) are all important.

There are several noticeable links with the previous problems or issues, hence the importance of properly sequencing the subjects.

The term "solid" refers to the entity's indebtedness.

IMP

- "Solid balance sheet at year-end, with equity totalling $26,338,280" — This statement would imply that SableTel has a strong balance sheet and its financial position is strong. a This is not the case at August 31, 2010. We know that SableTel has a considerable amount of debt and is relatively highly leveraged. This indicates a weak balance sheet rather than a strong balance sheet. After adjustments, SableTel has almost $6 of debt for every $1 of equity.

clear conclusion

link previous issue

few case facts ↓ of little importance

- The executive reporting document also includes a general statement that SableTel will "do even better in the future by increasing revenue and decreasing expenses." This is a very general statement and provides no information to the users of the executive reporting document on how SableTel might achieve these financial goals. The goals themselves are not very specific and provide little basis for the users to monitor SableTel's performance.

WAYS to achieve this

general statements; lack of detail

Since this case statement has not been explained, it is difficult to provide a pragmatic analysis.

IMP

- The executive reporting document indicates that Hurricane Baylee damaged a number of communication towers and disabled the mobile network. However, the executive reporting document does not contain any information on the implications for SableTel from a financial perspective and offers no information for the users on when the system may be back up and running (if ever). This is information that StarNova and by extension investors are surely to be interested in.

A heading such as "Hurricane" or "Baylee" could replace the first sentence.

financial impact

This is an unusual event that absolutely needs to be discussed.

IMP

- The executive reporting document indicates that the Wireless Technology Project will have a substantial impact in the short-term. There is no information on how the project may affect SableTel in the short term or even what SableTel means by "short term." We know that it will not be up and running until January 2012 from the presentation made by Dan. Therefore, any benefits from the new technology will not be experienced until at least that date. This may not be "short term" from an investor's perspective.

ST = 1 year One should pay attention to what is written.

Each statement in the reporting document is critically analyzed.

+/- IMP

- The executive reporting document also indicates that SableTel has made decisions in the past year that have decreased the company's overall risk. However, the risks that they have identified relate to health risks and not financial risks, which would be more useful for the readers. SableTel does not seem to grasp the risk concept from a financial perspective. b From a financial perspective it would appear that SableTel's risk has actually increased over the past year, as represented by its increased leverage. In addition to financial risks, SableTel would also face additional substantial risks such as technology, weather, and customer-related risks. These would all be relevant to users of the executive reporting document.

B51

link with earlier conclusions

Common sense requires that attention be paid to the specifics of the industry in which SableTel operates.

users' needs

hypothetical ↓ of little importance

- SableTel has indicated that they are not the defendants in any new environmental lawsuits. While this may be true, it implies that SableTel may be defendants in previous lawsuits. If this is the case, and the lawsuits are material, then SableTel should discuss these significant issues within the executive reporting document. Investors would be very interested in this type of information because it would affect their investment risk.

obtain information

Structure:
- Deficiencies
- Analysis: comments/explanations regarding deficiencies
- Suggested improvements

ATTENTION MUST BE PAID TO EACH WORD. WHAT IS NOT WRITTEN DOES NOT EXIST!

---

a It will be noticed that the expression "imply that..." is often used in the suggested solution. This is because the statements in the reporting document affect the way users see the situation. THE CANDIDATE MUST BECOME AWARE OF THE CUMULATIVE EFFECT OF HIS OBSERVATIONS IN ORDER TO BE ABLE TO MAKE AN OVERALL COMMENT.

b This is not the first time that the suggested solution brings up "deficiencies" in SableTel's management. Right from the beginning, the solution has indicated that the reporting document may in fact be misleading. It could be pointed out that the criticisms are not directly aimed at one person, but rather at the presentation in Exhibit II. ONE MUST SHOW CONSIDERATION FOR INDIVIDUALS.

Financial Review by management (IAS 1 par. 13): describe and explain the main features of the entity's financial performance and financial position, and the principal uncertainties it faces.

few case facts ↓ +/- IMP

- SableTel has indicated that they "continue to focus on evolving our core business" and they "have no significant new projects planned for the foreseeable future." However, we know that SableTel's strategic plan includes a very significant capital project (the Wireless Technology Project). This new project will cost a significant amount of money, and investors would surely be interested in the costs and benefits associated with this project. SableTel has not disclosed much information related to this project.

information for the investors

cost-benefit

minor ↓ of little importance

- Finally, SableTel would like StarNova's MD&A to thank a long-time employee of its organization for 25 years of dedicated service. While this may arise from good intentions, it is not clear how this information would be relevant to investors, especially at the StarNova level. SableTel should not provide information to be included in StarNova's MD&A that would not be of interest to investors.

This point is easily settled in a single sentence.

A CANDIDATE WHO PLANS OUT THE STRUCTURE OF HER SOLUTION WILL BE SURE OF PROVIDING AN APPROPRIATE RESPONSE WITHIN A REASONABLE TIME FRAME.

Some statements are misleading!

comment on reporting document ≠ redo MD&A

(There were several statements included in the reporting document prepared by Dan that were vague, if not completely misleading. The Board did not expect candidates to prepare an MD&A for SableTel. What the Board did expect was for candidates to understand the purpose of an MD&A and to recognize that what Dan had prepared was not appropriate. The MD&A should be a true and balanced representation of how the company performed during the past year and provide information about its future prospects to help prospective and current investors decide whether they want to invest or continue to invest in the company. [a] ***With that goal in mind, candidates should have been able to identify statements made by Dan that were incongruous. Most candidates had difficulty doing so. However, candidates were at least able to pick out some inappropriate statements made by Dan in the reporting document. The misleading statement most frequently addressed by candidates was the statement that no significant projects were planned for the future, whereas the WTP was clearly a significant project for SableTel on which they should be providing more detailed information to investors.)*** [b]

It is important to CAREFULLY READ EVERY WORD of the various case requirements.

B52

SableTel could make a number of substantial improvements to its executive reporting document in order to provide meaningful information to StarNova, and by extension to the investors of StarNova. For example, the executive reporting document is simply reproducing 2010 financial information that is readily available in the financial statements without providing any additional information or analysis. Financial information should be presented in an MD&A, but the purpose of the MD&A is to expand on this financial information and to explain to the user what the financial information is saying about the company.

overall conclusion with respect to the lack of information in the reporting document

Some suggested improvements to its executive reporting document are as follows:

- SableTel should provide relevant and meaningful financial information within the executive reporting document. This information should contain comparisons with the prior year and comparisons with the industry. Key financial information on the liquidity and capital resources of the organization should be presented. SableTel could develop financial indicators or ratios that assist users in determining the health of the organization and could monitor these indicators over time.

2. Key performance drivers

objective: describe and explain the financial statements

- SableTel should also provide additional information on its cash flow. This is important because SableTel has a significant amount of property, plant and equipment on its statement of financial position and as a result has a significant amount of depreciation buried in the various line items in its statement of comprehensive income. Additional information on its capital expenditures (capex) would also be helpful so that users could understand the cash flow to be expected from the entity in the future.

1. Core businesses and strategy

IAS 1: policy for investments

---

a CICA Standards and Guidance Collection, MD&A, Executive Summary.

b This statement is easy to identify, then to refute. NEVERTHELESS ONE SHOULD NOT CONFUSE EASINESS AND IMPORTANCE. The most obvious statements are not often--indeed they are rarely--the most important. One needs to go beyond one's first impression.

The suggested improvements to the reporting document are regularly accompanied by practical examples from the case itself.

CICA, Management's Discussion and Analysis[a]: The disclosure framework of the MD&A is presented in five parts:
1. Core businesses and strategy
2. Key performance drivers
3. Capability to deliver results
4. Results and outlook
5. Risk

- SableTel must strive to provide financial information that is accurate. Presenting misleading information can lead to mistrust and a loss of credibility for an organization. SableTel should present both good and bad financial information. It could also take the opportunity to explain to investors how it plans to improve its financial performance in the future. This would be provided with the overall strategic plan (such as "we plan to decrease our costs by 5% in the future through the use of our wireless technology, which will be implemented in 2012"). 4. Results and outlook

IAS 1: factors and influences determining financial performance

- SableTel should provide information on its risk profile (from an investor's perspective) and information to support its assertions on its risk profile. This risk profile would be primarily from a financial perspective. SableTel could also outline how it proposes to decrease its risk profile over time. This could be achieved through a targeted debt-to-equity ratio, for example. 5. Risk

IAS 1: funding/ratio of liabilities to equity

- SableTel should provide relevant, forward-looking information within its executive reporting document. There is no mention of the strategic plan that SableTel has developed for the future. Nor is there any significant mention of the Wireless Technology Project, which is a key component of SableTel's strategic plan. The executive reporting document provides management with the opportunity to communicate their vision for the future of the company. This is not evident within the current document. This vision could and should be presented over a longer time frame, as well. The current strategic plan only contemplates the next fiscal year, which is not a long time frame from a strategic point of view. Where does SableTel see itself in 10 years? 3. capability to deliver results p. 5

IAS 1: policy for investments

think ST-MT

- The executive reporting document could also contain strategies for dealing with any significant risks or concerns. For example, the document would provide SableTel with a great opportunity to explain to its users how it is dealing with the aftermath of Hurricane Baylee.

IAS 1: response to changes in the environment

- Finally, SableTel should not include irrelevant information that would not be useful for investors. It is unlikely that most investors would be interested in retiring employees unless it affects the future prospects of the company.

B53

MD&A ⟶ current and prospective investors

(Candidates could have focused on critiquing the misleading statements made by Dan in the existing reporting document or they could have focused on what information was missing from the document. Most candidates who addressed this indicator chose to critique the statements made by Dan. However, some candidates also clearly understood the type of information that should be included in an MD&A and raised some valid omissions. a ***Those candidates were rewarded for their added depth of discussion.)*** b

understand + raise

Criticism is not sufficient; suggestions for improvement must be provided, as required in Exhibit I.

---

a IN ORDER TO SUGGEST RELEVANT IMPROVEMENTS TO THE EXECUTIVE COMMITTEE, ONE FIRST NEEDS TO "TAKE A STEP BACK" AND REMIND ONESELF OF THE "USUAL" CONTENT OF A MANAGEMENT DISCUSSION AND ANALYSIS.

b The solution to this issue is presented in two parts: 1- comments on the reporting document and 2- suggestions for improvements. It needs to be pointed out that the natural reflex of the candidate is to identify a deficiency and to immediately recommend an improvement by "tempering or eliminating" one deficiency at a time.
In the present situation, this is not a very suitable approach. On the one hand, it must be recognized that the suggestions for improvements that may be put forward are applicable to more than one deficiency. On the other hand, it must also be taken into account that information is missing from the reporting document, including key financial information on liquidity. An analysis that is essentially focused on the statements found in the Exhibit II reporting document will not help to bring out this fact. ONE NEEDS TO TAKE A STEP BACK IN ORDER TO IDENTIFY THOSE SITUATIONS WHICH REQUIRE AN OVERALL VISION OF THE EVENTS.

It will be noticed that a good number of candidates have simply not understood the requirement, or alternatively have not really analyzed the deficiencies brought out. It is necessary to constantly ensure proper coverage in sufficient depth.

For Primary Indicator #5 (Performance Measurement and Reporting) the candidate must be ranked in one of the following five categories:	Percent Awarded
Not addressed — The candidate does not address this primary indicator.	5.3%
Nominal competence — The candidate does not attain the standard of reaching competence.	24.6%
Reaching competence — The candidate identifies some of the deficiencies in the executive reporting document.	29.8%
Competent — The candidate identifies some of the deficiencies in the executive reporting document and recommends improvements that would help readers understand the financial situation of SableTel or explains why the executive reporting document as presented is not useful.	39.9%
Highly competent — The candidate discusses several of the deficiencies in the executive reporting document, recommends improvements that help readers understand the financial situation of SableTel, and explains why the executive reporting document as presented is not useful.	0.4%

The context is very important. The CONTENT of the reporting document needs to be improved.

B54

(Candidates were asked to provide comments on the reporting document, including suggested improvements. Candidates were provided with the SableTel reporting document that Dan had prepared for the executive committee. The simulation explained that the reporting document should meet StarNova's MD&A requirements because it would be used to develop StarNova's annual report. Based on this direction, candidates were expected to critique the existing document since it contained obvious shortcomings.)

to criticize = to pick out and justify deficiencies

vague, misleading, insufficient statements → make the information more useful to the shareholders

(Many candidates struggled with what they had been asked to do. Some candidates had difficulty understanding exactly what the reporting document was and what they were supposed to do with it. Those candidates who understood the requirement were able to identify statements in the reporting document that were vague, misleading, or insufficient, and recommend changes to make the information more useful to the shareholders. However, many candidates incorrectly used Dan's comments in the reporting document to provide management or operational advice rather than critically analyze the document from a reporting perspective. Candidates are reminded that the MD&A is an important reporting tool, and they should be familiar with its contents.) [a]

useful theoretical concepts

Exhibit I is explicit. It requires that the candidate "comment on the reporting document" and "make suggestions for improvements." THIS ALREADY SUGGESTS THAT THERE ARE "DEFICIENCIES" TO BE IDENTIFIED. One will notice a direct reference to the "reporting document" in the heading of Exhibit II. The link must be established when reading the case.

---

a Comments:

- I believe that evaluating the importance of the deficiencies in the reporting document can be summed up as follows: there are seven important deficiencies, three of lesser importance, and two that are of little importance. The majority of the important deficiencies certainly need to have been analyzed. THE ANALYSIS MUST BE COMPLETE, THAT IS TO SAY ONE NEEDS TO EXPLAIN "WHY" IT IS A DEFICIENCY, AND THEN SUGGEST "HOW" TO IMPROVE THE PRESENTATION OF INFORMATION TO THE READERS. A number of case facts point the discussion to a consideration of the users' needs. As of the first page, one may note that the entity is publicly accountable, that the industry is strictly regulated, and that the Committee is "confused" by the results for 2010. Additionally, the CEO is unable to provide clear answers to the questions asked in the course of his presentation, in itself a worrying fact.

Structure:[a] - "P" Problem (or Deficiency)
- "I" Impact (or Analysis)
- "R" Recommendation

explicit requirement EXH 1

Primary Indicator #6	*(IV-2.1, IV-2.3, IV-2.6, IV-2.7, IV-4.1, IV-4.2)*
The candidate evaluates the strategic plan, recognizes that it is flawed, and suggests recommendations for improvement.	
The candidate demonstrates competence in Governance, Strategy, and Risk Management.	

IMP

Customer Losses [b] p. 16

One must not lose sight of the "strategic" aspect when discussing each of the subsequent elements.

Links could be established with the goals to bring the gross margin to 60% and to increase cross-selling. (p. 20)

During the year, SableTel lost two large customers, each with annual revenue exceeding $300,000. There has been no follow-up to determine why SableTel lost these customers.

The result is that SableTel has no idea why these customers left and has not identified potential problems within its organization or pricing strategy. Left unresolved, these problems may continue to grow and more customers may be lost.

The discussion should not be limited to the financial impacts of the customer losses.

SableTel should follow up on these large customer losses and determine the exact reasons it lost them. Once the reasons have been determined, SableTel can improve its systems or adjust its prices if necessary so that it does not lose additional customers in the future for the same reasons. Furthermore, no customer retention policies are documented in the strategic plan. The lack of a plan to retain customers could mean that current customers will be lost in the future. It is much more cost effective and simpler to retain existing customers then to obtain new customers.

retain current customers ⇆ obtain new customers

impact

A customer retention policy and plan should be implemented immediately. If a successful customer retention policy is instituted, current customers would be more likely to stay with SableTel, which would assist the sales team with the ability to achieve their sales targets.

B55

(Few candidates commented on the fact that SableTel had not followed up with the two large customers lost during the year or that it lacks a customer retention plan.)

IMP

Customer Visits p. 19

Several links can be made: - quotas (p. 19)
- new sales staff (p. 16)
- retirement long-time employee (p. 6)

The customer service department plans to visit all customers (big and small) once every five years. Sales staff will visit those customers that are close to SableTel's office first in order to keep travel costs down.

Since the title "Customer visits" is clear, one can go directly to the analysis.

practical aspect

While this may be a great way to enhance customer service, it is not clear that the benefits will exceed the costs. For example, visiting customers with annual revenues of $1,000 may not be worth the costs associated with the visit. The department has already indicated that they will need to hire 15 additional staff to meet this goal. The plan also calls for visiting locations "close to our main office in an effort to keep travel costs down." This is not an appropriate basis for determining which customers to visit. Therefore, while the objective of increasing customer satisfaction is a good one, the plan to achieve this goal appears to be flawed and not cost effective.

conclusion

analysis integrated with case facts

---

a This response structure is a general guide that constantly reminds a candidate of the essential part of her response. The structure must be used with discernment. It is sometimes necessary to provide an analysis that goes beyond the simple mention of the impact of the problem identified. It is sometimes necessary to come to a conclusion regarding the current situation before recommending one's suggestions for improvements.

b Personally, I prefer to set out the problem or deficiency as a heading. "Lost clients" constitute an event that needs to be taken into consideration, but it is not the problem per se. THE TWO DEFICIENCIES THAT NEED TO BE PICKED OUT ARE RATHER THAT "THERE WAS NO FOLLOW-UP" AND "THERE WAS NO CUSTOMER RETENTION POLICY." IT SEEMS TO ME THAT WHAT ABSOLUTELY MATTERS IS PROPERLY IDENTIFYING THE PROBLEM FROM THE BEGINNING.

simple practical solution → training

financial impact

Large customers with the potential for increased sales [R] should be visited first. This would likely provide SableTel with the most reward for its efforts. In general, SableTel needs to plan these visits more logically to ensure they are cost effective. As well, there may be alternative methods, to ensure that customers are satisfied, that are less costly. For example, SableTel could [R] call all of its existing customers or have all of its [R] customers complete a satisfaction survey. Employees [R] could also be trained to ensure that they are providing the best client service possible. Likely a combination of all of these methods, depending on the size of the customer and their potential for increased revenue, should be undertaken. a

This is a link with the goal mentioned above, that of retaining existing customers.

(This issue was the one most frequently addressed by candidates. Most candidates who correctly identified customer visits as an issue were able to explain why the current strategy was flawed and how it could be improved.)

The analysis of the subject "Customer visits" is easy to make; the case facts are clear.

IMP but few case facts

Standard Margin Pricing p. 20

SableTel appears to derive its pricing from a standard 60% margin, which [P] may or may not be indicative of the value of the product or service offered.

obj 60% (p. 20) current 45.8% (p. 46) industry 52.2%

[I] The implication of this is that SableTel cannot price products at a level above this margin. It is quite possible that some of its products and services could command a premium above this margin, but given the stated policy, SableTel could not realize this increased margin. This standard pricing policy issue [P] will become even greater if it is not adjusted once the benefits of the Wireless Technology Project begin to be realized in 2012, since the costs for SableTel are expected to decrease across all products and services.

"improve" margin by 5% (note 5)

One needs to think in both directions: above 60% and below 60% (discounts). Both situations are possible.

B56

I believe we [R] should review whether this method is appropriate. Another possible method is to [R] base pricing on competitive prices or value pricing. SableTel is in a competitive industry — telecommunications — which means that the market will drive the ability to achieve margins on product. Pricing [R] should be in line with the prices of competitors. The new policy of allowing some discounts with the approval of the Vice-President Marketing illustrates that SableTel is starting to realize that its prices need to be more flexible and more competitive. However, the non-standard pricing does not allow for the [P] circumstance in which SableTel may be able to increase its prices, driving margins higher while still remaining competitively priced compared with its competitors. This will be especially important when SableTel introduces its new wireless technology.

practical aspect

solutions

industry

The basic problem is the vagueness of the "pricing policy."

(About half of the candidates identified this issue, and most of them were able to explain its implications and propose a solution.)

Once the problem ("P") has being identified, it becomes easier to explain its impact ("I") and then to recommend a solution ("R").

+/- IMP

Sales Quotas p. 19

SableTel plans to increase sales by giving sales staff higher quotas and having senior sales staff lead by example. We already know that the sales staff was unable to meet their existing quota in 2010; p. 18, 16 therefore, it would appear unlikely that they'd be able to meet an even higher quota in the future. In addition, sales quotas need to be realistic in order for them to be a motivating factor. If the quotas are set too high, [I] the sales staff will be discouraged. A significant portion of their compensation is based on meeting quotas, so if these quotas are unrealistically high, [I] they might leave to work for a competitor of SableTel that offers a higher base salary.

conclusion

why

basic concepts in "Human resources management"

(Many candidates realized that increasing the sales quotas was likely not a good strategy for SableTel in light of other case facts.)

INTEGRATION

a We should not forget that we are accountants. Consequently, it is not our job to determine whether making customer visits is the right way of improving Customer Service or of doing marketing.

THE ANALYSIS, MAINLY FOCUSED ON THE COST-BENEFIT CONCEPT, OFFERS A FEW SUGGESTIONS, BUT ONLY IN A GENERAL WAY.

IMP **Plan to Increase Sales** p. 19

SableTel has also indicated that they plan to increase sales by hiring additional sales staff. Adding sales staff is not sufficient in itself to increase sales. SableTel needs a detailed plan. It needs to provide its sales staff with proper incentives and the proper tools to drive sales. For example, SableTel could provide its sales personnel with a targeted customer listing to help identify potential new customers. Customer lists for competitors may also be available. As well, it could develop a potential client list from customers that it has lost over the past two years that may be ready to return to SableTel. Finally, the sales department and the marketing department should communicate and determine as a team how to best increase sales. The objectives of these two departments are ultimately the same and sharing information between these two departments in particular would likely be very useful. [a]

link to "customer losses"

link "marketing" and "sales"

(Few candidates commented on the need for SableTel to come up with a detailed plan to increase sales.)

IMP This subject can be dealt with elsewhere.

Increase in Overhead Costs p. 19 [b]

unjustified decisions → losses for the entity

The 2011 budget prepared by SableTel indicates that SM&A expenses will increase by approximately $4.0 million in 2011. Most of this increase is likely due to the new staff that will be hired as contemplated in the strategic plan.

A candidate, reading through the case, who has picked up all those elements that will lead to a rise in costs may offer a conclusion that points to an effective increase of overhead costs in the future.

The plan calls for increased human resources, which results in increased overhead and will further increase the loss in 2011. After recasting the 2011 budget to take into account the problems that I have identified, there is no room for increasing overhead costs in 2011.

The plan should be adjusted to determine whether SableTel can do without the increased staff and operate more efficiently. More effective and efficient methods and procedures need to be identified and implemented to increase sales while holding the line or decreasing costs. Addressing the customer issues identified above could assist SableTel in maintaining and increasing revenues. Additional staff should not be hired at this point, and additional hiring should only be considered in the future when revenue warrants it. It should be remembered that the operating activities of SableTel currently result in a loss. (p. 39)

link to "customer losses"

(Very few candidates commented on the affordability of all the initiatives SableTel was proposing in their strategic plan. Strong candidates commented on the initiatives, thereby demonstrating integration across the indicators.)

Current ratio < 1.0 and required funding 21M

IMP **Executive Bonus Plan** p. 18

One of the goals of Human Resources for the year is to retain existing employees, which of course is a good thing. However, the only change noted that will help SableTel achieve this goal is to introduce a new executive bonus plan.

only executive group!

This new bonus plan is only relevant for seven employees (likely the executive group). It is unlikely that this program will have the desired effect on SableTel as a whole since most of the employees will not benefit from this program. Therefore, it is unlikely that SableTel will meet its goal of retaining existing employees.

comment on link between goals and ways of achieving

a The case does not include many practical facts with respect to this "plan to increase sales." One may also notice that the recommendations offered above, though certainly acceptable, are general and not closely connected to the case itself. They can be applied, as is, to many entities.

b This analysis is useful twice: when commenting on the strategic plan AND when evaluating the budgeted financial information. WE KNOW THAT THE SAME CASE FACT CAN SERVE MORE THAN ONE PURPOSE. Thus, when resolving a case, it is important to regularly ask oneself whether INTERRELATIONSHIPS CAN BE ESTABLISHED, on the one hand, between subjects in the same section and, on the other, between the various problems or issues.

justified recommendations

Further research needs to be performed to determine the costs and benefits associated with this plan and to ensure that Dan and the other senior executives at SableTel are not simply adding an unnecessary perk to their compensation packages. The plan will undoubtedly cost more to administer as well. Specific measurement criteria should be developed to determine whether the bonus plan is successful. Bonuses should be based on a number of criteria and financial objectives should play a large part in the bonus. If SableTel incurs a loss for 2011, then there may be no justification for any bonus. The board, or the compensation committee of the board, should also review this plan since Dan is likely in a conflict of interest with respect to it.

objectives → measurement criteria

It is important to bring out the stakeholders' "biases."

p. 18 There may be other ways to retain and improve the satisfaction of current employees, such as [a]

"list of…"

- an employee survey,
- a compensation survey,
- a work/life balance program, or
- similar lifestyle programs.

retention employees

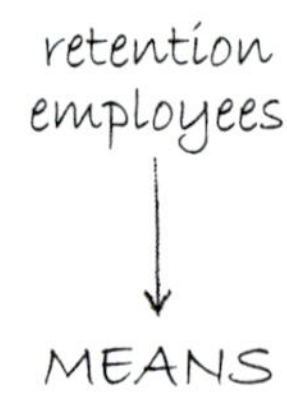

MEANS

(Most candidates recognized the shortcomings of the proposed bonus plan and made suggestions for its improvement.)

IMP

Compensation Policies [b] p. 19

Salespeople at SableTel are paid a base salary of $45,000, while comparable positions in the industry pay a base salary of $65,000. Dan has indicated that this is done to encourage the sales staff to make sales in order to increase their commissions.

One should try to move to the analysis faster.

There seems to be a large difference between the compensation offered to SableTel sales employees and the market. This may not be appropriate, and may account for the high turnover of SableTel sales staff and contribute to the lack of achievement of the sales targets. link p. 16

This policy should be reviewed to ensure that SableTel's compensation is achieving its desired results. If necessary, the base sales amount should be increased to ensure it is competitive with the industry. In conjunction with this, the sales compensation program should be reviewed to ensure that it is meeting its stated goals (in other words, increasing sales) while still maintaining its cost effectiveness.

ALWAYS justify REC'S

objectives → compensation

(Most candidates commented that SableTel's compensation policy appeared to not be competitive and may be contributing to its turnover issues. Candidates suggested alternative ways to structure the compensation package and often tied this discussion into their discussion of the proposed bonus plan.)

tie-up bonus plan

We can see that the concepts of "cost-benefit" and "efficiency" come up regularly in the suggested solution.

---

a This is a "list of…" ways presented as an enumeration. It would be a good idea to add one or two practical examples to illustrate the discussion. One could be to consult the sales staff when determining sales quotas.

b Several aspects to handle concerning the sales team. Myself, I would have analyzed them one after the other, in a structured manner, so as to be able to bring out interrelationships between them during their analysis. For example, sales staff might be tempted to go and work for competitors, consequent on their higher sales quotas. One should also tie in this discussion with current compensation policies.
Where possible, I find it easier to integrate related subjects into a single flow. However, the response should be diversified. Only discussing matters that concern the sales team, without taking into consideration other aspects of the strategic plan, would not be a good approach.

+/- IMP

IT Focus/Wireless Technology Project p. 18

One should be aware that this decision could disrupt SableTel's other activities.

The IT department has indicated that it will focus all of its resources on the Wireless Technology Project. This technology has not been proven yet because the feasibility study is still outstanding, so the IT department's time may be better spent elsewhere. Can SableTel afford to put all other IT projects on hold until the Wireless Technology project is complete? For example, having IT provide cross-functional access to files may help improve the coordination between departments and the company's overall performance.

cross-functional access (p. 22) + cross-selling (p. 20)

- technology as yet not proven
- effectiveness of IT department

(Many candidates either discussed specific concerns with regards to the Wireless Technology Project or the fact that the IT department's time was valuable and other potentially useful projects had to be sacrificed.)

The fact that the IT department will "focus ALL of its resources on the project" should attract the candidate's attention when he reads the case. Every word matters.

+/- IMP

Cross-Selling Program p. 20

Marketing plans to implement a new program in an attempt to cross-sell products and services at SableTel. The program requires an investment of $450,000 to modify the billing software. SableTel's IT department will develop the necessary software.

The advantages of this program are not explained in the case.

Resources need to be dedicated to this project if it is going to succeed. As well, there needs to be a cost/benefit analysis completed for this program or some type of "return on investment" analysis to ensure that the project is a good idea from a financial perspective. To perform such an analysis, SableTel will need to estimate incremental revenues and costs. It is also not clear if a "flyer" is the best way to proceed. As an alternative, a list of potential targets could be developed and given to the sales department for follow-up.

financial impact

link "marketing" and "sales"

(Few candidates discussed the cross-selling initiative proposed by SableTel.)

B59

IMP when elaborating a strategic plan

Access to Information p. 22

There is some indication that information sharing is discouraged within SableTel. Managers below the level of vice-president are only provided with information that directly relates to their own departments.

This lack of information flow inhibits management decision-making abilities. Managers need to know the vision and strategic plan of the organization and need to understand how their department fits in with the overall goals. If they do not understand their part of the plan, they will likely not implement strategies to achieve the plan. Decisions made in isolation may have impacts on other areas that are unknown, and without the cooperation of the management of other departments, projected benefits of the decisions may not be achieved. Also, the IT group seems to be focused on its development of customer products while ignoring internal customers and their need for reliable data.

THERE ARE SEVERAL INSTANCES WHERE IT RESOURCES ARE CALLED FOR. ONE SHOULD DETERMINE PRIORITIES AND BUILD A TIMETABLE.

Managers should be given information on the overall goals and objectives of the organization and how these will contribute to meeting the organization's vision. Managers should also be encouraged to develop plans that are consistent with the overall goals and objectives of the organization and should be held accountable for meeting these departmental goals in order to meet the overall organizational objectives.

REMINDER: Negative margin customers (p. 14)
IT: $1,130 M - Marketing: $0

(Many candidates recognized that SableTel's approach of limiting managers' access to information is not appropriate and may in fact be detrimental to the company.)

departmental goals VERSUS objectives of the organization

+/- IMP

Lack of Coordination between Departments This subject could be discussed at the same time as the previous one. They have a number of points in common.

SableTel has a philosophy of restricting the use of information and, as noted above, discourages communication between the departments. Further evidence of the lack of coordination between the departments is provided by the IT department and the marketing department with respect to the targeted advertising flyer program. p. 20 The strategic plan also appears to be formulated by each department independent of the other departments.

Indeed, we notice, on pp. 18 to 20, a number of goals from different departments.

The departments at SableTel appear to operate independently and do not share information or knowledge to ensure that the goals of the organization as a whole are achieved. This may lead to the departments developing departmental goals and objectives that are not congruent with the organization as a whole.

departments goals VERSUS organization goals

The departments need to communicate and develop goals and objectives as a team to ensure that the goals and objectives of the organization are met. This will assist SableTel in meeting its strategic goals and objectives and its mission and vision.

Mission + Vision ⟶ Strategic and Operational objectives

+/- IMP

(Few candidates commented on the lack of coordination between departments.)

One-Year Time Frame

It is a good idea to remember what is meant by a strategic plan in order to better understand the case requirements in the light of StarNova's needs.

The strategic plan as presented covers a one-year time frame — the 2011 fiscal year. The implication of a one-year time frame is that management at SableTel will focus on meeting the goals and objectives within the strategic plan over the next fiscal year and may not be focused on meeting long-term goals and objectives necessary to achieve its mission and vision (or the mission and vision of StarNova).

ST- MT as reporting doc (p. 53)

B60

SableTel should develop a strategic plan with a longer time frame. Normally, strategic plans are prepared for 5 or even 10 years and set out measurable goals and objectives. For example, StarNova has indicated that it expects all of its investments to generate a 15% return. Currently SableTel is not generating a return that is close to this amount. SableTel should develop a long-term strategic plan that will put it on the path to achieving this required return, and senior management should be held accountable for meeting the milestones within this strategic plan. a

obj of 15%

desired results ↓ MEANS

to be link with previous subjects: Compensation policies + Bonus plan

margin at 60%?

(Very few candidates commented on the short-term outlook taken by SableTel in developing its strategic plan.) b

---

a The task of the CEO is to provide the StarNova Executive Committee with the information it needs to understand SableTel's financial issues. It is also responsible for implementing the means required to reach the 15% return goal.

b As presented in the suggested solution, more than 13 subjects may be discussed as part of the evaluation of the strategic plan. It is clear that it would be impossible to deal with them all adequately within a time limit of approximately 20 to 25 minutes. A PRIORI, A CANDIDATE MUST ALWAYS ATTEMPT TO DETERMINE THE IMPORTANCE OF THE SUBJECTS IN ORDER TO FOCUS HIS DISCUSSION ON THOSE ELEMENTS THAT ARE THE MOST CRITICAL. ONE SHOULD REMEMBER THAT THE SUBJECTS THAT ARE EASIER TO HANDLE WILL NOT AUTOMATICALLY FIGURE ON THE LIST OF IMPORTANT SUBJECTS. Additionally, one does not necessarily have to follow the order of the slides as they appear in Exhibit VII. On the one hand, one must MAKE AN EVALUATION AS TO WHETHER THE PLAN PROVIDED IS ADEQUATE. To this end, pp. 18, 19 and 20 contain the goals of the six different Departments. On the other hand, ONE SHOULD CHECK WHETHER IT IS COMPLETE.
The importance of the various subjects was indicated while reading the suggested solution. There are six to eight important subjects: the amount of money at stake (or financial impact) is one aspect to take into consideration. One example would be the hiring of 16 additional salespersons who could each earn up to $85,000. Taking the case facts into account, when they are both numerous and practical, makes for a more detailed analysis. Thus, there will be less to say about "IT focus" than about "Customer visits."

For Primary Indicator #6 (Governance, Strategy, and Risk Management) the candidate must be ranked in one of the following five categories:	Percent Awarded
Not addressed — The candidate does not address this primary indicator.	0.2%
Nominal competence — The candidate does not attain the standard of reaching competence.	5.4%
Reaching competence — The candidate identifies some of the weaknesses in the strategic plan.	29.6%
Competent — The candidate describes some of the weaknesses in the strategic plan, describes the implications of the weaknesses, and recommends improvements.	64.3%
Highly competent — The candidate describes several of the weaknesses in the strategic plan, describes the implications of the weaknesses, and recommends improvements.	0.5%

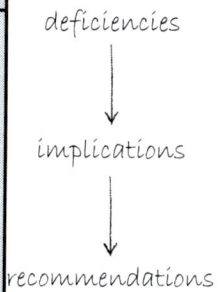

The candidates were successful as concerns this competency. Drafting is certainly helped by the use of a response structure such as P-I-R.

deficiencies → implications → recommendations

STRATEGIC point of view

(Candidates were asked to comment on the points raised in the 2011 strategic plan, including suggested improvements to the plan. Dan outlined many of his plans for 2011 in his presentation to the executive committee, and candidates were expected to recognize that a number of these were not good ideas from a strategic point of view.)

AS IS MADE CLEAR WHEN READING THE SOLUTION, THE IMPACTS NEED TO BE PRECISE AND TO TAKE INTO ACCOUNT THE SPECIFICS OF THE CASE.

(Candidates performed well on this indicator. Most candidates were able to identify and discuss several weaknesses in Dan's strategic plan and suggest improvements. Weak responses did not address the implications of some of Dan's proposed strategies or made impractical recommendations when attempting to resolve the issues.) a

B61

implications not addressed OR impractical recommendations

It will be necessary to mention the financial impact of the deficiencies on the strategic plan when evaluating the budgeted financial information and the likelihood of the result being achieved. SUGGESTED IMPROVEMENTS MUST BE LINKED TO THE CASE FACTS AND BE REALISTIC, AND PRACTICAL.

Candidates might decide to present the evaluation of the strategic plan and the evaluation of the budget together. However, since these are distinct requirements, I would suggest separate answers so as to ensure complete coverage of each aspect. The interrelationships between these two issues should be mentioned regularly.

strategic plan → budget

a Comments:

- AT THE "COMPETENT" LEVEL, ONE CERTAINLY NEEDS TO CORRECTLY IDENTIFY THE DEFICIENCIES, DESCRIBE THE CONSEQUENCES, AND END WITH SUGGESTIONS FOR IMPROVEMENTS. IN MY OPINION, A CANDIDATE WHO DOES NOT DISCUSS THE CONSEQUENCES OF THE DEFICIENCIES UNCOVERED CANNOT ACHIEVE THE PASSING STANDARD, EVEN IF HE PICKS OUT MANY OF THEM AND MAKES APPROPRIATE RECOMMENDATIONS. THE PRESENCE OF EACH PART OF THE RESPONSE STRUCTURE IS INDISPENSABLE.
- We know that "several" deficiencies" must be analyzed at the "Competent" level. Since six to eight subjects are more important than the others that need to be dealt with in approximately 25 minutes, I believe that analyzing five to six deficiencies would be reasonable. Additionally, one should certainly diversify the response by analyzing the goals of several of the six departments concerned. It would not be sufficient to limit the discussion mainly to what is going on in the Sales Department. At the "Highly competent" level, one needs to analyze "several" deficiencies, which I interpret as meaning eight or nine, to provide a complete response.

Primary Indicator #7 *(VIII-4.1, VIII-4.2)*

The candidate analyzes the financial budget provided for 2011 and concludes on whether the results are likely to be achieved.

The candidate demonstrates competence in Management Decision-Making.

We have been asked by John McReynolds to perform "an evaluation of the 2011 budgeted financial information" and to comment on "the likelihood of the result being achieved." a

The analysis that follows takes the 2011 budget as presented by Dan Wilson on slide 7 in his presentation to the EC (Column 1), makes reasonable adjustments to the financial statement line items (Column 2), and comes up with a revised or adjusted budget (Column 3). Note that some assumptions have been made, and further information should be obtained and analyzed before this budget is finalized. As well, the budget needs to be "married" with the other components of the strategic plan to ensure they are consistent.

Strategic plan goals ⟶ actions to be taken ⟶ Budget

All items are in thousands of dollars. b

Item Description	SableTel 2011 Budget (unadjusted)	SableTel 2011 Budget adjustments	SableTel 2011 Budget (adjusted)
Revenue **(Note 1)**	$ 75,400	$ (9,350)	$ 66,050
Cost of sales **(Note 2)**	33,930	(2,226)	31,704
Gross profit **(Note 2)**	41,470	(7,124)	34,346
SM&A and interest **(Note 3)**	37,250	(750)	36,500
Profit (loss)	$ 4,220	$ (6,374)	$ (2,154)
Depreciation (given)	$ 7,500		$ 7,500
Capital expenditures (given)	(32,000)		(32,000)
Cash flow c	$ (20,280)	$ (6,374)	$ (26,654)
Gross margin	55%	N/A	52% = industry

B62

a A clear title would be enough to introduce the subject. However, writing out the requirements in more detail may help certain candidates to better understand and specify what they need to do.

b This calculation may be presented in an exhibit. Personally I would present it after the qualitative analysis. I would draft the qualitative and quantitative parts of this issue in one go. By this I mean that, as the discussion moves forward, I would make the necessary adjustments to my calculation.
The structure of this calculation is similar to that presented in Exhibit 7 of the case (p. 21) with a view to providing the Committee with comparable adjusted financial information.
IT IS NOT NECESSARY TO REPRODUCE THE "NON-ADJUSTED" FIGURES. THE ADJUSTMENTS, TOGETHER WITH THE CALCULATION OF THE "ADJUSTED" FIGURES (2ND AND 3RD COLUMNS) ARE THE NEW AND RELEVANT ELEMENTS.

c The calculation of the cash flow is of limited usefulness, since the components (depreciation and capital expenditures) have not changed. Calculation of the difference in the profit (loss) ($6,374) speaks for itself. Consequently one can forget about this part, since the time allocated for resolving the issue is limited.

Given the requirement, it would be normal to determine that the financial impact is the key aspect of the discussion of this issue.

Assumptions and Support for Adjustments

IMP

Note 1 — Revenue

PERSONALLY, SINCE THEY ARE AVAILABLE, I WOULD ONLY DISCUSS THE ADJUSTED FIGURES.

Several case facts are brought up with a view to casting doubt on the budgeted revenue.

The forecast shows projected revenue increasing by 15.9% in 2011 (this is before we adjust the revenue for the government grant in 2010). In 2010, sales at SableTel decreased by 0.2% before adjustments p. 47 and by 4.4% after adjusting for the Industry Canada grant. As well, the average revenue increase within the industry is forecasted to be 1.5% for 2011. Therefore, it seems unlikely that SableTel will p. 11 increase sales by 15.9% over the next year. As well, SableTel has lost one of its long time sales staff p. 6 (Mr. Oldmun), which may result in customer losses. Further indications that sales may be lower in 2011 are that SableTel has lost two big customers in 2010 and the fact that its mobile network is currently disabled and likely not earning any revenues.

conclusion + impact

However, there are some factors that may mitigate decreased sales, including the implementation of the more flexible pricing policy that will likely increase the sales group's success. Also, the fact that many new sales people have been hired and may now be trained needs to be considered.

conclusion

After considering all of the above, I have projected that SableTel will increase sales by 1.5% over the next year, consistent with the forecast in the industry. a This requires a decrease in the sales projected of $9,350,000.

This conservative conclusion is sufficient in the present context of uncertainty with regard to the implementation of the strategic plan goals.

We will have to R monitor sales effectiveness closely over the next several months in order to determine whether these projections need to be revised further, since the increase of 1.5% may not materialize under the current strategy.

VERY IMP to interlink the facts.

(Most candidates recognized that the revenue growth forecasted by SableTel was overly aggressive given other case facts, and recommended a lower percentage. Few candidates discussed the other factors affecting the revenue projection, such as the one-time grant, the loss of customers, and the potential loss in revenue as a result of the damaged towers, failing to integrate their analyses.) b

B63

IMP

Note 2 — Cost of Sales and Gross Margin

It is difficult to predict what the gross margin and, as a result, the cost of sales will be over the next p. 11 year. On the one hand, competition is increasing and the industry gross margin has been decreasing over the past two years. On the other hand, SableTel is developing new technology that may significantly increase its margin. However, the Wireless Technology project will not be ready until 2012 and therefore will not affect the margin in fiscal 2011.

no impact

The Wireless Technology Project is one of the rare positive facts respecting the likelihood of the result being achieved.

It is generally recognized that the telecommunications industry is a competitive one. This case provides a lot of information with respect to this industry and one of the requirements is to evaluate SableTel relative to it competitors.

---

a The adopted assumption of a 1.5% increase, along with those that will come after, is realistic and reasonable under the circumstances. It is easy to work with and is based on case facts. In fact the assumption presented is the result of a necessary choice made from the following possibilities: a 15.9% increase, a 1.5% increase following that of the industry, the status quo, i.e. 0% (which is rarely a solution) or a drop in revenue of 0.2% or of 4.4%. It will be noted that the assumption adopted is simple, justified, and constitutes a compromise between the various possibilities.

b The case includes several facts that make one seriously question SableTel's ability to achieve the budgeted revenue.
Since the requirement to evaluate the likelihood of the results being achieved is an explicit one, candidates may have collected these facts throughout their reading of the case, jotting them down on a work sheet or a checklist, as in the example on p. 23.

obj 60% (p. 20) budget 55% current 45.8% (p. 46) industry 52.2% (p. 11)

Do not take unusual events into account: grant and obsolescence provision.

conclusion

I have estimated that the gross margin will be 52% in 2011. This margin is close to the industry average for 2010 and also approximates SableTel's gross margin in 2010 once the effect of the government grant is removed from the gross margin calculation. Note that SableTel's gross margin, after all accounting adjustments, would actually be less than 46%, but this includes a one-time charge for inventory obsolescence which we do not expect to repeat in the future.

The "unadjusted" gross profit of 53.1% would be a good conclusion as well, since it was earned in 2010.

It is also not clear what impact the "non-standard" pricing policy will have on SableTel. This has not been factored into my analysis, but it could have a substantial negative impact on margin for 2011. However, it is expected that any lost margin would be made up through increased sales, so the net effect may be minimal.

(Roughly half of the candidates commented on the gross margin projected by SableTel and supported why it needed to be adjusted).

IMP

Note 3 — Expenses

FS p. 8

SM&A and interest expenses in 2010 totalled $33,179,355 before any adjustments. This amount was artificially low due to the capitalization of Wireless Technology Project expenditures. For 2010, a more normalized expense total would have been approximately $42 million ($33 million plus the 2009 and 2010 research and development expenditures that were incorrectly capitalized in 2010).

$30,211,705 + $5,702,390 = $35,914,095 (adjusted SM&A)

Do not take unusual events into account: grant and impairment of Mobile network.

R&D
1- capitalization
2- expenses

One big question that remains is whether the Wireless Technology Project will meet the criteria for capitalization in 2011. Assuming that it does, the expenses for 2011 should be about $36.5 million: $42 million in 2010 less $9 million in R&D expenses (the expenses would be capitalized in 2011), plus 2% for inflation, plus additional staff (estimated at 31 new staff at about $60,000 per staff member), plus the new bonus plan estimated at $1 million. Therefore, we have decreased the budgeted expenses to $36.5 million for the year ended August 31, 2010, based on this analysis.

B64

15 Sales staff (up to $85,000 each) + 16 Customer Service staff (p. 19)

$60,000 per employee is an arbitrary, but realistic, assumption.

If the Wireless Technology Project expenditures are not capitalized, then the expenses would likely be closer to $60 million. Note that whether these expenses are capitalized or expensed will not have any effect on the cash flow for SableTel and on the amount of financing that SableTel requires. [a]

profit/cash flow

Finally, there is no mention that SableTel has included estimates for the following items in the SM&A total included in the budget projection: cost to repair the damaged towers; cost related to the new bonus plan; the revised CRTC fee; cost to implement the planned cross-selling program; etc. [b]

Since the case provides no fact concerning interest, I would discuss only the SM&A expenses.

(Most candidates commented on at least one element of the expenses, such as the need to include the revised CRTC fee or the impact of the treatment of R&D expenses. However, there were many other expense items that candidates should have adjusted for that often went unnoticed.)

Go back to all the places where "↑ costs" was written in while reading the case.

The additional Fees of $521,401 payable to the CRTC will be recorded in Cost of Sales.

---

a THIS COMMENT IS IMPORTANT BECAUSE THE BUDGET IS USUALLY PREPARED USING THE SAME STANDARDS AS THOSE FOR THE FINANCIAL STATEMENTS. However, one knows that the choice of an accounting policy never—or rarely—affects the cash flow. In the present situation, given the importance of the amount involved, I would make a separate presentation of the budgeted costs for the Wireless Technology Project.

b Once more, it is very possible that the candidates will have collected these facts throughout their reading of the case (p. 23). However, it would not be appropriate to "attempt" to calculate these expenses, since there are no facts that allow us to do this adequately! The consequent assumption would be both arbitrary and of medium usefulness.

few case facts → +/- IMP

Other Amounts

There is no budgeted "Cash flow statement."

No other amounts have been considered in the above budget from a cash flow perspective. For example, SableTel had a large amount of accounts receivable on its books at August 31, 2010. If it can turn these accounts receivable into cash in 2011 and reduce its accounts receivable balance to more acceptable levels, then the amount of financing required from StarNova may be reduced. Other working capital changes have also not been figured into the cash flow analysis and could influence the amount of funding required.

Of course, we can see that the balance of accounts receivable is high, but the case contains no other fact concerning this subject. That makes an in-depth discussion

OVERALL COMMENT on the adjusted budget

Summary of Adjusted Budget and Capital Requirements

N.B.: projections ≠ forecasts

The revised cash flow projections show that there will be a need for additional capital above the amount budgeted. The amount of funding required for SableTel for its 2011 fiscal year is estimated to be almost $27 million. The projections should be extended beyond 2011 to ensure that 2012 and future years will provide adequate free cash flow to justify the expenditures on the Wireless Technology Project. This work would need to be performed no matter which source of additional funding is selected.

ST/LT

EXPLICIT REQUIREMENT → EXPLICIT CONCLUSION

Is the Budget Likely to be Achieved?

1- deficit in cash flows from operating activities
2- capital expenditures for the project

The adjusted 2011 budget (p. 62) indicates that the budget as set out by Dan is not achievable and SableTel will not be profitable in 2011. Significant changes will need to be made in order for SableTel to become profitable. SableTel should take immediate actions to either increase sales or decrease expenses or both in order to become profitable. It cannot afford to wait for the benefits associated with the Wireless Technology Project, which at this point in time are not proven.

how

2012

Personally, I would have backed up these comments with one or two practical examples.

Should StarNova continue to support SableTel and its Wireless Development Project, then it must find a financing source to fund SableTel. Potential sources of funding that should be explored are funding from StarNova's other profitable operations, external funding (such as an issue of additional shares by StarNova), or debt financing based on the projected cash flows that will prove out the investment. SableTel could also generate additional cash flow by improving the collection cycle for its accounts receivable.

B65

solutions to meet need for funding

ALWAYS DISTINGUISH THE TWO ASPECTS: INVESTMENT AND FINANCING.

(Most candidates restated the budget, or qualitatively concluded on whether the budget was likely to be achieved, or did both.)

adjust the budget
OR
provide a qualitative conclusion

Here is the example of an adequate alternative response:

Exhibit X
Objective: To adjust the budget on the basis of more realistic assumptions
(in thousands of dollars)

Adjusted 2010 Revenue (p. 39)	$ 62,322	
+ Industry expectation 1.5% (Note 1)	935	$ 63,257
Gross Profit 52.2 % (Note 2)		$ 33,020
Unadjusted SM&A (p. 8) (Note 3)	$ 33,711	
+ Executive plan (p. 18)	1,000	
+ Additional employees (31 x $60)	1,860	$ 36,571

N.B.: Headings and references can be made even shorter.

For Primary Indicator #7 (Management Decision-Making), the candidate must be ranked in one of the following five categories:	Percent Awarded
Not addressed — The candidate does not address this primary indicator.	0.9%
Nominal competence — The candidate does not attain the standard of reaching competence.	15.8%
Reaching competence — The candidate attempts to analyze specific areas of the budgeted financial information that are not realistic.	33.8%
Competent — The candidate analyzes specific areas of the budgeted financial information that are not realistic and recognizes that the results are not likely to be achieved.	49.3%
Highly competent — The candidate analyzes specific areas of the budgeted financial information that are not realistic, recognizes that the results are not likely to be achieved, and makes adjustments to the 2011 budget.	0.2%

IT SEEMS TO ME DIFFICULT—EVEN IMPOSSIBLE—TO ACHIEVE THE "COMPETENT" LEVEL WITHOUT HAVING TAKEN INTO CONSIDERATION THE QUANTITATIVE IMPACT OF BUDGET ADJUSTMENTS.

a clear conclusion that this is "NOT LIKELY"

adjustments to budget – adjusted financial information p. 62

ALWAYS TAKING THE CASE FACTS INTO ACCOUNT.

(Candidates were asked to evaluate the 2011 budgeted financial information and the likelihood of the result being achieved. Candidates were expected to analyze the budget that had been prepared by Dan, contemplate whether the assumptions made by Dan were reasonable, and conclude whether the budget was achievable.)

For purposes of analysis, it is necessary to question the CEO's working assumptions.

B66

(Most candidates were able to indentify some of the flawed assumptions made by Dan in the preparation of his budget. The one most often cited by candidates was overly optimistic revenue growth. Most of the candidates who saw flaws in Dan's budget were able to use case facts to support the reasons why Dan's numbers were unreasonable. However, aspects of the budget that should have been questioned, such as the one-time grant and the impact of the damaged towers on both revenue and expenses, were often ignored by candidates. Overall, where most candidates fell short was that their analysis was too brief; some candidates just did not identify a sufficient number of the errors contained within the budget that Dan had prepared.) a

differentiate operating activities from non-recurring events

This is the last requirement in Exhibit 1 of the case. From experience, I know that candidates often lack the time to deal with the final subjects. THIS MAY EXPLAIN WHY APPROXIMATELY 50% OF THEM DO NOT PROVIDE A SUFFICIENTLY COMPLETE ANALYSIS TO REACH THE PASSING STANDARD.

---

a Comments:

- In order to master this competency, it is essential to have determined the likelihood of the result being achieved, since this is a specific requirement of the case. Also, given the nature and scope of the facts, the only valid response would be to conclude that the results are "not likely" to be achieved. In this particular situation, a different conclusion or tempered opinion would not be acceptable.
- Adjusted budget financial information is not required at the "Competent" level. However, one should not presume that the qualitative analysis takes precedence over the rest. It is essential to offer realistic assumptions. It may not be necessary to present everything in a fully organized table, but nevertheless it is important to discuss what adjustments are required and to quantify them, where possible. What, for example, will be the impact of hiring 31 additional employees? Indeed, I would say that a candidate who takes the time to quantify budget adjustments has chosen a speedier and therefore more efficient way of showing what impact more realistic assumptions can have.
- At the "Competent" level, I believe it is absolutely necessary to discuss Revenue, Cost of sales or gross margin, and one of the major Expenses. I believe coverage of the essential points, especially in relation to revenue, to be indispensable.

This competency requires that the candidate demonstrate his professional ability.

Primary Indicator #8	*(II-2, II-4, III-1.1 à 1.3, III-2.1, III-2.3 à 2.6 III-3.1 à 3.3, III-4.1 à 4.3, III-5.1)*
The candidate integrates information from various sources and explains why SableTel is not likely to be successful in the future without significant changes.	
The candidate demonstrates competence in Pervasive Qualities and Skills.	

It is necessary to see the interrelationships between the various events.

Integration

adjusted FS → recalculation of the Fee → accrued liability into FS

LINK FS + Audit

Many of the issues affecting SableTel are related and should not be considered in isolation. The following are some of the areas where one analysis may affect another analysis: [a]

SEE THE "CAUSE-TO-EFFECT" LINKS

- The CRTC Fee analysis (and the assurance concepts from this analysis) should be integrated into the adjusted financial statements. It is clear that SableTel has not calculated its 2009 or 2010 CRTC Fees correctly, and these must be corrected. Once these revised Fees have been audited, the revised amounts should be incorporated into SableTel's adjusted financial statements for 2010. In addition, the increase in the CRTC Fee should be included in the budget.
- The adjusted financial statements should be used when analyzing the financial condition and financial results of SableTel for 2010. The ratio analysis, and the comparisons with the industry ratios and with SableTel's 2009 financial statements, would be more meaningful using the adjusted financial statements. Again, the differences in the ratios between SableTel and the industry may also be explained, in part, by the adjustments made to the financial statements.
- The MD&A discussion (executive reporting document discussion) should use information from various parts of our response. The executive reporting document would be improved by using the adjusted financial statements since they provide the most relevant information for investors. As well, the executive reporting document could report significant items from the assessment of SableTel's financial condition and financial results for 2010 or from SableTel's variance analysis. It could reference various industry statistics to provide a useful comparison to investors. The document could also be improved by including additional information about SableTel's 2011 (and future) strategic plan and by providing future budgeting information.
- When reviewing and commenting on the strategic plan for 2011, different information could be used to support the analysis. For example, integrating the strategic plan with the 2011 budget analysis would be very helpful, as would using the adjusted 2010 financial statements when analyzing the specific information contained in the strategic plan. investor's point of view
- The adjusted 2010 financial statements could be used as the starting point for the 2011 forecasts since they provide the most relevant information on the financial results and condition of SableTel for 2010. The 2010 results could then be adjusted for items such as increased staffing levels or decreased margins, for example.

adjusted FS → variance analysis + ratio analysis → comments on MD&A

adjusted FS → comments on strategic plan → financial information in budget

LINK strat plan + budget

B67

As well, a number of other "high level" issues could be discussed in relation to SableTel's current operations and its future prospects. Adjusting the financial statements or the budget is a good way of demonstrating one's capacity for integrating information.

(The Board was pleased to see that most candidates provided an integrated response. Many used their adjusted financial statements when calculating ratios, considered the need to revise the CRTC Fee when preparing their adjusted financial statements or their budgets, and referenced their revised numbers when discussing the reporting document. Integration was one of the key skills the Board was evaluating with this particular comprehensive case.)

Integration is a key competency.

Interrelationships between the problems or issues

---

a THERE ARE FREQUENTLY INTERRELATIONSHIPS BETWEEN THE PROBLEMS OR ISSUES OF A CASE, AND THE CANDIDATE MUST CONSTANTLY LOOK FOR THESE LINKS AS HE WRITES HIS RESPONSE, MORE SPECIFICALLY WHEN HE COMES TO DRAFTING A CONCLUSION OR A RECOMMENDATION.

One needs to know how to pick out and build up those facts which point in the same direction.

implicit issue

Competence of SableTel Management a

There are many indications that senior management at SableTel does not have the skills required to return the company to profitable operations or put in place the tools to ensure it meets its potential in the future. There is also evidence that management at SableTel, particularly Dan Wilson, does not understand the details of the business and either intentionally or unintentionally is providing misleading information. This is evident throughout his presentation to the EC: he did not have the answers, or was making up answers as he went, to relatively simple questions. It is possible that Dan does not have the necessary skills for this position. conclusion

Evidence to support our assertion questioning the competence of management includes:

This is a "list of" facts that have one thing in common: they indicate a lack of competence as regards the reporting documents provided or the decisions taken by the management team.

- The purchase of $2.5 million of routers and modems in September 2009 when the annual cost of sales for routers and modems is less than $700,000. These products also have a short life, making this decision even more questionable. note 3 p. 10 p. 32 Inventory ⇆ Cost of sales
- A misunderstanding of the concept of "risk" from an investor perspective, which is evident in the executive reporting document. p. 51
- The lack of answers to relatively simple questions posed by the EC. ex.: p. 15
- Significant errors in the financial statements for 2010. p. 39
- The losses in 2009 and in 2010 and deteriorating results.
- Poor analysis of the variances for 2010. p. 42
- The poor preparation and support for the 2011 budget p. 65 and the 2011 strategic plan. p. 27
- CRTC calculations that are inaccurate, and the apparent lack of understanding of the seriousness of the letter received from the CRTC.
- Evidence that the control environment is not adequate (for example, the marketing and finance databases do not agree). p. 26
- The acquisition of Spacolli Enterprises Inc. in 2008, which did not appear to be carefully considered. p. 22

CORRECTLY ASSESSING THE RISK IS A KEY ASPECT OF BUSINESS CONTINUITY.

B68

OVERALL CONCLUSION

Overall, it would appear that the strategic plan presented by Dan is not well thought out, contains inconsistencies between departments, and is flawed in many ways. StarNova R may wish to consider hiring an external consultant who is familiar with the telecommunications industry to review and recommend changes to the strategic plan. WHY

Focus on finding solutions for the deficiencies and problems identified.

(Most candidates raised valid concerns with regards to Dan's performance and supported their concerns with several examples of his incompetence. While these discussions were generally very well done, some candidates went on to accuse Dan of fraud. Candidates should be cautioned that fraud is a serious accusation. Fraud implies that Dan's errors were intentional and deceitful in nature, whereas the case facts lead us more to believe that Dan may just not have the knowledge and judgment required to effectively run SableTel.) b

This type of comment needs to be well argued.

PRUDENCE IS NECESSARY WHEN AN ACCUSATION OF FRAUD IS INVOLVED!

Since many facts justify questioning the competence of SableTel management and of the CEO himself, one certainly expects the conclusion to be fully substantiated.

---

a ONE NEEDS TO SHOW CONSIDERATION WHEN OFFERING AN OPINION CONCERNING INDIVIDUALS. I SUGGEST REFERRING TO THE WORK DONE OR TO THE REPORT PRESENTED RATHER THAN TO THE PEOPLE THEMSELVES. ONE NEEDS TO SAY WHAT IS NECESSARY, BUT IN A PROFESSIONAL MANNER.

b We notice that most of the points listed correspond to earlier conclusions that followed the analysis of the various problems or issues.

Overall Conclusion In a long case, we often find an "overall" synthesis-type conclusion, generally on the last page of the response.

The 15% goal is very important for StarNova.

There are many indications that SableTel is not performing up to expectations and without significant changes will not meet the 15% return target in the future. a These indications include:

Is there any hope for SableTel?

This is a "list of" facts that have one thing in common: they demonstrate that SableTel's performance does not meet expectations, to wit the 15% return target.

- A CRTC Fee calculation that was not correct, and indifference from the SableTel management regarding this problem which could potentially have devastating implications for the company. PI#1 p. 25-31
- Financial statements that contain significant errors where adjustments are needed. All of these adjustments negatively affect SableTel, as well lending some support to the theory that these errors may have been intentional. PI#2 p. 32-41
- A financial condition that has deteriorated badly over the last year and is well below industry averages. This includes a high amount of leverage, indicating a financially risky operation. PI#4 p. 46-49
- A variance analysis (on the 2010 financial results) that was not informative and did not properly disclose the real variances inherent in the 2010 financial results. PI#3 p. 42-45
- A strategic plan that is inconsistent, not well thought out, and short-sighted. PI#6 p. 55-61
- An executive reporting document that is, at a minimum, not informative, and is potentially misleading. PI#5 p. 50-54
- A budget for 2011 that is not achievable given the current plans and the current financial situation of SableTel. PI#7 p. 62-66
- An investment of over $9 million dollars in the Wireless Technology Project when the feasibility of the technology has yet to be proven.

PI = Primary Indicator

We would like to draw to the attention of the executive committee the serious nature and the urgency of our concerns, and we R recommend immediate changes and further analysis for SableTel.

One should not forget that the operating activities of SableTel result in a loss.

(The Board was disappointed to see that more candidates did not comment on the overall performance of SableTel and the urgency of its current situation. However, while most candidates did not address these issues, strong candidates clearly highlighted their concerns with the overall performance of SableTel and questioned whether SableTel would be able to meet StarNova's 15% return target.)

B69

The present page contains a large number of comments that underline THE CRITICAL ASPECT OF SABLETEL'S CURRENT SITUATION.

We notice that the structure of the overall conclusion brings out the key element of each of the problems or issues covered by the seven previous primary indicators.

---

a The 15% return on investment goal was established as of the first paragraph in the case. It needs to be identified as an important specific of the context and, above all, should be referred to regularly when solving the problems or issues. Basically, StarNova is a public company whose objective is to make a profit and, consequently, its progress is a matter of interest to many investors, both current and prospective.
At the moment, SableTel's operating activities are running at a loss, and the analysis of the current situation does not suggest any improvement in the future. It has therefore become relevant to question the financial viability of this entity. What should StarNova do about SableTel? Should there be a loan of $21M? Should its operating activities be checked up on a more regular basis?
Moreover, once the analysis of the primary indicators has been completed, it becomes more than obvious that the case parameters need to be established as of the moment of reading the case (p. 23). These parameters constitute the basis for the resolving of the various problems or issues. Apart from the fact that StarNova is looking to a 15% return on investment, the industry in which SableTel operates is strictly regulated by the CTRC and the financial statements are prepared using IFRS.

ELEMENT 1: Integration of the problems or issues
ELEMENT 2: - Competence of SableTel management
- Ability to meet StarNova's expectations (15%; project)

This type of competence requires one to "take a step back" when dealing with the analyzed problems or issues as a whole.

It is not a simple matter to assess this type of professional competence, more especially when several elements are required.

For Primary Indicator #8 (Pervasive Qualities and Skills) the candidate must be ranked in one of the following five categories:	Percent Awarded
Not addressed — The candidate does not address this primary indicator.	0.0%
Nominal competence — The candidate does not attain the standard of reaching competence.	8.2%
Reaching competence — The candidate integrates some of the issues in the response or concludes that SableTel is not likely to be successful in the future without significant changes.	38.9%
Competent — The candidate integrates several of the issues in the response to conclude that SableTel is not likely to be successful in the future without significant changes.	52.4%
Highly competent — The candidate integrates several of the issues in the response to conclude that SableTel is not likely to be successful in the future without significant changes and provides a plan to address the concerns identified.	0.5%

precise meaning of the conclusion ←

It is important to say "how" it can be achieved.

It is not necessary to provide a section entitled "Integration" in the response, as on p. 67 of the suggested solution. Integration should rather be taking place throughout the analysis.

(There were two elements included in this indicator. 1- ***The first element required candidates to integrate issues throughout their response. Integration could be demonstrated in many ways, such as by using adjusted financial statements when calculating SableTel's ratios or including elements of the strategic plan in the revised budget.*** 2- ***The second element required candidates to take a step back and question issues underlying the entire simulation, such as Dan Wilson's competence and SableTel's ability to meet StarNova's expectations. Candidates were not directed to this pervasive indicator. However, the number of opportunities for integration and the variety of case facts should have led candidates to discuss both SableTel's overall performance and senior management's ability to effectively run the company.)*** Objective: To take the whole response into account.

When their sequencing in the response is adequate, the integration of the various problems or issues is easier.

(In general, candidates performed well on this indicator. The majority of candidates questioned Dan's competence and supported their concerns with specific examples from the case, such as Dan's lack of knowledge and poor judgment. Candidates also did a good job of integrating their responses, most commonly through the use of restated numbers in their ratio analysis and the inclusion of the CRTC Fee in their adjusted financial statements.) a

The use of adjusted figures in the analysis clearly demonstrates a capacity for integration

It is probably easier for a candidate to meet the requirements of Element 1 than those of Element 2.

---

a Comments:

- ELEMENT 1: To achieve the passing standard. THE CANDIDATE MUST INDICATE A NUMBER OF LINKS BETWEEN VARIOUS PROBLEMS OR ISSUES. The present case offers several opportunities to do so. If the marker picks up A CERTAIN NUMBER OF THESE LINKS, he will consider that the candidate has demonstrated sufficient competence.
- ELEMENT 2: In order to achieve the passing standard, I believe it is essential to question SableTel management competence OR its ability to meet StarNova's expectations. Besides, these two aspects being interrelated, some candidates will probably have dealt with both at the same time. AS A PROFESSIONAL ACCOUNTANT, IT IS IMPORTANT TO BRING TOGETHER THE VARIOUS FACTS THAT POINT IN THE SAME DIRECTION SO AS TO COME TO A PERFECTLY JUSTIFIED OVERALL CONCLUSION.
- At the "Competent" level, the candidate must offer a reasonable discussion with respect to each of the two elements involved. However, I would suppose that a really good discussion of one element—more especially of the second one—could compensate for a lack in the other.

SECONDARY INDICATORS OF COMPETENCE

Secondary Indicator #1	*(IX-1.1, IX-1.2, IX-2.3)*
The candidate discusses the relevant corporate income tax issues related to SableTel.	
The candidate demonstrates competence in Taxation.	

note 5 **Scientific Research and Experimental Development (SR&ED) Tax Credits and Expenditures** [a]

The 2010 financial statements include capitalized research and development expenditures in the amount of $9,160,250 ($5,702,390 relating to 2010 and $3,457,860 incurred in 2009) related to the Wireless Technology Project. These expenditures may qualify for SR&ED tax credits as defined in the *Income Tax Act*. It is not clear if SableTel has filed an SR&ED claim for this project. As SableTel is a wholly-owned subsidiary of a Canadian public company and is therefore not a Canadian Controlled Private Corporation (CCPC), SR&ED tax credits would offset income taxes payable and would not be refundable. SR&ED tax credits are only refundable to CCPCs.

The case contains no explicit information on this subject.

For SableTel, the investment tax credits will offset federal income taxes payable in the current, three previous, or next 20 years. As discussed below, there appears to be a loss-carryback available to SableTel for 2009. If that loss is carried back, it may wipe out all previous taxes. Then, the investment tax credits for SR&ED will be carried forward to offset 2010 and future taxes payable. Since it is unlikely that there will be any taxable income in 2010, the amounts would be carried forward. As noted above, the amounts will expire, therefore SableTel may want to consider reducing some of its discretionary expenses for tax purposes (CCA) in order to manage taxes payable to use up these amounts. [b]

tax planning

LINK with the fact that SableTel has incurred a loss. (p. 39)

B71

It should also be noted that the SR&ED expenditures go into a separate expenditure pool and can be used by SableTel in any taxation year. The expenditures in this pool never expire. This allows SableTel flexibility in using these expenditures to "manage" taxable income so that it can use other losses and tax credits that will expire.

why

impact

As well, the grant received from Industry Canada may reduce the eligible SR&ED expenditures if it directly relates to these expenditures.

The case contains no information about this. Nevertheless, it is a good integration idea; to be remembered for the next case.

---

a It should be noted that the analysis of SableTel tax issues is not on the Committee's list of requirements presented in Exhibit I. This may explain why such analysis is subject to a secondary indicator. One should also remember that the role to be played in this case is that of an accountant working within the Finance Department. In this context, one can point out that preparing income tax returns is not usually one of his main tasks.
Personally, given the information provided regarding the notice of reassessment, I would have taken a few minutes (max. 5) to discuss the matter.

b In the United States, businesses may qualify for the following business tax credits: Investment Credit and Increasing Research Activities Credit.

IMP

Spacolli Enterprises Inc. (Spacolli) Tax Losses a

SableTel received a notice of reassessment from the Canada Revenue Agency (CRA) denying the use of $500,000 in non-capital losses related to its acquisition of Spacolli in 2008. p. 22

The acquisition of Spacolli in 2008 appears to have been done so that SableTel could use the substantial tax losses that Spacolli had to offset future taxable income. However, the *Income Tax Act* contains rules governing the use of losses of acquired corporations. When there has been an acquisition of control of a corporation, like there was in the case of Spacolli, the acquiring corporation can only use the losses of the acquired corporation to offset income earned in the same or similar business, and the business of the acquired company that incurred the losses must be carried on after the acquisition of control with a view to a profit. It is likely that the CRA has denied the use of the Spacolli losses because:

1) the business carried on by SableTel may not be a same or similar business, and
2) the business of Spacolli was discontinued prior to the acquisition.

The two conditions that must be satisfied are discussed in relation to the case facts.

Spacolli was in the business of manufacturing and distributing cell phones. SableTel is in the business of providing telecommunications (phone and internet) services for its customers. On the surface, these seem like very different businesses, therefore it is questionable if SableTel could use the losses of Spacolli to offset income in SableTel. Additional details will need to be provided to determine if this is actually the case.

conclusion

check: similar business

Note that the letter from the CRA is dated July 15, 2010. SableTel has 90 days from the date of the reassessment to submit a Notice of Objection should it wish to challenge the reassessment. There may also be penalties and interest associated with the reassessment. These amounts should also be accrued (if not done so already). Penalties and interest are not tax deductible and will therefore be added back to income (loss) on SableTel's 2010 income tax return.

impact on FS

B72

Deemed Year-End b

clear answer OR short subject → go directly to the justified conclusion

At a minimum, there was an acquisition of control of Spacolli on January 1, 2008 (the amalgamation date). Both the acquisition of control and the amalgamation cause a deemed year-end for tax purposes, therefore tax returns should have been prepared with a December 31, 2007, year-end for both Spacolli and SableTel. We should ensure this was the case. This will necessitate a separate set of financial records as at that date as well.

The deemed year-end for SableTel caused by the amalgamation will count as one year in the carryforward of any losses or investment tax credits.

This page contains the main elements that derive directly from a consideration of the case facts relative to the notice of reassessment received by SableTel. They are key aspects of the Tax issue.

We notice that the suggested solution regularly mentions the impact of the tax issues on the financial statements.

---

a As a general rule, in the United States, the net carryover period of the net operating losses is back 2 years and forward 20 years.
However, in the context of an amalgamation of a parent company and a subsidiary, certain limits will apply. Although losses may be used to offset the future taxable earnings of the amalgamated entity, no loss carry-back is authorized.

b The United States have similar tax rules.

The present discussion could be integrated with that of tax credits on SR&ED, as is partially done in the suggested solution. In fact, one needs to analyze the two subjects simultaneously in order to minimize SableTel's tax liability.

Loss-Carryback

It appears from the data provided that SableTel had a non-capital loss in 2009 and may have another non-capital loss in 2010. These losses may be available to be carried back to the immediately preceding three prior years to offset taxes paid if those prior years were profitable. This should be investigated, with any expected refund reflected in SableTel's 2009 or 2010 financial statements. a

impact on FS

For Secondary Indicator #1 (Taxation) the candidate must be ranked in one of the following three categories:
Not addressed — The candidate does not address this secondary indicator.
Nominal competence — The candidate does not attain the standard of competent.
Competent — The candidate addresses some of the corporate income tax issues in sufficient depth.

Obviously, discussing only one tax question is not enough to achieve the "Competent" level.

(Some of the transactions that SableTel had entered into in the current year had tax impacts, the most significant being the potential scientific research and experimental development (SR&ED) credit related to the WTP expenditures, and the non-capital losses related to SableTel's acquisition of Spacolli. To demonstrate competence on this secondary indicator, candidates were expected to discuss some of these corporate tax issues.)

(Many candidates identified at least one of the tax issues facing SableTel, but only some of these candidates went on to discuss the appropriate tax treatment for the issues identified.) b

IT IS IMPORTANT NOT ONLY TO IDENTIFY, BUT ALSO TO DISCUSS.

2 IMP subjects:
→ SR&ED credits
→ non-capital losses

---

a We can see that, when resolving the Tax issue, there was a constant integration of tax rules with the case facts. We may also notice that the analysis of each subject is direct and that the conclusions are precise.
No need for a long discussion since the tax rules are clear.

b Comments:

- I believe it is essential that one integrate tax rules with case facts at the "Competent" level. A discussion that is of "sufficient depth" will most certainly deal with the two or three main elements specific to SableTel.
- In my opinion, "some of the tax issues" need to be dealt with in order to achieve the passing standard and should at least include the analysis of the new tax reassessment. This question is mentioned explicitly in the case and, given the unadjusted profit of $1,178,000 (p. 8), the $555,000 tax losses are not negligible. Although this is a basic notion, the matter of the deemed year-end needs to be taken into consideration.
- I also believe that one should—at least briefly—bring up the question of SR&ED tax credits. A candidate who decides to discuss the Tax issue in the present case needs to look into what may be distinctive and, given the importance of the Wireless Technology Project, it is quite natural that the SR&ED question should come up. We already know that such tax savings often add up to a very high amount to be taken into consideration when looking at the quantitative analysis of an investment project.

Structure: - Quantitative analysis - Qualitative analysis - Recommendation

Secondary Indicator #2 *(VII-3, VII-4.1, VII-5)*

objective of the analysis

The candidate analyzes the Wireless Technology Project to determine if SableTel/StarNova should continue to fund this project.

The candidate demonstrates competence in Finance.

SableTel is requesting funding of $21 million

Dan's presentation to the EC included some details on the Wireless Technology Project, which it appears is forming a significant portion of SableTel's strategic plan for the future. a p. 5

THE PAYBACK PERIOD IS A USEFUL MEASURE WHEN DEALING WITH RAPIDLY ADVANCING TECHNOLOGIES.

From a financial perspective we know the following: b

- SableTel has spent a total of $9,160,250 in 2009 and 2010 on this project. note 5
- SableTel plans to spend an additional estimated $20 million in 2011 to fund the remainder of this project. p. 15
- Once the project is complete, margins are expected to improve by 5% for all products and services. note 5

For the purposes of this analysis (in other words, whether SableTel should continue to fund the project), the costs that have already been incurred in 2009 and 2010 are irrelevant as they are sunk costs. Therefore, the only relevant costs are the estimated $20 million to be incurred in 2011. why

The benefits will be an estimated increased margin of 5% on all products and services. Using estimated revenue of $65 million (revenues for both 2009 and 2010 were approximately $65 million and revenue in 2011 is expected to be approximately $66 million), the increased margin on an annual basis would be $3,250,000. Dividing the $20 million in costs by the $3,250,000 in annual benefits gives an estimated payback period of 6.15 years.

B74

The grant received is ever-present in the analysis of several subjects.

Note that this analysis does not take into account the time value of money. The analysis also does not factor in the grant received from Industry Canada. If this grant must be repaid if the technology is not completed, then this should also be factored into the financial assessment. Thanks to the grant, the next cost of the project could be reduced from $20 million to $17.25 million.

When there is an investment to evaluate, you should consider the risks involved.

Some additional qualitative factors should also be taken into consideration:

practical aspect

1. SableTel operates in an industry in which technology changes quickly. Therefore, the timeframe to recoup the costs associated with a project such as this needs to be relatively short. A payback period of 6.15 years may not be acceptable in this industry.
2. It is possible that SableTel has already committed to some significant expenditures associated with this project. If this is true, then these amounts would need to be factored into the analysis (in other words, the sunk costs may increase and the $20 million of relevant costs may decrease, leading to a shorter payback).
3. The $20 million in costs is an estimate only and may increase or decrease as the project proceeds. This adds additional risk to the project from a financial assessment perspective.

committed expenditures = sunk costs

$ impact

---

a It should be noted that the analysis of the Wireless Technology Project is not on the Committee's list of requirements presented in Exhibit I. This may explain why such analysis is subject to a secondary indicator. However, since the competence of the SableTel management team has been questioned, I consider it relevant to ask oneself what the risks and benefit of this project are. The fact that the "weight" of this indicator, as concerns the evaluation of the case, is deemed to be "secondary" does not invalidate the relevance of the present discussion. Moreover, the analysis can be presented briefly.

b This summary of the case facts is not necessary. The information can be directly integrated into the analysis that follows. However, some candidates prefer to bring all the information together in one place in order to provide an overall portrait of the situation.

The financial impact (costs, margins, revenue) of the risks identified is mentioned regularly.

4. As with all projects in the technology area, there are substantial technological risks that the project would not lead to the desired outcomes. The technology is unproven, and the project may not generate the expected 5% increase in margin for all products and services.
5. In recent years, SableTel, and the telecommunications industry in general, has experienced decreasing sales. Decreasing sales mean that the benefits of the project would continue to diminish over time.
6. Taxes have not been factored into the analysis because SableTel is currently not taxable and may not be taxable for many years. If taxes were included in the analysis, this would decrease the benefits and increase the payback period.

$ impact

uncertainties

difficult economic conditions p. 6

One final note is that SableTel is expecting an independent feasibility study to be completed on the project within the next 60 days. This may mitigate some of the qualitative risk factors noted above and provide better information for this analysis.

p. 18

IT IS IMPORTANT TO TAKE A POSITION, EVEN WITH ONLY PRELIMINARY INFORMATION.

Recommendation

The quantitative advantage of improving the margins by 5% is the only positive point that was made.

I recommend that SableTel and StarNova wait for the feasibility study, which is expected within the next 60 days. Once that study is received, SableTel and StarNova should weigh all the costs, benefits, and risks to determine whether they should proceed with the project. From the preliminary information available, I would not recommend proceeding with the project since the projected benefits and payback of over six years do not justify the significant risks involved.

For Secondary Indicator #2 (Finance) the candidate must be ranked in one of the following three categories:
Not addressed — The candidate does not address this secondary indicator. **Nominal competence** — The candidate does not attain the standard of competent. **Competent** — The candidate performs a qualitative and quantitative assessment of the Wireless Technology Project to determine if SableTel should continue to fund this project.

Candidates usually manage a good investment project analysis.

conclusion required

B75

significant project for SableTel and StarNova

(SableTel had already invested a significant amount of money into the development of the WTP and planned to invest another $20 million in the coming year. The project was supposed to result in a 5% improvement in margins. Candidates were expected to perform a simple cost/benefit analysis to determine whether the WTP was a good idea and to discuss some of the relevant qualitative factors that would need to be considered when evaluating this project.)

cost-benefit analysis QUANT + QUAL $

(Most candidates questioned the feasibility of the WTP from a strategic point of view; however, very few candidates considered whether the promise of higher margins justified the high costs of the project. Those candidates who did address this indicator were generally able to perform a quick cost/benefit analysis and appropriately conclude whether or not to go ahead with the project.) [a]

The availability of the figures needed for the analysis is in itself a hint that suggests the candidate make a short calculation.

Taking the analysis into account, the project can either be recommended or not.

[a] Comments:

- THE REQUIREMENTS AT THE "COMPETENT" LEVEL ARE RELATIVELY CLEAR. THERE MUST BE A QUANTITATIVE ANALYSIS OF THE COST-BENEFIT OF THE PROJECT AND A QUALITATIVE ANALYSIS OF THE MAIN RISKS.
- My opinion is that there should be a discussion of the impact of at least three of the risks involved. Simply mentioning these risks is not enough.
- I believe it is essential to end the analysis with a conclusion or a recommendation. Should SableTel/StarNova go on with this project?

Overall comments

The time allotted for this case is sufficient, but it should be properly divided between the various problems or issues.

(Overall, the Board was relatively pleased with the quality of the responses on the comprehensive simulation. This was a highly integrated simulation, and the Board was delighted to see candidates attempting to take an integrated approach in their responses. The Board hopes that this continues.)

Candidates feel less comfortable with subjects that rarely come up in their cases.

Primary indicators easy to identify

(As in prior years, candidates were provided with five hours to respond, while the comprehensive simulation was developed to be a four-hour exam. There was no evidence of significant time constraints, which confirms the Board's belief that five hours provided the candidates with sufficient time to carefully read the simulation, plan their responses, and address the primary indicators. Most candidates addressed each of the primary indicators, but they struggled when asked to perform a variance analysis (Primary Indicator #3) and to comment on the reporting document (Primary Indicator #5). Although these competencies may not be tested as frequently as others, they remain important for entry-level CAs. Candidates seemed to be well prepared to address accounting issues in an IFRS context as demonstrated by their performance on Primary Indicator #2.)

When one looks at the suggested solution as a whole, the following elements become evident:

- There are almost never positive or strong points to be brought out in an analysis or evaluation. One needs rather to focus on "what is going wrong" and look for solutions.
- As the drafting of the response proceeds, the number of links to be made between the various subjects increases, since the solution becomes more and more complete. This confirms the need to correctly sequence the problems or issues as of the very start, by setting up a response plan. The StarNova case offers a large number of interrelationships between the problems or issues and, as a personal exercise, the candidates should ensure that they follow them all up.
- In order for the candidate to achieve the "Highly competent" level, the evaluation guide may require that an analysis take a specific element into consideration, for example by indicating that "a comparison with the approved budget would provide additional meaningful information" (p. 45) or by mentioning that the candidate must "provide a plan to address the concerns identified" (p. 70). It seems to me essential that candidates take the time to look at what is required at the "Highly competent" level and that they retain any ideas that could be of interest for the next case.
- Additionally, the "Highly Competent" level may require a quantitative analysis, such as adjustments to the financial statements for most of the accounting errors (p. 41) or adjustments to the budget (p. 66). In such situations, one should also note that the impact of the proposed adjustments should be indicated at the "Competent" level.

  Apart from this, THE "HIGHLY COMPETENT" LEVEL OFTEN REQUIRES A COMPLETE ANALYSIS OF A PROBLEM OR ISSUE CONTAINING NO MAJOR ERROR OR OMISSION. The depths to which one is required to go demands more time than what is normally allocated in the response plan. In other words, a candidate who spends too much time on a subject in order to achieve the "Highly Competent" level is thereby in danger of compromising his success in other subjects, due to a lack of time. One needs to provide a reasonable analysis of the various problems or issues, but not necessarily a perfect one! It is better to achieve the "Competent" level three times than to be "Highly competent" once and "Reaching competence" twice.
- It is often difficult for a candidate to work out a reasonable balance between quantitative and qualitative analyses. When studying the present evaluation guide, it is important, on the one hand, to take the time to identify the minimum calculations required to achieve the passing standard and, on the other hand, TO ACCURATELY ASSESS THE TIME TO BE ALLOTTED TO THE QUALITATIVE AND QUANTITATIVE ASPECTS RESPECTIVELY.

Assessment of a student response a

Date: September 14, 2010 b YE: August 31, 2010

To: Executive Committee of StarNova (SN)
From: CA, StarNova Finance Department

Subject: Report

Excellent idea to draw up a response plan.

My guess is that you took 70 minutes to read the case. A bit short, if you ask me. You need to make sure you have really understood the information provided, and that you have picked out the links between the case facts before you start writing.

Work required:

1. Performance evaluation/competitors (60 min)
   - Revise FS
   - Calculate ratios
2. Analysis of variances between 2010 and 2009 (20 min)
   - p. 17
3. CRTC audit plan (30 min)
   - Preliminary error estimate
   - Risk analysis
   - Procedures
4. Comments on 2011 strategic plan + REC (45 min)
   - Exhibit 7
5. Comments on activities + REC (20 min)
   - Exhibit 2
   - Exhibit 7
6. Budget evaluation and likelihood results being achieved (20 min)
   - Exhibit 7
7. Other: (10 min)
   - Taxation: 2008 Reassessment
   - Dan's knowledge GOOD!
8. Conclusion: (5 min)
   - Whether or not to go ahead with funding ($21M profit level 15%?)

Personally, I prefer to present a list of the main subjects to be discussed under Subject, on the Presentation page.

It's not such a good idea to try and present the analysis of the strategic plan before the one on the current activities. It's generally preferable to deal with the past before the future.

The audit plan is a very important issue. It requires both a quantitative AND a qualitative analysis. The 30 minutes allotted will certainly not be enough.

B77

20 min left!

Important point: Funding or not of the $21M requested by SableTel.

Subjects 4, 5 and 6 need roughly the same in-depth analysis. Offhand, nothing justifies planning to spend more than 45 minutes commenting on the strategic plan.

SN needs:

- 15% return on investment
- Subsidiary expected to comply with MD&A.

a This is a genuine student response, in fact he was a Chartered Accountant candidate, in the last term of his degree in Accounting. He simulated the case "StarNova" on a computer within the allotted time of 5 hours. For presentation purposes, the marker's comments are written in the font used here. Sometimes those comments could be presented more concisely.

b The response plan is structured and concise. Time is divided up reasonably well between the main problems or issues. Taxation and investment in the project are sufficiently identified as subjects of lesser importance.
On the other hand, there is not much point in writing the references to the case exhibits under each problem or issue, especially since Exhibit 7 is a reference common to several of them.

Performance evaluation

Taking the time to really identify the problem is a good idea.

FS adjustments: [a]

You need to sequence your subjects better; the analysis of "R&D expenses" should come before that of the "Grant."

Grant

You are dealing directly with the financial statements presentation. You should start out by asking yourself whether you need to record this grant. The analysis of an accounting issue should be done step by step.

Problem:
A grant has been recorded as revenue, while in fact it's used for technological development.

IAS 20-12 Government grants shall be recognised in profit or loss on a systematic basis over the periods in which the entity recognises as expenses the related costs for which the grants are intended to compensate.

Bring out the link between the accounting standard and your analysis more clearly.

This isn't the case here BECAUSE the money is recorded as revenue. THEREFORE, it's recorded under the wrong heading. [b] clear and precise REC

24 Government grants related to assets, including non-monetary grants at fair value, shall be presented in the statement of financial position either by setting up the grant as deferred income or by deducting the grant in arriving at the carrying amount of the asset.

already said

For a complete response, see impact on net income.

Right now the whole grant is recorded for as revenue. The two policies suggested don't have any direct impact on profit, but only on the statement of financial position. With a deferred credit, we recognize a liability and assets are higher. There is no liability to be set against the assets.

YOU HAVE CORRECTLY DESCRIBED THE TWO WAYS OF MAKING THE PRESENTATION, BUT YOU HAVEN'T ANALYZED THEM! I WOULD LIKE YOU TO JUSTIFY YOUR CHOICE OF ONE OVER THE OTHER.

Conclusion:
We recommend that you use the policy which lowers the assets because it doesn't record a liability. OK

Impact: An amount of $2,750,000 is recorded as a reduction of the Wireless technology project intangible assets and the same amount has to be removed from the revenue.

Excellent idea to describe impact.

You treat R&D expenses as if they were to remain capitalized, which is not certain. That is why the R&D expenses should be discussed first.

No point in wasting time with "italics" and "bold-face" options, unless it really helps you remain focused!

Inventory

Correctly identified problem, but could be put in less words. A heading such as "Obsolescence Provision" would do.

Problem:
SN inventory becomes obsolete very fast. Taking into account the 2010 inventory increase, you might need to set up an obsolescence provision.

IAS 2-9 Inventories shall be measured at the lower of cost and net realisable value.

reasonable number of abbreviations

---

a When we look at the way the analysis of accounting issues is drafted, we come to realize that the student uses the following response structure: "Problem-Analysis-Conclusion-Impact." In the present situation this analytical structure is efficient.

b Students tend to present or sum up theoretical concepts—such as an accounting standard—in a first paragraph. Then, in the next one, they analyze what is going on in the case. Such an approach does not clearly indicate the integration of theory and case.
The student writes: "This isn't the case here...." But since the word "This" is not explained, the marker is required to make the link with the concept of "recognition on a systematic basis over the periods." He must then decide what weight he will give to the ideas expressed, and that makes his assessment task difficult.

Since SN inventory has a 12-month life, you may need to treat it as obsolescent. So, the cost being higher than the NRV, a provision must be set up.

Theory well applied to the specifics of the case.

a good use of case figures

As at August 31, 2010, inventory levels stand at $3.2M, compared with $883K in 2009, a difference of $2,336K. That's close to the amount of inventory purchased in September 2009. Since only $200K of the $2.5M inventory was used up in one year, there's a pretty good chance that the remainder is obsolete, because none of it was used in 2010.

This will not affect the evaluation of your response, but remember that inventory is "sold," not "used."

Conclusion:

We need an obsolescence provision, BECAUSE the inventory spent close to 12 months in the warehouses without any sales.

a reasonable assumption; well linked to the case facts

Impact: You should record $2.3M as an obsolescence provision, because this will bring you back to your 2009 inventory level (always supposing that the 2009 inventory level is OK for inventory turnover).

Your analysis of the inventory issue is excellent.
You could certainly write this section in a more succinct manner.

R&D

The case target year is 2010. The main discussion should therefore cover 2010 costs. The current year is usually the most important.

Problem:

This is the most important accounting issue! To discuss first!

Costs already expensed in 2009 were reversed and capitalized in 2010.

Costs already expensed cannot be reversed and capitalized later. If the costs were expensed in 2009, this was because they didn't meet the development criteria, so they had to be expensed. Since the criteria for capitalizing development expenses in 2010 have been met, you can't adjust expenses retrospectively in order to capitalize them.

For a complete analysis, you need to call on theoretical concepts: changes in accounting estimates or error? (IAS 8)

Conclusion:

B79

Don't capitalize 2009 expenses.

... and those for 2010? You take it for granted that the costs can be capitalized, but they can't! I suggest that you revise the case in order to identify those facts that put the capitalization of these costs back in question. For example, SableTel has not yet received the feasibility assessment of the project. (p. 18)

Impact: The amount of $3,457,860 should not be capitalized as an intangible asset.

Review conclusion and impact: write rather about what needs to be done...

Expenses (extraordinary event)

IFRS do not allow presentation of extraordinary items. (IAS 1 par. 87)

Problem:

Following the hurricane that damaged the Mobile network, no accounting adjustment was made.

OK

Given that 60 of the 340 communication towers were damaged and no longer work;

conclusion justified using the case facts.

Given that the towers no longer work and have to be replaced, they should no longer be recorded as assets in the book of accounts.

This is an important subject that deserves to be looked at in greater depth. Try and work out the steps of the discussion.
1- impairment? 2- individual asset/cash-generating unit 3- recoverable amount.

Conclusion:

Derecognize the towers and expense the same amount in a profit-before-income-taxes item.

Impact: $2.1M must be expensed and PP&E must be reduced.

60 x 35 = 2.1M; important to say that you are getting rid of 60 towers, and not of 340!

Evaluation ratios:

See exhibit 1

Very good idea to present an overall conclusion after the ratio analysis. Comparing ratios over time, and with the industry, is perfect! You can take advantage of this to establish interrelationships with other problems or issues.

Conclusion:

The company is in a difficult situation; its financial position and profits have gone down over the year. Additionally, compared with the industry, the company ratios are down.

Right now, the company cannot offer 15% return on investment, because it is running a deficit and can't even pay the interest on its debts!

Excellent return to StarNova's target goal. Had you calculated the return on equity, your response would have been more complete.

Analysis of variances between 2010 and 2009

The main 3 variances have been identified.

Reasonable effort to resolve this issue.

Revenue:

The variance in revenue was not caused by the loss of 2 clients, who would make a difference of $100K, but rather by other significant factors.

Good use of case information.

The word "grant" is sufficient.

First of all, there is a government grant that is currently mistakenly recorded under revenue; therefore $2,750 must be deducted from revenue.

The real variance is $2,854,518 and not $100K.

Most of this difference is caused by the drop in long-distance services, which have fallen from close to $5M ($28M- $33M). The gross margin has dropped (Exhibit 2).

Place the reference to the exhibit earlier, near the heading.

Good analysis of Revenues.

On the other hand, the other services offered by SableTel are up, compared with 2009, and the cumulative increase is roughly $2.15M ([65M-28M-2.75M] - [65.17M-33.07M]).

Gross profit:

Good justification of your figures. Since you have an Exhibit for this section, all your calculations could be presented in the same place.

See Exhibit 2, changes in GP.

Administration expenses:

Apart from R&D expenses, there are many other case facts to be taken into consideration (e.g.: sales staff turnover) Needs looking at again.

Administration expenses have not dropped because of cost containment in marketing, but because of expenses recorded as intangible assets in the amount of $5.7M in 2010 and $3.4M in 2009. If we suppose the expenses to have gone down by $2.78M, this means a real decrease of $0.48M (5.7 - 3.4 = 2.3 - 2.78 = 0.48) in expenses compared with 2009.

Refuting the Chief Executive Officer's statement was an excellent idea.

Dan's explanation isn't completely true: the drop in expenses is mainly due to the capitalization of R&D.

I suggest you make an overall comment on the variance analysis. You could also establish a link with your previous conclusion on "Evaluation ratios."

This is the most important issue of the case. Should be presented first!

CRTC Audit Plan — The risk analysis usually comes first.

<u>Materiality:</u>

Materiality should be deemed low, because the CRTC uses our figures as its fee basis. So, given the fee review situation (3rd notice) and the threat to revoke our license, we cannot afford another notice based on invalid data.

Good link with report users.

<u>Risks:</u>

The risks are relatively high, BECAUSE: — relatively??? According to what you say in the previous paragraph, they are considered high. Don't soften down your conclusion!

The risks linked to the use of the audit work are properly identified.

- CRTC is threatening to take away our operating license and, should that happen, SableTel could find itself non-operational, which would be dangerous. OK
- Changes effective August 31, 2008 with respect to calculation and fee rate.
- Contradictory information from IT dept on the one hand and Marketing on the other, regarding customers with negative margins. OK
- Exclusion of transactions between related parties. We are in danger of assessing them differently from the CRTC (CRTC standards aren't the same as IFRS as regards assessment of transaction amount).
- Exclusion of transactions with non-Canadian entities, i.e. risk of different exchange rate being used. ? I cannot see what risk there is if you exclude these transactions.
- Risk of coming across revenues other than telecommunications amongst the net revenue. OK
- Risk of undervaluing sales or overvaluing expenses in order to bring down CRTC Fees. OK

It is an excellent idea to take the specifics of the calculation formula into consideration.

<u>Approach:</u>

Since we are not going through an audit, we don't need to look at the systems and controls of SableTel. All the same, we could do with some assurance as regards the risk areas mentioned.

WRONG! The work of internal audit can be based on internal controls.

<u>Timing:</u>

We have two-and-a-half months to carry out the audit and review the fees. That should be time enough.

<u>Procedures:</u>

Since this is a major requirement, you should analyze it in greater depth. For starters, the number of procedures listed is insufficient.

- Check out the CRTC notices as respects the amounts asked for and the years that have to be covered by the review notice. WHY?
- Contact the CRTC (telephone, Internet) to find out what the eligible revenues and expenses are, along with the fee rates. That way we can confirm our calculation basis. Exhibit IV?
- Carry out tests on the IT and Marketing departments' data bases to confirm which one has the right information. For example, we can pick a client, look at the full amount billed vs all costs related to this client (run the info through both data bases) and then compare them and see if the information is correct. Good: a practical procedure. You need to track the amounts back to the invoices.
- Take the detailed client list (with sales $) and check that the transactions made with related parties are excluded from the revenues used to determine CRTC Fees. OK, but start by identifying these related parties.
- Take the list of all the suppliers and check that they are not included in expenses, by looking at the year's transactions and deducting their amounts from the total expenses. To check over the amounts, look at the supplier's bill and confirm the occurrence and value of the transaction.

I don't understand the last procedure. US supplier? Related party?

<u>Preliminary error estimate:</u>

See Exhibit 3.

To make sure you don't forget anything, your best bet would be to structure your discussion by going back over each component of the fee calculation. Amongst other things, you haven't enough procedures dealing with Revenue.

Remember to mention impacts!

The fee represents an amount higher than the previous calculation.

YOU NEED TO DRAW UP YOUR PROCEDURES VERY PRECISELY. WHAT IS YOUR OBJECTIVE? HOW DO YOU INTEND TO ACHIEVE IT? A LINK WITH THE ASSERTIONS WILL HELP YOU WORK OUT A SPECIFIC PROCEDURE.

Comments on activities:

Structured presentation of the ideas.

Comments:

Be more precise: "reporting document" or an "MD&A"

As regards the activities report, a number of the points raised are debatable:

Excellent

- The sales figures are not as robust as he claims, since there has been a significant drop in long-distance services, which make up the largest % of the company's sales. On top of that, if they are maintained, it's partly thanks to a grant.
- Net income is not on the positive side once the accounting adjustments have been considered. In fact, SableNet made a loss in 2010. well linked to previous sections
- The cost of sales has not really been contained, because of a drop in the gross margin of its most important service, i.e. long-distance. OK
- One might need to question part of the $16M liquidity figure, because there was a sharp increase in accounts receivable in one year, which probably suggests some bad debt expenses among them. OK
- The Technology Project does not appear to have generated increased sales, but simply a 5% drop in expenses. a little more explanations would help...
- Consequent on the Hurricane, the SableTel Mobile network is no longer functioning in Nova Scotia, and we still don't know if they intend to repair the damaged towers. OK
- He claims he has achieved his objectives of lowering risks by changing the cafeteria menus and installing hand sanitizers at strategic locations. But such measures do not eliminate the danger of work injuries. What is more, it doesn't lower the company's operational risks.
- The fact that there are no significant new projects is a risk in itself, BECAUSE it means the company doesn't add to its value and can come under threat from new technologies developed by competitors. OK should be linked to current project
- It is not relevant to use the MD&A report to thank an employee who has been with our company for 25 years. What do you mean by "not relevant"?

Recommendations:

- The Wireless Technology project grant needs to be discussed, because this could be important for shareholders, since WT will also belong to IC.
- Provide information regarding hurricane losses.
- Discuss market share variations as concerns the different product lines.

GOOD!

The recommendations are clear, practical, and show that you understand what an MD&A is all about.

Excellent response to this requirement.
Key elements made clear.
A good number of elements are identified and justified.
Very good use of the case facts.

Once you have resolved this issue, you could take "a step back" and write an overall comment on the "usefulness of the reporting document as a whole."

Comments on 2011 strategic plan:

IT:

Problem:
The Wireless network is expected to be up and running as of January 1, 2012, i.e. not in 2011. Additionally, every effort as regards this project will be made in 2011, but there is no guarantee of this, since a third-party report is currently under way.

On top of it all, if the company is to secure its objective of decreasing costs by 5%, it will need to make major savings if it is to enjoy a 15% return on investment. Moreover, in order to generate profits at the current level of activity, i.e. $30M, the project costs must be brought down by $1.5M. Therefore they must not go beyond $10M, a much lower amount than the $20M asked for project completion.

1.5M comes from where?
I need to know the source of your figures.

Excellent idea to consider the financial impact.

Impact:

- The project will not really be profitable, therefore risk of unnecessary indebtedness.
- IT employees will be focusing exclusively on this project, which means there will be no development of other projects = business continuity at risk if the wireless technology project is no longer feasible.

Problem not precise enough
↓
Recommendation not precise enough

Recommendations:

- Review the usefulness and profitability of the Wireless Technology project.
- Avoid focusing only on this project, and start developing other technologies. *OK*

HR:

Adequate response structure.
No need to write "Problem-Impact-Recommendations."
You can also abbreviate to "P-I-R".

Problem well identified

Problem:

- Bonus plan to increase employee retention, but limited to executive staff.

Impact:

- Those who benefit may not necessarily be the ones who matter, because at the present time the turnover of both sales and marketing dept staff is high and it will not be them who benefit from this plan. This means you're going to the wrong place if you want to increase retention. *Excellent*

Recommendations:

- Forget this plan, or at least don't limit it to only 7 people. Extend it to the rest of the company. *OK*
- Bring the amounts down, because $500K to $1M is much too much considering the employees' current salaries, i.e. $75,000 to over $100,000 per employee. *OK*

Customer service:

You'd do better to write something like:
"No study was made of the effectiveness of client visits."

Problem:

- The first clients to be visited will be those located near the main office.

Impact:

- Clients near the main office are not necessarily important; so maybe you're not necessarily aiming at the right clients!

Excellent

OK

Recommendations:

- Make a selection of those clients who represent big money. *OK*
- Turnover should be more frequent than once per 5 years for major clients.

Comments on 2011 strategic plan:

Sales:

Review the identification of the problem for each of the subjects in this issue: there's a lack of precision.

Problem:

- Sales staff quota has been increased, but salaries haven't.

Impact:

- Risk of maintaining high turnover, since basic salary is below that of competitors ($45,000 < $65,000) and the quota increase could see sales staff quitting, because they will no longer be able to meet their quotas and their salaries will drop. *Excellent*
- Current quotas aren't being met; increasing them will mean their being reached even less.

Good. You have attempted to find a solution for each problem brought up.

Recommendations:

- Increase basic salaries, because they are below industry norms. *OK*
- Maintain stable quota levels, because it's hard enough to reach them as it is; or bring quotas down to make them achievable. *OK*

Marketing:

Problem:

- Implementation of a non-standard pricing policy. *What is the problem?*

Impact:

- A discount won't make clients buy more, since purchase volume is dictated by their needs. This means no increase via your current clients.

Recommendation:

- Offer discounts to clients who bring NEW customers to SableTel. *Not really linked with the gross margin.*
  For example: a client bringing in a new $100,000 per-year customer will be entitled to a 10% discount.

Structuring your response in line with the various departments at SableTel has allowed you to discuss a reasonable number of different items.

Budget evaluation and likelihood of results being achieved: *EXCELLENT Opinion clearly stated and justified.*

It is unlikely that the budget target will be met, since:

- Sales increase has been overstated. The budget provides for a 15% sales increase whereas analysts are looking at 1.5%. *OK*
- Wireless Technology project related expenses cannot necessarily all be capitalized. In fact none of them may be, if the report we'll be getting within the next 60 days indicates that it is not feasible. This would mean adding $20M to the costs. *not very clear*
- The budget does not take into account revenue losses in Nova Scotia and the expenses linked to the restoration of the mobile network. *good*
- *Your analysis is really insufficient. This is an important issue and I wonder if you did indeed allow 20 minutes to deal with it, as indicated in your response plan. In fact, you seem to have allocated more, (and indeed too much) time to a less important issue on the next page, i.e. taxation.*

I know what you mean, but don't forget that accounting treatment does not impact cash flows. Nevertheless, an outflow of 20M should be expected.

ALSO, SINCE YOU HAVE ALL THE FIGURES REQUIRED, YOU SHOULD AT LEAST PROVIDE A "SHORT" CALCULATION THAT WOULD ADJUST BUDGET INFORMATION. MAKING THESE ADJUSTMENTS WILL FACILITATE THE DRAFTING OF YOUR CONCLUSION AND DEMONSTRATE YOUR CAPACITY TO INTEGRATE PREVIOUS PROBLEMS OR ISSUES.

Other:

Taxation: 2008 Reassessment

The acquisition resulted in an acquisition of control. Therefore:

Spacolli: inactive company p.22

Your application of these two criteria to the case is incomplete, to say the least. Make more use of the case facts in order to determine whether the criteria WERE or WERE NOT met.

"capital loss" or "business loss"? Should be specified!

Losses are usable only if:

1. The company continues to operate with a view to a profit --> which has not been the case;
2. The company earns income in same or similar business --> which could have been feasible.

The *Income Tax Act* includes rules that forbid the use of tax losses incurred by companies bought up simply for that purpose. (limitations rules)

Since the amalgamation was carried through legally, there's nothing you can do to avoid paying back the tax reductions you took.

not precise enough

** If the amalgamation had never taken place, you could have transferred the company's earning assets and then used the losses (obviously, the two above conditions would need to be met).

There is no point in spending time on something that doesn't apply to the present situation.

Dan's knowledge

Dan doesn't appear to be aware of what is taking place in the company, BECAUSE:

- He doesn't know why he wants $20M funding.
- He is unaware of the real reasons for the FS changes.

An excellent idea to raise this issue. However, you COULD and you SHOULD list more elements in order to better flesh out such an important comment. After all you are dealing with the SableTel CEO!

Recommendation:

- Replace Dan by someone more competent.

Agreed. Personally I would recommend that you assess the situation a bit more, or offer some training before "replacing the CEO." One must show people some consideration.

OVERALL CONCLUSION:

The company is currently unprofitable, since it is incurring losses. Additionally, its market position is negative.

GOOD. You should offer more justification of what you put forward, using the conclusions of the main sections of your report.

The project being undertaken by SableTel does not meet the level of profitability you require from your investment, i.e. 15%, because the 5% cost saving does not generate enough to provide a 15% profit margin on a $20M loan. Based on the current level of activity, you shouldn't be investing more than $10M.

Where does the 10M come from?

Presenting an overall conclusion is an excellent idea, but it could certainly be more elaborate.

You are heading in the right direction, but you should remember that this is a good place to bring out the interrelationships between the various problems or issues, along with the "CAUSE AND EFFECT" LINKS.

Exhibit 1

Several ratios calculated. Return on equity?

Objective: Calculation of company ratios compared with industry

Based on unaudited data

Calculated: (in thousands of $)

You give a conclusion on the performance of each ratio by comparing them with those of the industry. This is a good approach. However, given all the ratios on this page, your conclusion is too short. To say that it is "above" or "below" just isn't enough.

Margin analysis:

Gross profit

	2010	2009
Revenue	65072	65177
Grant	-2750	
Adjusted revenue	62322	
CGS	-30715	-30592
Margin	31607	34585
%	0.485723506	0,530631971
Industry	0.522	0.53

A good link with your conclusion about the accounting treatment of the grant.

In 2010, the gross profit was lower than industry.

It would have been better to calculate one or two ratios less. This would have given you the time to better interpret the others.

Selling expenses

	2010	2009
Expenses	30212	32995
%	0.484772632	0.506236863
Industry	0.405	0.403

The selling expenses % is falling; but it remains above industry.

Operating profit

	2010	2009
Gross profit	31607	34585
Costs	30212	32995
Damage	2100	
Inventory	2300	
R&D	3458	
Operating profit	-6463	1590
%	-0.103	0.0244
Industry	11.70%	12.70%

An adequate presentation. The calculations were well structured. You didn't need to repeat the industry ratios each time.

The operating profit is well below that of the market. *industry?*

A/R turnover

	2010	2009
Sales	62322	65177
A/R	15865	6789
Turnover	3.928269776	9.600382972
Industry	6.7	6.9

Exhibit 1 (cont.)

Accounts receivable were doing better than the industry in 2009.
GOOD But there was some control slippage in 2010, because turnover was lower in the industry.
Possibility of collection problem in receivable, because the amount has more than doubled in 1 year.
You'll need to consider an A/R analysis with a view to a provision.

On this page you "interpret" more, which is a good thing. You need to provide an ADDED VALUE analysis for the users of your report.

ST liquidity

Current (Comment: In 2010, I adjust inventory -$2.3M)

A good link with the accounting section.

	2010	2009
Cash	351	8321
A/R	15865	6789
Inventory	919	883
Total	17135	15993
Current liab	22266	16518
Ratio	0.769558969	0.968216491
Industry	0.8	0.8

In 2009, higher than the industry, but lower.
In 2010, therefore danger to ongoing operations.

The word "danger" should be explained.

LT solvency (Comment:)

	2010	2009
Operating profit	-6463	1590
Interest expense	2968	2878
Ratio	-2.177560647	0.552466991
Industry	8.1	8.3

It is not the fact that it is below 1 that matters most, but the fact that it is negative and much lower than the industry ratio. Since ST is incurring a loss, the calculation of this ratio for 2010 is less useful.

Below industry over the 2 years.
Therefore, no way of meeting interest charges because below 1.

Growth

	2010	2009	% difference
Revenue	62322	65177	-4.38%
Industry			-2.60%

GOOD Loss in growth exceeds that of the industry. This means less sales and the company loses part of its market share.

Link this to the increase of 1.5% expected by industry analysts.

Conclusion:

Compared with the industry, I believe the company is in a mess, because in 2010 most of its ratios were negative compared with those of the industry.
THEREFORE the company is in a difficult situation.

I would suggest that you provide a more complete conclusion in one place only, either in the qualitative analysis or in the quantitative analysis.

Exhibit 2

Objective: To calculate gross profit variation

Unaudited data AND? If you don't mention the impact or the consequences, this is not very useful.

Calculations (in thousands of $)

adequate calculations; well presented

	Sales 10	CGS 10	% in 10
Long-distance	28051	11943	0.574239778
Local access	24568	11067	0.549535982
Mobile	4239	2204	0.480066053
Internet	3789	1002	0.735550277
Internet - Routers	1676	679	0.594868735

	Sales 09	CGS 09	% in 09	Difference
Long-distance	33069	12562	0.620127612	-0.045887834
Local access	23679	10684	0.548798513	0.000737468
Mobile	3963	2087	0.473378753	0.0066873
Internet	2898	795	0.725672878	0.009877399
Internet - Routers	1568	619	0.605229592	-0.010360857

Conclusion:

GP decreased between 2010 and 2009, mainly because of a drop in long-distance, the company's major revenue, and also because of the rise in costs.

Since you have made your calculations by product line, your interpretation should take this into account. Here, as in the text, you are essentially analyzing the long-distance services.

I notice that your quantitative analysis is excellent, but I wonder whether you haven't spent too much time on this part at the expense of the qualitative analysis. For example, the evaluation of the budgeted financial information has been neglected.

Exhibit 3

THERE ARE or THERE ARE NOT any negative margin customers. And, in the affirmative, the amount must be accurately determined. You cannot justify an assumption on the basis of SableTel's preferences. The Fee calculation formula is clear and must be complied with.

objective: To calculate the amount of the error

Based on unaudited amounts

We are not taking into account clients with negative margins, because it is possible that there are no clients with negative margins.

Therefore, we are not using the $1.13M, because this would lower the fee amount, which goes against what we wish to do. ???

We have to hope that if there is an adjustment, it will be downwards, simply because we must avoid having our license revoked.

"to hope"?
You have already indicated the danger of their license being revoked in your response.

Calculation:

	2010	2009
Revenue:	65,072,224	65,176,742
Adjustments:		
Grant	(2,750,000)	
Related	(1,357,850)	(1,458,760)
Adjusted revenue	60,964,374	63,717,982
Costs:	30,714,869	30,591,682
Adjustments:		
CRTC Fee	(3,817,484)	(3,842,785)
Non-Canadian supplier	(897,500)	(788,000)
Adjusted costs	25,999,885	25,960,897
Basis for calculation:	34,964,489	37,757,085
Fee rate	0.12	0.12

Fee calculation formula fully understood.

12% and not 10%, BECAUSE rate was changed in August, 2008.

True, but since this information is stated clearly in the case, you don't need to justify it.

	2010	2009
CRTC Fee	4,195,739	4,530,850
Fee as previously calculated	3,817,484	3,842,785
Preliminary error estimate	378,255	688,065

You have fully understood that it was necessary to make a "PRELIMINARY estimate of the error."

Total fee amount requiring correction over the two years: $1,066,319.88

The figure can be rounded

Conclusion:

SO?
Impacts must be discussed.

The fee payment requires an adjustment for 2009 and 2010 in the amount of $1,066,320 to cover the two years.

B89

EVALUATION GUIDE – SABLETEL (5 hours) [a]

Primary Indicator #1: Assurance ***The candidate provides an audit plan, recalculates the CRTC Fee, and provides auditing procedures to test the accuracy of the Fee calculation.***

The candidate...

Highly competent	Competent	Reaching competence	NM*	NA*
discusses audit planning issues AND makes a reasonable recalculation of the Fee AND provides some relevant audit procedures. *The Approach needs reviewing.*	discusses audit planning issues *OK* OR makes a reasonable recalculation of the Fee *OK* AND provides some relevant audit procedures.	discusses some of the audit issues surrounding the CRTC Fee calculation. *insufficient number of procedures*		
0.3%	51.5%	41.5%	6.7%	0.0%

Overall Risk *OK* Preliminary Materiality *OK* Approach *X* Preliminary Estimate of Error *GOOD*
Revenue: Classification Revenue includes services not included ____ Classification Related party revenue *incomplete*
Costs: Accuracy Foreign exchange amounts ____ Classification Non-Canadian costs ____ Classification Related party costs ____
Negative margin customers: Accuracy Database *OK* Accuracy Identified/recorded appropriately ____
Fee rate: Accuracy Calculation ____ *a little about the suppliers*

Primary Indicator #2: Performance Measurement and Reporting ***The candidate discusses the significant accounting issues related to the 2010 financial statements.***

The candidate...

Highly competent	Competent	Reaching competence	NM*	NA*
discusses most of the relevant accounting issues AND adjusts the financial statements for most of the accounting adjustments.	discusses some of the relevant accounting issues *almost* AND discusses their impact on the financial statements *OK* *2010 R&D costs not analyzed, though it is an important subject*	identifies some of the relevant accounting issues.		
0.5%	68.9%	26.5 %	4.0%	0.1%

Inventory: Obsolescence Provision *excellent* Deferred Research and Development Costs ____ Industry Canada Grant *incomplete*
Impairment of Mobile Network *incomplete* Adjusted Financial Statements ____
Accounting Errors: CRTC Fee/2009 R&D ____ Deferred Revenue ____

* NM: Nominal competence – The candidate does not attain the standard of reaching competence. NA: Not addressed – The candidate does not address this indicator.

a This "shortened" evaluation guide, used to inform the student of how he is assessed, is based on the indicators of competence on pages 25 to 76. It could, of course, be more concise and limited to one or two pages, as necessary.

EVALUATION GUIDE – SABLETEL (continued)

Primary Indicator #3: Management Decision-Making ***The candidate performs a variance analysis on the 2010 financial statements.***

The candidate...

Highly competent	Competent	Reaching competence	NM*	NA*
analyzes the areas of variance that provide relevant information to the executive committee AND recognizes that a comparison with the approved budget would provide additional meaningful information.	analyzes areas of variance that provide relevant information to the executive committee. The various types of revenue have not been analyzed. on the right path	attempts to analyze areas of variance that provide relevant information to the executive committee.		
0.0%	13.9%	25.1%	56.4%	4.6%

Sales: Long-distance OK Other ____
Cost of Sales and Gross Margin: Long-distance few Routers and modems ____ Other ____
Expenses: Selling and marketing incomplete R&D costs ____ Other Variances ____

Primary Indicator #4: Finance ***The candidate calculates financial ratios to determine the financial condition and operating performance of SableTel relative to its competitors.***

The candidate...

Highly competent	Competent	Reaching competence	NM*	NA*
calculates relevant financial ratios, including a full range of ratios related to the financial position (i.e. balance sheet) and the operations (i.e. income statement) of SableTel AND performs a meaningful analysis comparing SableTel to industry.	calculates relevant financial ratios for SableTel OK AND except for ROE performs a meaningful analysis, comparing SableTel to the industry. almost	calculates relevant financial ratios for SableTel.		
0.4%	36.0%	57.2%	5.8%	0.6%

Profitability ratios NO! Margin Analysis (Gross margin, SM&A, Operating profit) incomplete
Turnover OK Short-Term Liquidity incomplete Long-Term Solvency incomplete
Growth Ratios OK CONCLUSION incomplete Other comments ____

You are on the right path. But you need to "interpret" the ratio calculations a bit more, especially the Return on equity because of the 15% return target.

* NM: Nominal competence – The candidate does not attain the standard of reaching competence. NA: Not addressed – The candidate does not address this indicator.

EVALUATION GUIDE – SABLETEL (continued)

Primary Indicator #5: Performance Measurement and Reporting ***The candidate identifies weaknesses within the executive reporting document as presented and recommends improvements.***

The candidate...

Highly competent	Competent	Reaching competence	NM*	NA*
discusses several of the deficiencies in the executive reporting document OK AND recommends improvements that help readers understand the financial situation of SableTel OK AND explains why the executive reporting document as presented is not useful.	identifies some of the deficiencies in the executive reporting document EXCELLENT AND recommends improvements that would help readers understand the financial situation of SableTel OK OR explains why the executive reporting document as presented is not useful.	identifies some of the OK deficiencies in the executive reporting document.		
0.4%	39.9%	29.8%	24.6%	5.3%

Loss to Profit: OK Robust revenue: OK Reduction in operating costs: ____
Cost of sales contained: OK Strong liquidity: OK Solid balance sheet: ____
Increasing revenue/Decreasing expenses: incomplete Implications of Hurricane Baylee: OK
Impact of Wireless Technology Project: incomplete Financial risks: OK Lawsuits: ____
Evolving core business: OK Thanks to an employee: OK SUGGESTED IMPROVEMENTS: OK

Primary Indicator #6: Governance, Strategy, and Risk Management ***The candidate evaluates the strategic plan, recognizes that it is flawed, and suggests recommendations for improvement.***

The candidate...

Highly competent	Competent	Reaching competence	NM*	NA*
describes several of the weaknesses in the strategic plan AND describes the implications of the weaknesses AND recommends improvements. almost	describes some of the weaknesses in the strategic plan AND describes the implications of the weaknesses AND recommends improvements. EXCELLENT	identifies some of the weaknesses in the strategic plan.		
0.5%	64.3%	29.6%	5.4%	0.2%

Customer Losses: ____ Customer Visits: OK Standard Margin Pricing: incomplete Sales Quotas: OK
Plan to Increase Sales: ____ Increase in Overhead Costs: ____ Executive Bonus Plan: OK
Compensation Policies: OK IT Focus/Wireless Technology Project: OK Cross-Selling Program: ____
Access to Information: ____ Lack of Coordination between Departments: ____ One-Year Time Frame: ____

* NM: Nominal competence – The candidate does not attain the standard of reaching competence. NA: Not addressed – The candidate does not address this indicator.

EVALUATION GUIDE – SABLETEL (continued)

Primary Indicator #7: Management Decision-Making ***The candidate analyzes the financial budget provided for 2011 and concludes on whether the results are likely to be achieved.***

The "Reaching competence" level is not too demanding, since you have not analyzed many areas.

The candidate...

Highly competent	Competent	Reaching competence	NM*	NA*
analyzes specific areas of the budgeted financial information that are not realistic AND recognizes that the results are not likely to be achieved AND makes adjustments to the 2011 budget.	analyzes specific areas of the budgeted financial information that are not realistic AND recognizes that the results are not likely to be achieved. OK	attempts to analyze specific areas of the budgeted financial information that are not realistic.		
0.2%	49.3%	33.8%	15.8%	0.9%

Restating budgeted financial information: __________
Revenue: few Cost of Sales and Gross Margin: __________ Expenses: few Other amounts: __________
Summary of Adjusted Budget and Capital Requirements: __________
Likelihood of the results being achieved: OK

Primary Indicator #8: Pervasive Qualities and Skills ***The candidate integrates information from various sources and explains why SableTel is not likely to be successful in the future without significant changes.***

The candidate...

Highly competent	Competent	Reaching competence	NM*	NA*
integrates several of the issues in the response to conclude that SableTel is not likely to be successful in the future without significant changes AND provides a plan to address the concerns identified.	integrates several of the issues in the response to conclude that SableTel is not likely to be successful in the future without significant changes. Concern with integration. CEO's competence and 15% return target considered.	integrates some of the issues in the response OR concludes that SableTel is not likely to be successful in the future without significant changes.		
0.5%	52.4%	38.9%	8.2%	0.0%

Integration: Links ACCT/ratios; Links variances and reporting document
Competence of SableTel Management: OK (1-3 examples missing)
Overall Conclusion: OK (not enough explanations)

* NM: Nominal competence – The candidate does not attain the standard of reaching competence. NA: Not addressed – The candidate does not address this indicator.

EVALUATION GUIDE – SABLETEL (continued)

Secondary Indicator #1: Taxation ***The candidate discusses the relevant corporate income tax issues related to SableTel.***

The candidate...

Competent	NM*	NA*
addresses some of the corporate income tax issues in sufficient depth.		

Scientific Research and Experimental Development (SR&ED) Tax Credits and Expenditures: ____________

Spacolli Enterprises Inc. (Spacolli) Tax Losses: ____________

Deemed Year-End: ____________ Loss-Carryback: incomplete; not enough integration

Secondary Indicator #2: Finance ***The candidate analyzes the Wireless Technology Project to determine if SableTel/StarNova should continue to fund this project.***

The candidate...

Competent	NM*	NA*
performs a qualitative and quantitative assessment of the Wireless Technology Project to determine if SableTel should continue to fund this project.		

Qualitative analysis: few Quantitative analysis: incomplete Recommendation: not precise enough

p. 83

TO REMEMBER:

- All your analyses end with a recommendation or a conclusion.
- Your response calculations correspond to the goals expressed and were well presented.
- You are always seeking to use the case facts in your analyses. Well integrated.

TO IMPROVE:

- Have another look at the determination of the priorities so that you can give a high profile and consequently greater depth to the most important subjects.
- Make greater use of the results of your calculations. Simply making them is not enough; you need to use them to illustrate "what is going wrong" and to justify your own arguments. You have to interpret calculations!
- Take a bit more time so that you can better identify the problem that needs to be discussed. When the problem or issue is badly defined or not precise enough, it makes it more difficult to offer a relevant solution. More especially, have another look at the analysis of the accounting issues.

* NM: Nominal competence – The candidate does not attain the standard of competent. NA: Not addressed – The candidate does not address this indicator.